THE CALIFORNIA GOLD RUSH

BY JOHN WALTON CAUGHEY

HISTORY OF THE PACIFIC COAST

BERNARDO DE GALVEZ IN LOUISIANA

MCGILLIVRAY OF THE CREEKS

CALIFORNIA

HUBERT HOWE BANCROFT, HISTORIAN OF THE WEST

THE CALIFORNIA GOLD RUSH (GOLD IS THE CORNERSTONE)

AMERICA SINCE 1763

IN CLEAR AND PRESENT DANGER:
THE CRUCIAL STATE OF OUR FREEDOMS

A HISTORY OF THE UNITED STATES (with Ernest R. May)

LAND OF THE FREE (with John Hope Franklin and Ernest R. May)

SCHOOL SEGREGATION ON OUR DOORSTEP (with LaRee Caughey)

THE PUEBLO WATER RIGHT OF LOS ANGELES
HISTORICALLY CONSIDERED

THE AMERICAN WEST

TO KILL A CHILD'S SPIRIT:
THE TRAGEDY OF SCHOOL SEGREGATION IN LOS ANGELES

EDITED BY JOHN WALTON CAUGHEY

THE EMIGRANTS' GUIDE TO CALIFORNIA
By Joseph E. Ware

THE LOS ANGELES STAR, 1851-1864
By William B. Rice

RUSHING FOR GOLD

ROBERT OWEN, SOCIAL IDEALIST
By Rowland Hill Harvey

EAST FLORIDA, 1783-1785, A FILE OF DOCUMENTS
By Joseph Byrne Lockey

THE INDIANS OF SOUTHERN CALIFORNIA IN 1852:
THE B. D. WILSON REPORT

SEEING THE ELEPHANT:
LETTERS OF R. R. TAYLOR, FORTY-NINER

SIX MONTHS IN THE GOLD MINES
By E. Gould Buffum

THEIR MAJESTIES THE MOB

CALIFORNIA HERITAGE:
AN ANTHOLOGY OF HISTORY AND LITERATURE
(with LaRee Caughey)

THE CALIFORNIA GOLD RUSH

JOHN WALTON CAUGHEY

With vignettes by W. R. Cameron

UNIVERSITY OF CALIFORNIA PRESS
Berkeley, Los Angeles, London

UNIVERSITY OF CALIFORNIA PRESS
BERKELEY AND LOS ANGELES
CALIFORNIA

UNIVERSITY OF CALIFORNIA PRESS, LTD.
LONDON, ENGLAND

PAPERBACK EDITION, 1975
ISBN: 0-520-02763-9

THIS BOOK WAS ORIGINALLY PUBLISHED IN THE CHRONICLES OF
CALIFORNIA UNDER THE TITLE *Gold is the Cornerstone*.

PRINTED IN THE UNITED STATES OF AMERICA

3 4 5 6 7 8 9

TO

ELMER BELT

WHO ONCE DID
SOME PROSPECTING
ON MY ACCOUNT

Preface
to the Paperback Edition

UNDER *a more fanciful title,* Gold is the Cornerstone, *this book broke ground in 1948 as a comprehensive view of the discovery at Sutter's Mill, the rush at first local but soon worldwide, the work and life in the mines, and the social, economic, political, and cultural consequences which created a new California. Published originally in the Chronicles of California, the book was an element in the celebration of the centennial.*

Since then many additional documents have come to light or to publication and several excellent studies have issued. Accordingly, the bibliography is now extended. Information now available would have permitted a wider selection of anecdotes, for instance, on the experiences of the overland forty-niners. But it seems to me that the overall construct of this book still stands, and I am gratified that the publisher is willing to reissue it unchanged.

J. W. C.

Los Angeles, 1974

Preface

THE AUTHOR *of every book must feel surprised that his subject has waited for him. How does it happen that no one else has tackled it, or at least that no one has written in the exact fashion that to him seems indicated?*

When I first thought of writing on the gold of California, I must confess that I had minimum hopes of finding anything new to do. The literature on this topic began to pile up in 1848 and has been growing steadily ever since. In the shadow of so vast an accumulation of writing, could any questions remain unanswered, any approach untried? My basic assumption, however, was that the most useful contribution would be a comprehensive view, beginning with the discovery, the first season of prospecting, and the rush by land and sea, and going on to measure the economic, political, social, and cultural outgrowths. That is the sort of book this is; and to my pleasant astonishment, it seems to be the pioneer effort to deal thus broadly with its subject.

Writing from a vantage point a hundred years removed from the onset of California's gold excitement, I have had the benefit of an abundance of firsthand accounts and scholarly studies of various phases of the rush and its aftermath. To these writers I am much indebted, and likewise to the modern custodians of their knowledge—bookmen, collectors, and librarians. Friends and students have helped me toward a better grasp of the subject. Several of the full-page illustrations, as indi-

cated, are reproduced through the courtesy of the Henry E. Huntington Library. One is from the collection of the late C. C. Pierce. The chapter-head vignettes, done with careful attention to authenticity, are from the skilled hand of William Ross Cameron. To these friends I am obliged.

On the multitude of problems that arise in converting a manuscript into a book Samuel T. Farquhar and August Frugé were most helpful. In the formulation and expression of my ideas I got valued criticism from Louis Knott Koontz, James Gilluly, Harold A. Small, and, in particular, from my wife.

J. W. C.

Los Angeles, 1948

Contents

Illustrations

Introduction

HISTORY, as a nonexperimental science, is confronted by an irrevocable past in which whatever has happened has happened. To the extent that evidence and testimony are available, the student of history can play back the record. Except in his imagination, however, he is not at liberty to play it back with any variations, such as sparing Lincoln to complete a second term in the White House, or persuading Roosevelt not to seek a third. Mankind's past, even as yours and mine, is immutable, and we are not privileged to recast it. Yet oftentimes it is a temptation, and may even be useful, to wonder what might have been.

Concerning California, for example, much ink has been spilled in idle speculation on the fate of the land if Drake had found gold in his Nova Albion, or if the Spaniards, Russians, or Mexicans had made the discovery. A more significant inquiry would be to ask what if California had been ushered into the American family without a gold spoon in her mouth.

A hundred years later, gold mining was one of the least of the state's activities. At that time California's annual payments of federal taxes far exceeded what she once remitted in bullion, all the gold she had mined would buy only a small fraction of the total oil production, less than twenty orange crops, only eight or ten years' output of motion pictures, only a part of a year's airplane manufacture, and no more than a couple of years' agricultural yield.

But take away the initial bonanza of gold and how much less rapid and how different would the state's rise have been? With the drowsy pastoral epoch much prolonged, with Anglo-American people and ways only gradually coming into the ascendant, the tempo and doubtless the nature of her development would have been much less spectacular. In time she might have overtaken Oregon, but it is not likely that she would have drawn the first Pacific railroad or have become the first metropolis of the West. Notwithstanding special advantages of resources, climate, and position, it seems certain that at least for another generation or two she would have languished in comparative neglect, relieved by only a leisurely upsurge of population increase and economic growth.

California's real past is infinitely more vibrant. Her pioneers erected a framework for a most imposing structure, and they did it with gold for the cornerstone.

CHAPTER I

The Mill on the American

ALTHOUGH chemists and apothecaries have another sign for gold, the popular symbol is 1849. In that year Argonauts from the ends of the earth converged on California and engaged in an orgy of gold gathering that ranks as the greatest of all mining rushes. It all began in an accident, early in 1848, at a sawmill on the south fork of the American River.

As that year opened, California did not impress as a land for which great things were in store. Its political future was clouded, its economic prospects strictly limited, its population small, miscellaneous, and discordant. Yet in the metal that underlay the Sierra foothills and lined the mountain stream beds a force lay dormant that would bring the sleepy province suddenly to life.

The Spaniards, with a superlative record of treasure finding in Mexico, New Granada, and Peru, had first chance to uncover California's gold. That they muffed the chance is one of the ironies of history. Yet it is perfectly understandable. The early voyagers explored merely the coast, and the colony planters who came more than two centuries later—soldiers, padres, and ranchers rather than prospectors—likewise emphasized the coastal district. Hard at work erecting an imperial outpost, they lived out the five decades of the Spanish period with only occasional and superficial contacts with the gold-bearing interior.

Nor were the local Indians any help. In their general backwardness, sometimes maligned as the most abysmal on the continent, they were quite unmindful of the wealth about them. They discovered no mines to the California Spaniards, as more accommodating Indians had done elsewhere for Columbus, Balboa, Cortés, and Pizarro.

Mexico, the next mistress of California, likewise overlooked the gold. In turmoil after the long, bitter struggle for independence and beset by uncertainty in political philosophy, she looked on the province as one of little worth.

In sum, it consisted of a score of missions strung out from San Diego to the shores of San Francisco Bay, supplemented by four decrepit military posts, two struggling towns at San José and Los Angeles, and perhaps a dozen ranchos. The population, other than Indians, amounted to less than three thousand. Except through its strategic value as a military outpost the province had not paid its way. Mexican neglect, accordingly, was almost inevitable.

In this period, nevertheless, California registered important growth. Taking advantage of the relaxed controls, Britishers and Americans entered the province and demonstrated how cattle raising could be made to show a profit. The pastoral advantages of California grasslands had long been recognized. The new departure was a matter of sending cowhides round the Horn to market in England and New England and tallow to the soap and candle makers in Peru and Chile. Beef remained largely a waste product, but cattle raising flourished, pressure rose for the breakup of the mission holdings, which was soon accomplished, and ranching spread into the interior, practically to the region soon to be called the Mother Lode. With the increased prosperity, the "foreign colony" grew, though always mingled with the Spanish-speaking residents. Traders were joined by men from the whaling fleet, by beaver trappers from the Rocky Mountains, and in the 1840's by pioneer settlers of the covered-wagon type. In grand total they numbered less than a thousand, but they were highly adaptable, ambitious, and worldly wise; and midway in the Mexican period they had gained control of many of the ranchos, had engrossed the internal as well as the external trade of the province, and had achieved economic annexation to the United States.

These foreigners were individualists all; none more so than John A. Sutter, a Swiss who arrived in 1839 by way of Indiana, Santa Fe, Oregon, Hawaii, and Alaska. He had never amounted to much elsewhere, and his biographers do not depict him as endowed with particular talent. But he represented himself to the governor as a man of importance and had no difficulty getting a grant of eleven square leagues, about 50,000 acres, on the lower Sacramento. Such grants, of course, were routine. Enlisting the neighboring Indians and any hands that came along, Sutter began improving his property. He brought in cattle; he set out fruit trees and planted wheat. When the Russians moved away from Bodega Bay he bought most of their portable equipment, a launch, threshing floors, and a number of antiquated but serviceable cannon. The former tied in with his projects for a flour mill, a tannery, a distillery, a sawmill; the latter, with the fortification of his headquarters, which already had a wall and uniformed sentries. His military preparations are excused by the exposed location of his grant. Unquestionably it also gratified his vanity to translate his rancho into a principality—he called it New Helvetia, as though it were a country. His fort dominated the Sacramento Valley, and, especially after being publicized by John C. Frémont, it was the lodestar for American overland emigrants.

For several years Sutter's affairs ran along uneventfully, therein sharing the pattern of pastoral calm that characterized California life. The year 1846, however, brought several interruptions. Frémont was a visitor, and, after the Hawks Peak affair, moved north toward Oregon. In June a group of discontented, alarmed, and ambitious Americans near Sonoma, stimulated by the hovering presence of Frémont and his sixty fighting men, staged the Bear Flag Revolt. Before their aims could be realized, or even made clear, word came that the United States and Mexico were at war. Commodore John D. Sloat timidly implemented a part of the American war plan by taking possession of Monterey, the Bear Flaggers were assimilated, and the rest of the province was brought under American control. Southern California flared into rebellion and was not put in line again for several months. Meanwhile, troop units and naval reinforcements had been dispatched to assist in taking or holding the province, including a hundred dragoons from the Army of the West, a larger detachment in the Mormon Battalion, overland from Fort Leavenworth to San Diego, and a still larger force of volunteers, round the Horn from New York.

There was civilian migration also in 1846 and 1847, including the most famous of all overland groups, the Donner party, which met disaster in the Sierra. In volume, however, the military movements were considerably larger, and by the end of 1847 the soldiers and sailors assigned to the California station were more than twice as numerous as the American residents of earlier vintage.

Meanwhile, California had a stopgap military government such as is customary in occupied territory. At war's end captured provinces are sometimes returned to their original owners, but in Sloat's proclamation and in the war aims of the Polk administration this one was clearly earmarked for retention. Its status, so to speak, was that of lying in escrow, pending the final say of the treaty makers, but with annexation practically a foregone conclusion.

Encouraged by this prospect and also by the flow of Americans into the province and by the availability of skilled and willing workmen, many of them discharged members of the Mormon Battalion, Sutter redoubled his efforts toward becoming miller and lumberman. The gristmill that he started to build at Natomo, not far from his fort, represented the larger investment. History is infinitely more interested in the sawmill.

After much searching, its site was picked by a certain James Wilson Marshall, a moody and eccentric fellow, a carpenter with a knack for things mechanical, though never a great success in his own affairs. A native of New Jersey, he had traveled west on the Oregon Trail, and in 1845 had moved south to California. Because of his beard, his peculiarities, and his rank as foreman, Marshall is usually thought of as an old codger. Actually he was thirty-five. Sutter, whom frontiersmen regarded as an "old gentleman," was only ten years his senior.

On the south fork of the American River, some forty-five miles above the fort, Marshall came upon a park-like widening of the mountain valley. To the north the mountains rose abruptly. To the south lay more softly rounded hills, well wooded with oak, balsam, and pine. The valley itself had a good stand of sugar pine. The Indians called the spot Culuma, or Coloma, meaning "beautiful vale," yet the beauty Marshall saw was not that of vista or landscape, but of the water power that could be impounded and the convenient stand of timber. These, as he measured them, were Coloma's best assets. He was not even discouraged that the stream below was too turbulent for rafting sawn lumber.

Sutter inspected the site, approved it, and on August 27, 1847, entered into a partnership with Marshall to build and operate the mill. With a crew consisting of the Wimmer family—Mrs. Wimmer was to act as cook,—several Indians, and a number of Mormons, Marshall set out for the mill site the next day. First step was to make camp by erecting two cabins; then work on the mill itself got under way.

That something so complicated as a sawmill should be contrived in the wilderness, two score miles from even such rudimentary civilization as existed at Sutter's Fort, challenges the imagination. That it should be done by dead reckoning and rule of thumb, without benefit of exact survey or detailed specifications and with only the simple tools of woodsman, carpenter, and smith, doubtless appalls the more sheltered elements of today's civilization. Projects the like of it, however, were common on the American frontier. And Marshall's mill was held down to a simplicity that would fit the means available.

Where the river swung wide around a bar he planned a log-and-brush dam and a headgate. Across the base of the peninsula-like bar, past a double pine that was to be the landmark of the site, a dry channel would be deepened and made into the race. The mill itself, of hewn and handsawed timber, would straddle the upper end of the race. Its timber would be prepared on the site, as would also the wooden-pegged flutterwheel, approximately twelve feet in width and diameter. The axle, crank, and pitman irons were forged at the fort. Less skill but more labor would go into digging the race, but with oxen, plows, scrapers, and blasting powder this part of the task was also pushed along. Many of the details of the work can safely be left to surmise: the labor turnover as old workers left and new ones arrived, the complaints about Mrs. Wimmer's cooking, her ire when the boys would not answer the breakfast call, Henry Bigler's Christmas sermon, the disappearance of six bottles of brandy consigned to the Wimmers, and the occasional tension between the crew and the boss of the mill, who was a man of little humor. For so isolated a work camp such incidental frictions were no more than normal.

About mid-January, although the machinery of the mill was not yet fully installed, a test showed that the lower end of the race needed deepening to provide a more rapid runoff. Accordingly, workers were assigned to dig and blast by day, and by night the water was turned in to scour out the channel.

On the morning of January 24, as was his custom, Marshall walked down to inspect the tailrace. Well down it, about 200 feet from the mill, he chanced to see a glittering particle lodged on the bedrock of the channel. He saw more, some mere flakes and others as large as a grain of wheat. He collected these specimens, held them in the dented crown of his slouch hat, and excitedly rushed up to the mill, shouting, "Boys, I believe I've found a gold mine."

The boys were both skeptical and curious. Azariah Smith fished out a five-dollar gold piece, part of his mustering-out pay. Marshall's find had the right color. When bitten, and when pounded on the anvil, it behaved properly. They all went down to the tailrace to try to find more. Another couple of mornings of prospecting increased the pile to two or three ounces. Yet they were not stampeded; the prosaic work on the mill continued.

In Marshall, however, the gold fever had already found a victim. Unable to contain his excitement, he took the accumulated dust and posted off to the fort. Bursting in on his employer, he demanded to see him alone, behind locked doors. He called for two bowls of water and a stick and piece of twine to make a balance. Instead, Sutter went to the apothecary's shop for a pair of scales. Returning, he neglected to lock the door. Marshall pulled a cotton rag from his pocket, but just as he was about to unroll it, the door opened and in came one of Sutter's clerks. Much upset, Marshall hastily concealed his mysterious bundle, but when the clerk had gone and the door was safely barred, he brought it out again and showed the gold.

Nothing could have surprised Sutter more. He and Marshall applied every test their ingenuity and the *American Encyclopedia* could suggest. They sent for *aqua fortis*, which had no effect on the metal. Balancing some against silver coins, they submerged the scales and found that the gold pan sank heavily. Sutter was ready to admit that it was gold. And of course he wanted to know all about where it came from and how Marshall had found it.

Despite a pelting rain, Marshall insisted on hurrying back to his mine and, incidentally, to the mill. Sutter waited for the weather to clear, then he too went up to Coloma. The story goes that the millhands prepared for his coming by salting the race with all the gold thus far gathered, and that one of the Wimmer youngsters spoiled the fun by picking up most of the nuggets. Even so, Sutter was impressed. It behooved him, he thought, to get the Coloma Indians to give him and Marshall a three-year mining lease.

On the other hand, he foresaw disaster for his current enterprises—his gardens, farms, industries, and mills—if his workmen heard about the mountain treasure and turned to prospecting. He persuaded Marshall and his men to promise to stay on the job another six weeks. And to spare the emotions of his employees elsewhere, he requested secrecy.

Secrecy, of course, was a preposterous hope. At the fort the length and mysteriousness of Marshall's conference with Sutter had set the people there to wondering. They concluded that he had found a quicksilver deposit such as the one discovered near San Jose a couple of years earlier. Sutter himself imperiled the secret by his move to get the lease from the Indians and confirmation from the governor. He also made frequent allusions to his secret, he confided it to John Bidwell and Henry Lienhard and perhaps to others, and he wrote the news to his neighbor Mariano Guadalupe Vallejo at Sonoma.

Furthermore, to carry his request to the governor he unwisely chose Charles Bennett, a Mormon who had accompanied him to Coloma. En route, Bennett fell in among men keyed up at the prospects for a coal mine near Mount Diablo. He could not resist topping their story, and he had samples for proof.

A few days later, Jacob Wittmer, arriving at the saw-mill with a load of supplies, was greeted by one of the Wimmer urchins with the boast, "We have found gold up here." Old Jacob was so emphatic in his disbelief that Mrs. Wimmer came to the rescue of her son's honor, not only by exhibiting some of the gold, but also by giving the teamster a sample. Back at the fort, Jacob helped the secret along its natural course. Entering Smith and Brannan's store, he ordered a drink and in payment offered dust which he said was gold. Smith suspected chicanery, whereupon Jacob referred him to Sutter, who had no choice but to admit that it was the real thing.

In retrospect it seems strange that, with all the spilling of the secret, no prospectors showed up at the diggings until more than a month after the discovery, and then only by special invitation. One reason doubtless was that from the sixteenth century to the eve of '48 many responsible persons had asserted that there was gold in California. The list includes Sebastián Vizcaíno; José Antonio Carrillo, provincial delegate in Mexico; Richard Henry Dana, in *Two Years Before the Mast;* and John Bidwell. Yet only once had there been actual color to substantiate the claim. That was when a certain Francisco López happened on placer gold in San Feliciano Canyon in the mountains about forty miles north of Los Angeles. His discovery touched off a modest rush. The placers gave employment to a few score men for a few years and produced the first California gold sent to the United States mint. But before 1848 the deposit had played out. This entire record tended to dampen enthusiasm about the province as a gold producer. Furthermore, in the first weeks neither Marshall, nor Sutter, nor anyone else had reason to believe that the Coloma placer was more than a local and superficial deposit. This fact helps to explain why the sawmill hands were willing to promise to stay by their jobs for six weeks and why they kept that promise.

Another evidence of the casual attitude toward the discovery in the first weeks is the imprecision with which it was recorded. In after years Marshall, Mrs. Wimmer, Bigler, and Brown each tried to reconstruct the story. As to the physical scene, Marshall displayed a good memory—he made sketches and diagrams low in artistry but high in accuracy. Yet when he tried to fix the date of the discovery, the best he could do was to place it "between the eighteenth and the twentieth"—which naturally was interpreted to mean the nineteenth. He endorsed one of his sketches with that date, which found its way into history, for a generation, and onto the first monument erected to mark the site.

In their reminiscent testimony Bigler and Brown complicate the story by asserting that, on the afternoon preceding the real find, Marshall sent for a pie tin and began panning for gold in the tailrace. Neither asserts pointblank that he found any. Bigler makes the date the twenty-fourth; Brown, the twenty-third. It is possible, as Aubrey Neasham remarks, that Marshall looked for gold on the afternoon of the twenty-third and that he talked about it. The most dubious feature of the anecdote is the pie tin. The record is clear that through the ensuing six or eight weeks the only gold-prospecting tool was the knife—when Sutter visited the camp he distributed pocketknives—and it is reasonably certain that panning was introduced some weeks later by Isaac Humphrey, veteran of the Georgia diggings.

For the peace of mind of historians and any others who may be concerned about the exact date of the discovery there fortunately exist two contemporary diaries which, together with Sutter's, fix the time with fair exactitude. On January 30 Azariah Smith made this entry: "This week, Mr. Marshall found some peace of (as we all suppose) Gold, and he has gone to the Fort for the purpose of finding out." On January 24 Henry Bigler noted: "This day some kind of mettle was found in the tail race that looks like goald, first discovered by James Martial, the boss of the mill."

Although one informant mentions Bennett as the discoverer, and although Mrs. Wimmer once insisted that Marshall heard about gold from her husband, who had been told about it by one of her sons, no reasonable doubt remains that Marshall was the discoverer or that the time was the morning of January 24.

The mill builders, as has been said, kept on with their task. Yet before and after work, on Sundays, and on days when work was rained out, they turned prospector. At first, all their searching was along the tailrace, but on the second Sunday, February 6, Bigler and James Barger crossed the river and with knifeblades picked eight or ten dollars' worth from the opposite bank.

The next Saturday, Bigler took his gun as if to go hunting, went downstream half a mile, waded across, and picked up a few flakes. Under the same pretext he revisited the spot the next day and found half an ounce.

He returned the following Sunday and was rewarded with an ounce. February 22 turned out to be a holiday, thanks more to a snowstorm than to George Washington. Again Bigler took gun in hand to "hunt." This time the river was up. Without a fire, he had to do some prodigious jumping and threshing about to thaw out once he had waded across. His discomforts were soon forgotten, however, when he found a bullet-shaped nugget worth $6.00 and many smaller flakes and grains. Returning to camp by way of the log raft maintained at the dam, he had to confess to his now suspicious comrades what he had been up to. Untying a corner of his shirttail, he displayed his day's take, which on their improvised scales they made out to be $22.50.

A day or two earlier, Bigler had written to some of his Mormon Battalion cronies who were at work on the flour mill. He told them about the find, asking them not to broadcast the news, but inviting them to visit Coloma. Three accepted: Sidney Willis, Wilford Hudson, and Levi Fifield. They arrived at the mill site late on the twenty-seventh of February. The next morning Marshall and the other veterans escorted them to the tailrace, where Hudson, with beginner's luck, found a six-dollar nugget. Using their knives, they worked over the tailrace for another two days and then felt impelled to go back to Natomo.

On the way, Willis and Hudson did some prospecting, and at a bar about halfway down they found a small amount of color. It was enough to make several of the other Mormons want to be taken up to this place. At length Willis and Hudson obliged. To their surprise, the pickings proved excellent. Mormon Bar, Mormon Island, and Mormon Diggings—the place names of the locality—thus became the second proved placer.

Mid-March was signalized by the completion of the sawmill. The first log was sawed on March 11 and the planks were applied to heightening the forebay. Further deepening of the tailrace improved the performance, and on March 22 Sutter's Fort got delivery of planks from Coloma. Their task completed, the Mormon builders of the sawmill began to leave. By the end of April not one remained, and Marshall was sawing with a crew consisting of teamster Horace Loy, blacksmith James Gregson, and a few Indians. Mrs. Gregson had succeeded Mrs. Wimmer as cook.

Once paid off by Sutter, Bigler and his companions returned to the mountains as gold seekers. The flourmill workers also quit their work, even though it meant forfeiting their back pay, and headed up the American River. In this exodus of a score or so of men, mostly Mormons and former employees of Sutter, the gold rush may be said to have had its beginnings. In April and May, Sutter's diary records the transit of other gold seekers: on April 3 Isaac Humphrey, who had talked with Bennett and seen his samples in San Francisco; on April 7 Sam Brannan, with plans for a store at Coloma; on April 11 a Dr. Bates and John Sinclair; about April 15 Baptiste Ruelle and his family; on April 19 Major P. B. Reading and E. C. Kemble. Soon the whole world would join in.

The initial heavy draft, however, was from the personnel of Sutter's employ. His workmen gone, he could not complete the flour mill. His tanners quit, leaving 2,000 hides to rot. He was able to hold his Indian help long enough to get his wheat crop cut, but the estimated 40,000 bushels went to waste because there was no one to thresh it. All his fine plans of producing flour, lumber, leather, blankets, shoes, saddles, barrels, and the like, and of heading a feudal principality, came tumbling down as his workmen vanished and strangers thronged through New Helvetia. Temporarily he profited through rents, and revenue from trade; in fact, he got out of debt —for him a most unusual sensation. But the long-term results were disastrous to the empire he had sought to build, and his fort was reduced to a way station on the road to the mines.

The most poignant reversal of fortune was at Coloma. There, just as the sawmill was ready to begin cutting, just as the mechanical difficulties in its construction had been overcome, just as the months of toil and investment seemed about to bear fruit, Sutter and Marshall had to shut down. There was a market for lumber; indeed, in mid-May Brannan hauled three wagon loads from Sutter's Landing up to Coloma. But no wages could keep men lumbering when gold lay all about. The instrument of discovery thus fell a victim to the overpowering force that it had unloosed.

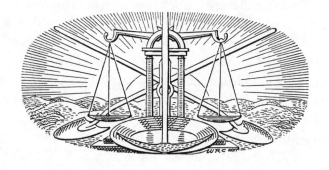

CHAPTER 2

The Forty-eighters

FAR FROM being gullible or credulous, the Californians in the early months of 1848 took to heart the old Spanish proverb, "no es oro todo que reluce"—"all is not gold that glitters." Even after admitting that it was gold that Marshall had found, they doubted that it would amount to much.

Thus the men at Coloma kept on building the mill. Thus Bigler's invited guests proved the gold fields and trudged back to the Sacramento. Nor did Sutter and his fellow "keepers of the secret" rouse an immediate throng of prospectors. When Bennett passed through San Francisco in mid-February, he exhibited his pouch to many persons, yet only Isaac Humphrey responded by going to Coloma.

Similarly, the California press was decorously cautious about so much as mentioning the gold discovery. Not until March 15, a month after Bennett's visit, did it acknowledge the news. Then, inconspicuously on its back page, the *Californian* reported: "GOLD MINE FOUND. In the newly made raceway of the sawmill recently erected by Captain Sutter on the American fork gold has been found in considerable quantities. One person brought thirty dollars' worth to New Helvetia, gathered there in a short time." Here was accurate reporting, but unfortunately the paper went on to editorialize the story and to rob it of its punch. "California no doubt is rich in mineral wealth," opined the editor; "great chances here for scientific capitalists." And then, as anticlimax and crowning inaccuracy: "Gold has been found in every part of the country." San Francisco's and California's other weekly, the *California Star*, followed suit on the eighteenth.

In his issue of the twenty-fifth, Editor E. C. Kemble of the *Star* noted that gold had become "an article of traffic" at New Helvetia. But what the country really needed, as he saw it, was more plowing and planting and some silver mines. A week later, in an article by V. J. Fourgeaud on "The Prospects of California," the *Star* mentioned gold, but bracketed the American River diggings with the placero "a few miles from the Ciudad de los Angeles" and dwelt primarily on agricultural and commercial resources.

On April 15 Kemble announced that he was going off to "ruralize among the rustics of the country for a few weeks." He headed for Sutter's Fort and Coloma, toured the diggings, which then were paying well, and was back by May 6 with this staccato report, commendably enthusiastic, but about the wrong things: "Great country, fine climate; visit this great valley, we would advise all who have not yet done so. See it now. Full-flowing streams, mighty timber, large crops, luxuriant clover, fragrant flowers, gold and silver."

Kemble's writings epitomize the April attitude. Most San Franciscans, for example, had heard reports of gold. Many had seen samples. But only a few struck out for the mountains, and they stole away in order to escape ridicule, or else, like Kemble, pretended to have some other reason for going. By all odds the most calculating of the excursionists was Elder Sam Brannan.

Less than two years a resident in the province, he had forged ahead rapidly. It helped, of course, that he had come at the head of two hundred Latter-day Saints out of New York by Cape Horn. He also claimed ecclesiastical jurisdiction over the Mormons of the battalion, including those who were at New Helvetia and the diggings. Yet, apart from his rank as a cleric, Brannan had qualities of energy and acumen that were making him one of California's leading businessmen. His interests included hotel, newspaper, and store at San Francisco, and the partnership with Smith at Sutter's Fort.

Through the latter connection came reports of American River gold that suggested a further business opportunity. Early in April, Brannan left to investigate. He was at Sutter's Fort on the seventh, then on to Coloma, which he chose as a likely site for a store. Before the middle of May—James Findla puts the date as May 12—he was back at San Francisco with a quinine bottle of the precious dust and a great zeal to spread the news. Flourishing his hat, holding high the glistening bottle, he promenaded the streets, bellowing, "Gold, gold, gold from the American River."

Brannan's motives may have been strictly ulterior. The more prospectors took to the hills, the larger would be the volume of business at his several stores. Some writers insinuate that his enthusiasm was entirely synthetic, that he was merely drumming up trade. On the other hand, he was a thoroughgoing extrovert, a man of easily aroused enthusiasms, and a lover of the limelight. It is conceivable that he was merely the compliant medium through which a superior power acted.

At any rate, his antics had electrifying effect. The town that had shrugged off the earlier intelligence suddenly went wild. All would rush at once to the diggings. Editor Kemble vainly tried to stem the tide. On May 20 he fulminated against the gold mines as "all sham, a supurb [*sic*] take-in as was ever got up to guzzle the gullible." But how could such phrases compete with "Gold, gold, gold from the American River"?

By sloop, lighter, and many a lesser craft the San Franciscans set sail for the diggings. On horseback and on foot they rounded the southern or northern arms of the bay and hurried toward the mines. By June 1 Larkin reported San Francisco half emptied, and by the middle of the month three-fourths of the 800 townspeople had gone, business was at a standstill, real estate slumped to give-away prices, the alcalde's office closed, the newspapers had to suspend, and San Francisco took on the appearance of a ghost town.

The contagion spread to ships in port. Sailors granted shore leave ran off to the diggings. Those held on board lowered boats and rowed away. The master of the *Flora* tried to forestall desertion by ordering his ship out to sea, but his sailors mutinied, overpowered the watch, and made their escape. The captain of a Hudson's Bay Company ship was more philosophical and perhaps wiser. When his crew deserted, he followed their example, leaving his wife and daughter as anchor watch. Thus early, San Francisco Bay began to accumulate its ghost fleet of abandoned ships. In '49 the fleet was augmented by a number of hulks that had barely made it to California and were not worth sailing away. In the beginning and in the majority, however, the ships left at anchor were good ships robbed of their crews by the irresistible pull of gold.

The wave of excitement rolled out to San Jose and Monterey, and even to Santa Barbara and Los Angeles. The spread was not instantaneous and the force of the wave was somewhat diminished by distance. Alcalde Walter Colton dates its arrival at Monterey as of May 29, and he records some skepticism persisting into June. Southern California did not respond until July or August. Before the end of summer, however, the whole province was contributing generously to the flow of man power to the diggings. The military was by no means exempt. The pittance of soldier's pay and the threat of court martial could not compete with what the gold fields offered. Desertions multiplied, and by mid-July Colonel-Governor Mason was left without even a cook. All of which fulfilled the prophecy which the expiring *Californian* had printed as news in its edition of May 29: "The whole country from San Francisco to Los Angeles, and from the seashore to the base of the Sierra Nevada, resounds to the sordid cry of *gold!* GOLD!! GOLD!!! while the field is left half planted, the house half built, and everything neglected but the manufacture of shovels and pickaxes. . : ."

A few perverse spirits resisted the mania. Colton describes one man at Monterey who insisted it was all a hoax. Don Luis Peralta, according to Hubert Howe Bancroft, advised his sons to stay by their farms and ranches, since God had obviously reserved the gold for the Americans. Most dramatic among the unbelievers unquestionably was a contingent of Latter-day Saints, many of them original participants in the mining along the American. They had planned, as soon as the passes over the Sierra should be open for travel, to depart for the Mormon headquarters at Salt Lake. The gold discovery tempted some to remain in the service of Mammon, but forty-six, including William Coory and his wife, rendezvoused at Pleasant Valley, not far from the site where Placerville soon would rise, and prepared for the difficult trek across mountains and desert. On July 3 they started the hard climb along the divide between the American and the Cosumnes. Their departure illustrates a strength of religion and of the authority of Brigham Young that is almost incredible.

In his diary, J. H. Carson records the more normal reaction. As he peeked into a returned miner's well-filled bag, he writes, "a frenzy seized my soul; unbidden my legs performed some entirely new movements of polka steps—I took several—houses were too small for me to stay in—; I was soon in the streets in search of necessary outfits; piles of gold rose up before me at every step; castles of marble, dazzling the eye with their rich appliances; thousands of slaves bowing to my beck and call; myriads of fair virgins contending for my love—were among the fancies of my fevered imagination. The Rothschilds, Girards, and Astors appeared to me but poor people; in short I had a very violent attack of the gold fever."

Out of San Francisco Bay on May 31 the schooner *Louisa* carried news of California's gold to Honolulu. Despite two pounds of the metal dispatched on this schooner, Hawaii preserved its equilibrium. The Honolulu *Friend* relegated the news to page six, and the *Polynesian* prosaically remarked that California merchants might now be able to settle accounts due. Later reports from the mainland led to a substantial exodus, beginning about the middle of July. Those who went were not merely waterfront loiterers, but included a number of prominent members of the island community.

From Hawaii, Hudson's Bay Company men relayed the news to the Northwest Coast, where its principal effect was on the American settlers in the Willamette Valley. A few of these Oregonians took ship for California. More elected pack train or covered wagon by land. By fall two-thirds of Oregon's able-bodied men had gone, among them Peter H. Burnett, who was to be California's first elected governor.

Mexico got the news fairly promptly, and toward the end of summer her northwestern provinces, Sonora in particular, were contributing a substantial flow of prospectors. The men of Sonora included many skilled miners. They preferred the southern diggings, and they left the name of their state on its principal town.

Still later in the year, smaller delegations of gold seekers arrived from Chile, another land rich in mining experience; from Australia, then suspect because of its history as a penal colony; and from China, soon to be recognized as a tremendous reservoir of able-bodied and capable laborers. These entrants from the farther reaches of the Pacific basin confirmed the cosmopolitan pattern already characteristic of California. The Atlantic world, which would supply most of the later Argonauts, did not get or accept the news in time to deliver any gold seekers in 1848. That season was a Pacific monopoly and through its early months a California monopoly.

Meanwhile, what of the diggings? The hesitant beginnings have already been charted: the discovery; the casual prospecting along the tailrace; a fortnight later, Bigler's move half a mile downstream and across the river; and after another month, the further spread of gold gathering to Mormon Bar. For at least six weeks the locale was limited to the south fork of the American, the only implement was the knife, and the work was almost exclusively that of gathering particles that erosion had exposed.

Gradually the tempo quickened. New recruits joined the labor force. New techniques were imported or invented. Prospectors ranged afield, making new strikes and starting local rushes, and before long the mining area had mushroomed out from Coloma and the American to stretch to the Feather on the north and to the Tuolumne on the south. By midsummer it embraced practically the entire area that was to be mined by a much larger army in 1849.

Fairly early in the process, technological evolution displayed itself in the form of simple devices for gold washing. According to one reminiscent account, the first such gadget was an Indian basket. Some miner—his name is lost to history—found that by washing a few quarts of gold-bearing gravel in a basin-shaped basket he could get rid of the dross and retain the gold. Suddenly there was a great demand for Indian baskets; the price, Bigler says, advanced to fifteen dollars apiece.

For lack of a basket, other miners, according to this same informant, resorted to a tin pan or a hollowed-out wooden bowl. Elaborating the story further, he credits a certain Alexander Stevens with transforming a bowl into the first rocker. His bowl was heavy and round of bottom, and he found it simpler to rock than to shake it. Also, by slanting it slightly he could make it self-emptying. In rudimentary form this was the subsequently popular rocker.

The more generally accepted account is that Isaac Humphrey, the Georgian, introduced panning when he arrived at Coloma. The gold pan, usually with its sides sloping toward a flat bottom, had a long and honorable history, reaching back not merely to the American Southeast, but across the Atlantic to the Old World. Humphrey unquestionably panned for gold, and the novices round about him were quick to copy. The wooden bowl, furthermore, sounds like a translation of the *batea*, standard equipment in Mexican prospecting. Indian baskets very probably entered the picture as substitutes for pan or bowl rather than as precursors of these implements.

Humphrey also is honored as the first to use a rocker. This machine was a short trough with a handle for rocking and jostling, a hopper at the upper end to sort out the larger rocks, and with cleats across the floor of the trough. The operator shoveled pay dirt into the hopper and bailed in water, which would flush toward the lower and open end of the trough. The same mechanical principle that settled gold to the bottom of the pan was counted on to trap it at the cleats. The rocker, or cradle, let much gold escape, but cradling was faster than panning and on that account was immediately popular. The rocker, like the pan, had been a standard device in gold mining long before the California field opened.

For the confusion of the record it should be admitted that John Bidwell names a certain Jean Baptiste Ruelle as the original cradler. The evidence in general points more in the direction of Humphrey. The place, pretty clearly, was on the south fork of the American; the time, most probably in April.

Still other devices came into early use. Bigler, who quit the diggings in the exodus of the Mormons, says that he and Brown tried bed-sheet mining. From a Sonoran they learned how to spread a sheet on sloping ground, apply a layer of pay dirt, and splash with water until only the gold remained. Sheets or blankets were also the equipment for dry washing, a dusty winnowing method by which the dirt was tossed in the air in the hope that wind would carry away what was lighter and worthless.

Once introduced, the pan and the rocker spread rapidly. Yet they did not completely displace the older means. A surprising number of forty-eighters preferred to keep on poking around with a knife. Throughout the gold rush, as a matter of fact, new techniques had an astonishingly hard time gaining ground against the less efficient but oftentimes simpler methods already in vogue. Nevertheless, criticism is unrealistic if it assumes that the gold seekers were concerned with improving total production. This was private enterprise. Each miner was trying to add to his own personal pile, and as quickly as possible.

Applied intelligence did result in enlargement of the mining area. John Bidwell, for example, visited Coloma in early April, soon after Humphrey and Ruelle had arrived on the scene. He noted not merely the methods they were using, but the kind of soil they were working, which reminded him strongly of gravels near his rancho at Chico, north of the Buttes. Returning home, he organized an expedition, prospected several locations along the Feather, and went to work with his Indian retainers at a spot soon named Bidwell's Bar. A visit to Coloma in April likewise convinced P. B. Reading that there was gold on his rancho in the upper Sacramento Valley. He and his Indians began mining along Clear Creek.

On the middle fork of the American a party of Mormons were the pioneer miners. Where the forks unite it was John Sinclair with fifty Indians. At Dry Diggings, later called Hangtown and still later Placerville, it was William Daylor. At Weber Creek it was a group outfitted by Charles M. Weber of the French Camp rancho and Stockton. John Potter and Samuel Neale led the way to Potter's Bar and Adamstown on the Feather. Jacob Leese and his associates from Sonoma opened up the valley of the Yuba. All these were old-timers, pre-discovery neighbors of Sutter, and Californians of six months' to ten years' standing. They dominated the scene in the early summer. And the region they stressed was that of the eastern tributaries of the Sacramento, a district later spoken of as the northern diggings.

Interspersed among them were, of course, an increasing number of prospectors from San Francisco, San Jose, and Monterey, and, as the season progressed, a few overland immigrants, who had set off without knowledge of the gold discovery, and a larger number of out-of-state Argonauts, especially from Oregon. Early-season descriptions remind that many who went to the gold fields did so as excursionists, with only enough equipment for camping briefly. In other words, many persons who responded to the call of gold were far from grasping its full import. They outfitted themselves for a short fling at gold mining, and many had to go back and prepare again for a longer stay.

Yet, despite primitive methods and inadequacy of supply, this was an epoch of superlative success. Wherever these prospectors went along the American, the Bear, the Yuba, and the Feather, they found wonderful caches of gold. The most likely spots, they soon learned, were nestled against the bedrock, where water flowed or had flowed and where a boulder or an irregularity in the rock formation made a natural trap. Occasionally, the deposit had been washed clear. More often, there was a surface covering that had to be removed. Two or three feet down was as far as they usually bothered to go in the northern diggings in 1848, though at Foster's Bar, late in the season, a gravelly clay twelve feet below the surface was being worked.

The success stories pile one on another. Bidwell found color in every pan along the Feather. Job Dye with a gang of Indians in seven weeks on this stream collected 273 pounds—at the going rate, something like $40,000. The Sonoma crew that led the way to the Yuba is credited with $75,000 in three months. At Parks Bar, named after a latecomer to the district who was conspicuous because accompanied by his wife, and at Long Bar, also on the Yuba, the miners are alleged to have made $60 a day. In a ravine north of Coloma a David Hudson cleared $20,000 in six weeks, and a lad named Davenport got seventy-seven ounces one day and ninety the next. Rich Dry Diggings, later Auburn, on the north fork of the American, boasted a $16,000 return on five cartloads of pay dirt, and day's earnings ranging from $800 to $15,000. At Hangtown Dry Diggings, William Daylor and Perry McCoon made $17,000 in one week, and claims were said to yield three ounces to five pounds a day.

Southward to the tributaries of the San Joaquin, Indian prospectors led the way. The two men chiefly responsible were Charles M. Weber of the French Camp rancho and José Jesús, a former neophyte at Mission San José. Weber got José to send twenty-five robust Indians to the diggings along Weber Creek. There he gave them a short course in the techniques of gold gathering and sent them home to the Stanislaus with a promise that any gold they brought to his store would be redeemed in goods. When they came back, it was with gold in quantity, and coarser than any yet seen. Coarse gold would be easier to salvage; more enticing, it was believed to point the way toward the source of all the gold. The news, therefore, touched off a rush to the southern diggings.

Weber's men deserted Weber Creek in favor of the new El Dorado. Sutter transferred his crew of Indians and Hawaiian Islanders to a new location that came to be called Sutter Creek. Many others affixed their names on the map of the southern diggings: John M. Murphy at Murphy's Camp, Dr. Henry P. Angel at Angel's Camp, William Knight at Knight's Ferry, Don Pedro Sansevain at Don Pedro Bar, and J. H. Carson and James Wood on Carson and Wood creeks. The name of Sonora on the Tuolumne commemorates its Mexican discoverers.

At least two new sites were spotted by trailing Indians back to their diggings. It was thus that J. H. Carson made his strike on Carson Creek. And Antonio Coronel has a similar story about how Benito Pérez shadowed other Indians to Cañada del Barro on the Stanislaus. Coronel is the authority for even more remarkable anecdotes. On his first day at Cañada del Barro he claims to have collected forty-five ounces. Near by, Dolores Sepúlveda found a twelve-ounce nugget. Another neighbor, Valdes by name, struck a pocket containing enough gold to fill a towel, and this claim, sold to Lorenzo Soto, yielded another fifty-two pounds in a week. Even more remarkable was the pocket unearthed by still another companion, a Sonoran known as Chino Tirador. In a short day, and using only a horn spoon, he scooped up a tray load of clean gold that was almost more than he could lift. Although not the largest to circulate, Coronel's are stories of remarkable successes. His account was not put in writing until three decades later, and may have grown in the telling, yet he was an honorable man, subsequently mayor of Los Angeles, and presumably a reliable informant. All agree that the southern diggings excelled in pockets and nuggets.

In the bustling excitement of gold hunting, most of the forty-eighters did not bother to record the scene. A few wrote down their recollections without undue delay, notably E. Gould Buffum by January 1, 1850, and J. H. Carson in 1852. Others such as Antonio Coronel and Agustín Janssens dedicated reminiscences when solicited by Bancroft in the 1870's. In some respects, however, the most satisfactory over-all descriptions of the gold fields of '48 are those in the official reports by Thomas O. Larkin, United States consul in Mexican California, and by R. B. Mason, colonel and military governor. Resting on personal inspections, they are careful, considered, responsible statements on the status of the diggings.

From San Francisco on June 1 Larkin addressed a preliminary report to the Secretary of State. For two or three weeks, he said, men had been bringing gold to town to exchange for supplies. All told, he estimated such receipts at $20,000. According to his informants, the placers along the American and the Feather, where two or three hundred men were at work with shovel, pan, basket, and bowl, were yielding from ten to fifty dollars a day per worker, and many persons still in the diggings had accumulated five hundred to a thousand dollars each. Out of his own observation he went on to describe the excitement at San Francisco, the sudden rise in wages, the booming market in shovels, and the depopulation of town and port.

On June 28 Larkin amplified this report on the basis of a trip to the mines on the American. In the vicinity of Mormon Bar he found fifty tents pitched. The one in which he put up sheltered eight miners, who had two cradles in operation and counted their gains at better than fifty dollars a day apiece. Another man panned eighty-two dollars in a single day. Larkin found no one who had mined steadily for as long as a month—a fact which he tried to explain in terms of the nature of the work and the inadequacy of supplies,—but he met a great many who had averaged an ounce a day. He estimated that more than a thousand, perhaps two thousand, men were at work. As yet, however, there was no way of telling how extensive or rich the gold deposit was. Every Mexican who had seen it said that there had never been such a placer in Mexico, and Larkin predicted that the ground would afford gold for many years, perhaps for a century.

Mason's report, although not written until August 17, was based on a July excursion, likewise to the American. He tarried at Sutter's Fort to help celebrate the Fourth. By that date Sutter had only two mechanics in his employ, a wagonmaker and a blacksmith, each at ten dollars a day. His merchant renters, however, were paying him handsome fees. At Mormon Diggings Mason saw the hillsides strewn with brush arbors and tents, and two hundred men busy with baskets and pans or preferably with cradles. Average earnings he set at twenty-five dollars a day. At Coloma he found several parties at work, "all of whom were doing very well." Marshall talked to him about the discovery, and some of the miners showed specimens weighing as much as four or five ounces. On Weber Creek he met Antonio María Suñol with a crew of thirty Indians, and Weber conducted him on a tour of ravines which had yielded $12,000 and $17,000. A miner of three weeks' experience showed him $2,000 worth of gold. Larkin had reported one-dollar shovels selling for ten, lumber at $500 a thousand, and pans worth twenty cents in the States commanding a half ounce to an ounce. Mason says he saw a miner pay Weber an ounce and a half for a fifty-cent box of seidlitz powders.

As senior officer in the province Mason pondered the question of how the government might derive a revenue from the mining of public lands. Tentatively he proposed a licensing system, or perhaps sales in twenty- or forty-acre plots. A problem even more acute was that of desertions. The Sonoma post, he admitted, had lost 26 men, San Francisco 24, and Monterey 24, and he was at a loss how to stop it. No officer, he pointed out, could live in California on his pay; and one soldier on three weeks' furlough had earned $1,500 in the mines, more than the government would pay him for five years' enlistment.

Mason estimated 4,000 men as the working force in the mines, half of them Indians, which tallies reasonably well with Larkin's figure. He put daily production at $30,000 to $50,000. He agreed with Larkin that California gold mining had just begun. In fact, he was less worried that the diggings would play out than that the metal would be found in such abundance as to lose its value.

Through August, September, and October the complement of gold seekers increased and spread out over more of the Mother Lode country. Gradually and belatedly a system of supply was developed to cater to their various needs. The process quite naturally was the reverse of what would have characterized a military maneuver: the army of gold seekers went ahead and after they had advanced there was a tackling of the problems of supply.

Storekeepers such as Smith and Brannan at Sutter's Fort, Brannan at Coloma, Weber at French Camp, William Knight at Knight's Ferry, and Syrec at Mokelumne Hill, spearheaded the advancing frontier of commerce. They operated in flimsy tents or crude shacks. Their stocks began with the necessities—flour, ship's biscuit, jerked meat, salt pork, whisky, picks, shovels, boots, shirts—and added whatever else could be had. Their goods were bought from what was available at San Francisco, transported by sloop or schooner to the Sacramento embarcadero, and then taken in hand by wagon freighters or packers for delivery in the diggings. The high charges of the freighters are what is usually noted—it cost Buffum $300 to have three barrels of flour, one of pork, and two hundred pounds of small stores hauled fifty miles. Possibly the more fundamental fact is that launches and other small craft began a regular plying of the waters of the bay and delta and that teamsters and packers entered the Sierra foothills in force. California farmers had no great supply of grain to offer, but near-by ranchos were drawn upon for beef, and other enterprisers shipped in flour and lumber from Oregon and general cargoes from Hawaii.

In retrospect it appears that the fantastically high prices that prevailed in the diggings were only partly due to shortages and transportation charges. To a great degree they sprang from the habits of reckless spending that became epidemic among the gold-happy Argonauts. When Buffum arrived at the diggings in November, 1848, he balked at paying sixteen dollars for a coarse striped shirt. A month later at Coloma, he and his partner nonchalantly breakfasted on a box of sardines, hard bread, butter, cheese, and two bottles of ale, for which the bill was forty-three dollars.

Buffum's narrative exemplifies other characteristics of the diggings toward the end of '48. At Foster's Bar on the Yuba he and his companions found the workable bars entirely covered by claims. At Weber Creek, which he mistakenly calls Weaver's, they started to erect a cabin, but instead decided to buy one for $500. In a week they earned twice that amount and were happy with earnings of an ounce a day until they heard of much better diggings on the middle fork of the American. Scrambling across the mountains to this new strike, Buffum found some pockets and crevices that were exceedingly rich. One yielded twenty-six ounces; another, five ounces in a single washing; still others, twelve and a half and sixteen and three-quarters ounces. But before they could exploit the spot further, the winter rains began. The stream rose four feet and threatened to overflow their camp site. Ruefully, they broke camp and returned to the cabin on Weber Creek.

Prospecting a small ravine in this neighborhood, Buffum took out $190 and had hopes of working out the whole ravine undisturbed. The next morning, however, he found himself "suddenly surrounded by twenty stout fellows, all equipped with their instruments of labour." They "helped" him turn the ravine upside down and carried off most of the gold that it yielded.

In the first half of January four feet of snow put a stop to all mining at his camp. Later in the winter Buffum was laid up with fever, swelling and bleeding gums, and swelling and blackening of the legs. He took it to be rheumatism and treated it accordingly, only to find that what he really had was scurvy. Finally he found relief in a diet of bean sprouts and potatoes. The congested diggings, the winter interruption, and the onslaught of sickness were thoroughly typical of mining experience as the season of 1848 came to a close.

Thanks to the individualism that was rampant and to the mercurial character of the forty-eighters the statistics for the year can be no more than approximate. Certain contemporaries, for example Alcalde Colton at Monterey, exaggerated the number of gold seekers who rushed to the diggings. Later writers tended to follow this error, though Bancroft strove to reduce the figures to something more reasonable: a few score in March, a few hundred in May, a few thousand in June and July, and no more than eight or ten thousand by the end of the year.

The amount of gold realized has also baffled the experts. The *Quarterly Review* set it at $45,000,000; an often-quoted modern calculation whittles it down to $245,301. Both appear to be wide of the mark. The officially recorded export for the year was $2,000,000, to which must be added the undeclared exports, the amounts that remained in the miners' pokes, and the substantial sums garnered by the freighters, the store-keepers, the saloonkeepers, and the gamblers. John S. Hittell, J. Ross Browne, and Bancroft prefer ten millions as the estimate of gold produced in 1848, and, all things considered, it seems a logical figure. An ounce a day is mentioned over and over as the average earning of the forty-eighters, to which must be added local instances of much larger earnings and occasional finds of much greater quantities. The whole tenor of the narratives of '48 is that gold was abundant, that the miners were picking it up by the handful.

Also, the forty-eighters appear to have been as happy and good-natured as they were prosperous. A pick or a shovel sufficed to mark a claim. Belongings left in camp were unmolested; even bottles or bags of gold were left unguarded in tent or cabin. The gold fields lay beyond the effective arm of the law, but in the "state of nature" that prevailed in '48 the roseate theories of Rousseau seemed to find fulfillment. Many explanations have been hazarded: that human nature is good; that these men were too prosperous to be criminal; that it was simpler to gather gold than to steal it; that the un-crowded diggings produced no friction; that all these men bristled with arms and thereby deterred crime; that they were Californians, neighbors, and therefore kindly disposed toward one another. Whatever the reasons, the forty-eighters enjoyed their picnic and set an example unfortunately not hewed to by the Argonauts of forty-nine and the 'fifties. In many other respects, however—in dress, claim law, mining method, and manner of camp life,—these first California gold seekers carried out a dress rehearsal of '49.

CHAPTER 3

Gold Fever

NEWS OF gold percolated eastward about as rapidly as distance and the timetables of travel would permit. Copies of the *Star* of April 1, 1848, with the feature article on "The Prospects of California," were hustled across the plains in the keeping of a man named Gray and reached Missouri about the first of August. A St. Joseph paper is cited by Ralph P. Bieber as printing excerpts, as did the St. Louis *Missouri Republican* on August 8, and after it many newspapers throughout the country, but none included mention of the gold on the American River. Similarly, a letter from Larkin, enclosing a clipping of the *Californian*'s first notice of the discovery, though it reached the Department of State on August 2, lay neglected in the files.

The New York *Herald*, therefore, had the honor of breaking the news. On August 19 it printed a letter dated San Francisco, April 1, and written by one of the

New York volunteers. He was, he said, "credibly informed"—presumably through reading the San Francisco papers—that thirty dollars' worth of gold had been found "in the bed of a stream of the Sacramento," and he predicted for California "a Peruvian harvest of the precious metals." Readers of the *Herald*, perhaps noticing the date line, paid this item scant attention.

On September 12 the New Orleans *Daily Picayune* ran a story based on a Mexico City interview with Lieutenant Edward F. Beale, who was en route to the national capital with dispatches from Commodore Jones and Consul Larkin. California prospectors, according to Beale, were making seventy dollars a day with no other implement than a spade. San Francisco and Monterey were depopulated. Prices had skyrocketed, but this mattered not where gold was so plentiful. The writer opined that California was "destined to become probably the richest and most important country on the continent." Two days later the Philadelphia *North American* carried a letter from Walter Colton with a glowing account of the simplicity of mining, the rush to the diggings, the inflated prices, and the spectacular yield. It set the number of miners at 5,000—too many for July 2; the area at 100 miles by 50—somewhat too large. But at the end it struck the proper note: "Your streams have minnows in them, and ours are paved with gold."

Like sentiments ran through many other California notes printed in eastern papers in the following weeks. A Colton letter in the New York *Journal of Commerce*, for example, said that prospectors were skirmishing through the diggings and picking up gold "just as 1,000

hogs, let loose in a forest, would root up ground-nuts."
"Some," it continued, "get eight or ten ounces a day,
and the least active one or two," while one man, with
sixty Indians working for him, had been making "a
dollar a minute."

The increasing frequency of such entries may indicate
that the editors were becoming convinced. There are
hints, also, that a few persons made ready to go to the
land of gold. The vast majority, however, looked upon
these wild tales from the Far West with a suspicious eye,
and, from time to time, editors advised their readers to
discount what was being said. Even Lieutenant Beale's
arrival with the dispatches from Larkin, reported in the
Washington *Daily Union* of September 17, did little to
dispel unbelief.

Yet the barrage of letters softened resistance, and so
did the specimens of gold that began to arrive. A St.
Louis paper certified receipt of one such sample on September 28. Another, remitted by Larkin, was assayed at
Washington on October 6 and pronounced 17 or 18
carats fine. Still another was displayed by Mormons at
Council Bluffs and, on November 22, was tested by a
chemist at St. Joseph, who declared it pure gold. All
this was not enough to induce gold fever, but the crisis
was at hand.

From Monterey at the end of August, Colonel Mason
had dispatched a courier to the Adjutant General at
Washington with official reports on his tour of the
diggings. The courier, Lieutenant Lucien Loeser, had to
use such means as offered, and he followed a roundabout
route. A schooner carried him to Payta in Peru, thence

by British steamer he proceeded to Panama, crossed the Isthmus, took passage to Jamaica, and thence to New Orleans, where he filed a telegraphic report to the War Department. Apparently he did not get to Washington until December 7.

Meanwhile, President Polk had received a duplicate copy of Mason's report. By its care and precision the document impressed him as reliable, as indeed it was. Furthermore, it seemed remarkably good news about a province just wrested from Mexico in a war that had been none too popular in the United States and for which he was generally held responsible. Mason referred to the gold as a hundredfold counterpoise for the cost of the war. Under the circumstances Polk needed no such prompting to hail it as a patent justification of the war. Here was news that should have feature billing in his report to Congress on December 5.

Translating Mason into Presidential language, Polk proclaimed: "It was known [!] that mines of the precious metals existed to a considerable extent in California at the time of its acquisition. Recent discoveries render it probable that these mines are more extensive and valuable than was anticipated. The accounts of the abundance of gold in that territory are of such an extraordinary character as would scarcely command belief were they not corroborated by the authentic reports of officers in the public service, who have visited the mineral district, and derived the facts which they detail from personal observation."

Then, as always, Presidential endorsement carried weight. On December 7 it was dramatically substantiated by the arrival of Lieutenant Loeser bearing a tea caddy crammed with 230 ounces, 15 pennyweights, 9 grains of virgin gold. Colonel Mason had dipped into the civil fund to purchase this concrete evidence of California's golden harvest. At the capital it was a sensation. It was placed on display at the War Office. The Secretary of War announced that some of the flakes and nuggets would be preserved, some would be coined, and the rest cast into medals "commemorative of the heroism and valor of our officers." The official assay confirmed Washington opinion that it was high-grade gold; it averaged 0.894 fine. For the nation, Loeser's tea caddy touched off the gold mania, very much as Brannan's quinine bottle had done for San Francisco. It appeared that visible gold was better than words, yea, than many fine words.

How the gold fever swept the Atlantic seaboard, jarred staid New England, coursed through the Ohio Valley, and up and down the Mississippi, how it spread to Canada, jumped the Atlantic to England, invaded the European continent, and stirred France and Germany, the Baltic peoples, and the Mediterranean—is an outstanding example of the contagion of ideas. True enough, not everyone in all these states and nations joined the rush to California. Some resisted the impulse. Some were too old to go, or too young; some too rich to be interested, others too poor to be able to make the move. Yet the gold fever was no respecter of rank or privilege or condition, and all accounts agree that the suddenly accepted news ignited a most remarkable excitement.

A more opportune time for propagating gold fever could hardly have been devised. The American people had just carried off a national election. They were on the rebound, too, from a war in which a major objective had been territorial expansion southwestward. The war, and just before it the Oregon Treaty, had made the nation transcontinental, to the great encouragement of the epic process of moving the frontier of settlement ever westward. Many veterans, just released from the services, found readjustment difficult and life at home humdrum. They were ripe for new adventures. So too were their immediate juniors who had not been eligible for uniformed campaigning in '46. The revolutions that swept Europe in 1848 and the repressions which followed added to the general restlessness of the times. The volume of migration to America increased sharply, and directly or indirectly many of these immigrants contributed to the rush to California.

A favorite topic of conversation, California gold also was the theme of sermons throughout the thirty states. The newspapers, even those that had flouted the earlier reports, jumped on the bandwagon with letters, news stories, and unbridled comment about the richness of the diggings. In the New York *Tribune*, for example, Horace Greeley hailed the advent of the Age of Gold and predicted that within four years the aggregate of this metal in circulation would be increased by a thousand million dollars. The papers also echoed statements such as a Mr. Atherton made in a "Gold Lecture" at the Tabernacle in New York. The reports, he said, were by no means exaggerated; "the supply of gold was absolutely inexhaustible; and . . . *one hundred thousand* persons could not exhaust it in *ten or twelve years.*" Miners earned "from an ounce to a thousand dollars per day." He had heard of one man making $12,000 in six days, and of another getting thirty-six pounds in a single day, and he saw no reason to doubt these reports. The largest nugget he had seen was a seven-pounder, 19¾ carats fine. The gold area was as large as the state of New York, and "one handful of the earth where gold is found yields," he said, "half an ounce of pure gold, on an average." Retailing such stories, the newspapermen helped to whip up an enthusiasm in which they often found themselves carried along.

Many editors and ministers "shelved their books and papers to join foremost in the throng" headed for California. Their companions, according to Bancroft's classic list, were: "the trader . . . , the toiling farmer, whose mortgage loomed above the growing family, the briefless lawyer, the starving student, the quack, the idler, the harlot, the gambler, the hen-pecked husband, the disgraced; with many earnest, enterprising, honest men and devoted women." The extremity of their optimism is illustrated by one of Stewart Edward White's characters, who said he knew that most of the talk was wildly exaggerated. He was too wise to believe all the stories he had heard, did not expect to find them true, and hoped only for a modest success. "In fact," said he, "if I don't pick up more than a hatful of gold a day I shall be perfectly satisfied."

How far the gold mania intruded on the customary routines of business is illustrated in a comment of the

New York *Tribune* on January 30, 1849: "A resident of New York coming back after a three months' absence, without having heard of the California fever, would be almost doubtful of the identity of the place. He would find it impossible to account for the remarkable activity in certain branches of trade which are not usually subject to sudden change. He would wonder at the word 'California,' seen everywhere in glaring letters, and at the columns of vessels advertised in the papers as about to sail for San Francisco. And finally, he would be puzzled at seeing a new class of men in the streets, in a peculiar costume—broad felt hats of a reddish brown hue, loose, rough coats reaching to the knee, and high boots. Even those who have watched the gradual progress of the excitement are astonished at its extent and intensity. The ordinary course of business seems for the time to be changed. The bakers of sea-bread keep their ovens hot day and night, turning out immense quantities of the article, without supplying the demand; the provision stores of all kinds are besieged by crowds of purchasers; manufacturers of India rubber goods, Gutta percha, oil cloth, etc. have very large demands to supply; the makers of rifles, pistols and bowie knives can scarcely furnish as many of these articles as are called for; and even the venders of quack medicines and all kinds of nostrums share a part of this windfall of business. . . . In fact, goods of every description sell just at present, and articles which have been long unsaleable, are packed up and sent away. . . . The business part of the city presents a spectacle of extraordinary activity. Boxes, barrels and bales crowd the sidewalks, and hundreds of drays convey to the wharves the freight now being stored away in seventy vessels for the Gold Region. . . ."

The urge to go to California, as the foregoing comment indicates, was exceeded only by the desire to sell something to the prospective gold seekers. Advertisements of the period bear testimony. In addition to the standard stores of provender and bottled goods, work clothes, tents, and camping equipment, they offered: "Slakin's celebrated six-barrelled Revolvers"; "California Goods . . . particularly recommended to gentlemen about starting for California; Colt's and Allen's Revolving Pistols, Allen's Self-cocking do . . . , Bowie Knives . . . , Belt Hatchets and Axes . . . , Jenk's Patent Carbines and Rifles"; "Money Belts, made exclusively for gold"; and "superior Wax Taper Matches, in round wooden boxes perfectly safe and portable."

The prudent miner was likewise offered his choice of an amazing variety of mining machinery, operated by cranks, gears, belts, and chains, steam-powered, water-powered, and hand-driven, patented and unpatented, machines for digging and dredging and washing, most of them contraptions of fearful complexity. A few may have proved their worth; the great majority were destined to be junked when brought into actual competition with the simpler technology of the diggings.

Even at the gentler level of letters the gold fever was responsible for production of a line of goods catering to the departing gold seeker. To recapture what such a person would know about California as he prepared for his journey in the winter of '48 or the spring of '49, we have to subtract all the concepts and publicity that have

48

since attached to Hollywood, the Rose Bowl, the chambers of commerce, the orange, and the tourist. California was then a remote and mythical land, known to some through the travel writings of Richard Henry Dana and John C. Frémont, known to a few others as a destination for covered-wagon emigrants, and more recently associated with American aims and operations in the war against Mexico. In that respect it had entered the national consciousness somewhat as the Philippines did in 1898 or the Solomons in the period of the Second World War. A diggers' handbook, with hints on how to get there and what to expect to find upon arrival, looked like a publication that would sell. The thing was attempted, not once or twice, but twenty-five or thirty times in 1848 and 1849.

At New York late in 1848 Joyce and Company brought out a thirty-page opus entitled *The Emigrant's Guide to the Gold Mines: Three Weeks in the Gold Mines, or Adventures with the Gold-Diggers of California, in August, 1848, together with Advice to Emigrants, with Full Instructions upon the Best Methods of Getting There, Living, Expenses, etc., etc., and a Complete Description of the Country, with a Map and Illustrations.* Fifteen pages present a letter signed by Henry I. Simpson, who claimed to be of the New York Volunteers, purporting to describe his experiences in the diggings. He says that he and Charley H——— and two others went to the mines late in August. They encountered Indian diggers; also Suñol and Company, Holmes, and Weber. Rich finds were being made all about; Simpson claims to have been in on a haul of

$50,000; the river beds, he says, were lined with gold "to the thickness of a hand"; but for some reason he did not tarry long or set himself seriously to mining. The next nine pages set forth the so-called description of California which the publishers had "caused . . . to be prepared by a gentleman recently familiar with the country." The last four pages outline six ways to go to California: the Isthmus, Cape Horn, the Rocky Mountains, Nicaragua, Acapulco, and Guadalajara. Obviously this was a pretty flimsy guide book. It was priced at twenty-five cents, or twelve and a half without the map, which Bancroft remarks cuttingly was the better buy.

Another one-bit guide of December vintage, this one in thirty-two pages, had the ambitious title, *California, from Its Discovery by the Spaniards to the Present Time, with a Brief Description of the Gold Region, Its Present Position, together with a Few Hints to Gold Hunters and a Guide to Those about to Visit That Country.* It announced itself to be "by a traveller," since identified as C. E. Kells. It leans heavily on S. Augustus Mitchell's accompaniment to his map of Texas, Oregon, and California (1846). Like the majority of the subsequent guides, its backbone is Mason's report, and this serves to date it in December.

J. Ely Sherwood, through George F. Nesbitt of New York, stationer and printer, offered a forty-page brochure, *California: Her Wealth and Resources,* etc. etc., etc. From government sources he extracted Larkin's and Mason's reports and all that Polk had said about the discovery. He gleaned stray letters from the local press, threw in a report by the director of the mint, an Aspinwall memorial for a railroad to the Pacific (at the Isthmus), some suggestions, also scissored from the newspapers, on how to get to California, and closed with "Song of the Gold Diggers," a parody on Hood's "Song of the Shirt."

Still another assemblage of extracted material, without mention of who wielded the scissors and without clear statement of place or date, bore the title *California Gold Regions* . . . It is usually assigned to Boston in December, 1848.

The best of the year's crop was clearly G. G. Foster's *The Gold Regions of California* . . . , published by Dewitt and Davenport of New York, eighty pages for a quarter. Foster used the standard passages from Mason, Larkin, and Colton. He had informative letters from Christopher Allyn and A. Ten Eyck. In addition, he had gone to the books of Greenhow, Darby, Wilkes, Cutts, and Frémont, and particularly to Thomas J. Farnham's *Travels*, John T. Hughes on Doniphan's expedition, and William H. Emory's *Notes*. This was commendable research. Yet, directions on how to go are confined to the last three pages, which mention Darien, the Cape of Good Hope (presumably in error for Cape Horn), the Panama steamers, the Vera Cruz–Acapulco route, and, under the Hughes-Emory influence, the overland path via Independence, Santa Fe, the Gila, and San Diego, which was far from the most direct overland route.

At New Haven, on January 1, 1849, one Sidney Roberts addressed himself *To Emigrants to the Gold Region: A Treatise, Showing the Best Way to California.*

... In the short compass of twelve pages, infused with the fervor of a religious tract, which it was, Roberts raised "serious objections to going by sea, doubling the Cape, or crossing the isthmus," and countered with nine arguments for using the Mormon trail, from Council Bluffs to Salt Lake: (1) oxen, horses, and wagons are available; (2) the climate is salubrious; (3) the Mormons have made a road and offer facilities for recruiting; (4) the Mormons are hospitable; (5) companies of Mormon travelers will assist in curbing Indian danger; (6) a stopover is feasible at Salt Lake; (7) wagons and animals will be useful in the diggings; (8) since California is highly productive, emigrants should take seeds; and (9) the eight preceding arguments are facts. He might have added that another Mormon, William Clayton, as long ago as the preceding March, had published at St. Louis *The Latter-day Saints Emigrants' Guide,* a detailed description of the trail as far as Salt Lake. Roberts' booklet was actually a prospectus for the Joint Stock Mutual Insurance Merchandizing Company.

Other 1849 publications include: *The Gold-Seeker's Manual* (London), by David T. Ansted, professor of geology at Kings College, an exposition of the theories and technicalities of gold mining, with some indebtedness to Frémont and Humboldt, as well as to Larkin and Mason; *California and Its Gold Regions* ... (New York), by Fayette Robinson, author of *Mexico and Her Military Chieftains;* and *Guide pratique* (Paris), par Jules Rossignon, professor of physical science at the university and director general of powders and saltpeters of the Republic of Guatemala. Knowing little or nothing remark that the Rio Grande was not navigable and that the array of place names was intended to suggest the Mexican caravan route north of the Grand Canyon, a little-used route most often designated the Old Spanish Trail.

For 1849 add *Das Goldland Kalifornien* (Leipzig); *Route from the Gulf of Mexico and the Lower Mississippi Valley to California* . . . (New York), by Robert Creuzbaur; *The Emigrant's Guide to New Mexico, California, and Oregon* (New York), by mapmaker J. Disturnell; *California and her Gold Regions* (Philadelphia), by A. J. H. Duganne; *Nach Kaliforniens Gold u. Quecksilber-District* (Leipzig), by Friedrich Gerstäcker; *Accompaniment to the Map of the Emigrant Road from Independence, Mo.* (New York), by T. H. Jefferson; *Emigrants' Guide to the Gold Mines of Upper California* (Chicago), by E. S. Seymour; *Notes of Travel in California* (New York), by John C. Frémont and William H. Emory; *Guide to the Gold Regions* (London), by William Thurston; *Manuel des émigrants de Californie* (Paris), by Miette de Villars; and *The Digger's Handbook* (Sydney), by D——— L———, in one surviving copy elaborated to "Damned Liar."

Among all these efforts at guidebook writing, the palm clearly goes to Joseph E. Ware of St. Louis. He had never been to California and was a newspaperman rather than a plainsman. Consequently, the expertness that he had to offer was that of the lamp and the study rather than of the trail itself. By judicious reading, by sifting and reorganizing, and by generous lifting from better-informed writings, he fashioned a compact description of the most favored route to the diggings, the main highway from Missouri to the Platte, South Pass, the Humboldt, and the Sierra Nevada.

For instructions on outfitting wagon trains he drew on Lansford W. Hastings; for the trail from Missouri to Fort Laramie he depended on Edwin Bryant and Frémont; from Laramie to Bear Valley, Clayton was his mainstay; along the Humboldt he followed Bryant; and over the Sierra he relied mostly on Frémont. These were travelers all. By judiciously compounding their information and adding thereto a large map based on Frémont, Ware produced the most informative of all the guidebooks issued at the beginning of the gold rush. Setting out to follow his own guide to the diggings, he was stricken by cholera on the first leg of the journey, was abandoned by his companions, and perished miserably.

In addition to the guidebooks, hack-written or scissored, and hastily or conscientiously prepared, publishers cast about for other means of capitalizing on the prevalent gold fever. Some had older titles that they could reprint—Bryant's *What I Saw in California,* for example, was in its seventh printing before the year was over. Others snapped up California narratives when they were offered, such as Theodore T. Johnson's *Sights in the Gold Region and Scenes by the Way . . .* (New York, 1849). Still others, as was the custom then, looked for foreign titles that could be pirated.

Tin Pan Alley, as Owen Coy has pointed out, fell in step with "The Gold Digger's Waltz," "The Golden

Drag Waltz," "The San Francisco Waltz," and "The Sacramento Gallop." A New York publisher issued a work called *Outline History of an Expedition to California,* which proved to be a cartoon narrative by "X. O. X." of the "Get All You Can Mining Association." At Cincinnati, meanwhile, under the staid title *The Journey to the Gold Digging Region,* J. A. and D. F. Read pictured the experiences of the raucously heroic Jeremiah Saddlebags, while in London cartoonist A. H. Forrester illustrated the exploits of one "Mivins" in *A Goodnatured Hint about California.*

At London also appeared *Four Months among the Gold-Finders in Alta California, Being the Diary of an Expedition from San Francisco to the Gold Districts* by J. *Tyrwhitt Brooks, M.D.* "The book is well written," says Bancroft, "and the author's observations are such as command respect." Too true. Immediately popular, it was promptly reissued in New York, and, in translation, at Amsterdam, Hamburg, and Paris. Historians have reckoned it one of the best descriptions of the northern diggings in '48 and have relied on it heavily. In 1893, however, in a book entitled *Glances Back Through Seventy Years,* Henry Vizetelly disclosed that J. Tyrwhitt Brooks was a fabrication and his experiences synthetic if not fictional. On the basis of notices from California, two London journalists, Vizetelly and David Bogue, had gotten into the fevered spirit of the times and perpetuated this amiable fraud.

CHAPTER 4

By Panama

How to get to California? For those whom the gold fever claimed, that was the question. Argonauts in England and Europe would have to go halfway round the world to get to the land of gold. Those in the States, in the winter of '48–'49, faced as difficult a problem.

Geography and history, nevertheless, offered several answers. Beginning in the 1790's, Boston fur ships, China-bound, had rounded Cape Horn or threaded the passage of the Strait of Magellan on a long sea route that passed through California waters. Since the 'twenties, whalers and hide traders and ships of the navy had plied this same course. The Atlantic seaboard—New England and New York, in particular—thus had equipment and know-how for sailings to California. The catch was that on this track of 17,000 or 18,000 miles voyages ran five or six or eight months. What assurance was there that the California gold would last that long?

Another option was to go overland. Jedediah Smith had blazed such a trail in 1826. Other intrepid beaver trappers followed and in the 'forties their paths were widened by pioneer settlers in covered wagons, by government agents such as Frémont, and by the marching soldiers of the Army of the West. Here also was a catch. The overland trails were not reckoned open for travel until April or May, which would not land one in the diggings until August or September. Again rose the question, would all the gold be gone?

The third main pathway of the gold rush—the broken-voyage route, with a land crossing at Panama, Nicaragua, or Mexico—had not been so popular before 1848. Yet the two official dispatch bearers had traveled this way, Beale by Mexico and Loeser by Panama. Some Argonauts may also have remembered that, on the eve of the war, when President Polk wanted an urgent message delivered to California, courier Archibald Gillespie went by Vera Cruz, Mexico City, Mazatlán, and Hawaii.

Furthermore, the Panama route had two great advantages over its competitors. It was an all-year route. Over it one could start for California immediately and hope to arrive in a matter of weeks, in plenty of time to get to the mines as the season of '49 opened. And, best of all, the Panama route boasted public transportation; one could engage passage on the steamers of the United States Mail Steamship Company and the Pacific Mail.

The inspiration and the initiation of this service antedated the gold rush. Commercial men, notably William Henry Aspinwall of New York, had urged it for the sake of trade with Latin America and the Pacific Coast.

Improved mail service to sparsely settled California and Oregon was a talking point, though not of much weight with members of Congress who saw no constituents west of the Missouri. The real persuasion came from the navy, which faced a changeover from sail and saw in a line of merchant steamers a chance to give its officers some experience with the new pattern of seafaring. This was the argument that got a federal subsidy in 1848 for the carriers on the Atlantic and Pacific runs.

For the Pacific three 1,000-ton paddlewheel steamers were built, the *California, Panama,* and *Oregon.* Larger vessels, the *Ohio* and *Georgia,* were on order for the Atlantic, but permission was gained to start operations with a smaller ship, the *Falcon.* On October 6, 1848, the *California* left New York to take up her duties in the Pacific. She was heavily laden with supplies, spare parts, and 520 tons of coal. By way of Rio, the Strait of Magellan, Valparaiso, Callao, and Payta, she headed for Panama. No one could be sure just when she would arrive, but with the general idea of connecting with her at the Isthmus the *Falcon* sailed from New York on December 1.

Some ninety-five passengers were aboard—not a real case of gold fever in the lot. But within a few days Polk and Loeser were to work their magic, and by December 11, when the bark *John Benson* sailed for the Isthmus, a number of her sixty passengers were confessed gold seekers. At New Orleans, too, in the following week, the *Falcon* encountered mounting excitement. She took aboard some routine passengers, among them General Persifer F. Smith, who was to relieve

Mason in the California command, but gold-minded travelers competed for the remaining places and ran the list to 193. Other ships took the southward track and before the end of January had discharged more than seven hundred persons at the Isthmus, many with through tickets, and all hoping to be accommodated.

Reminiscences of these voyages dwell on seasickness, which exacted a heavy toll; on the makeshift accommodations, for arrangements were as yet by no means perfected; on the good-natured camaraderie of the travelers; and on their determined efforts with flannel shirts, boots, revolvers, and knives, to dress and act the part of Californians from the very outset. Elisha Crosby recalls how they rushed to the rail and unlimbered their revolvers whenever a dolphin was sighted. He also tells of the panic on his ship, the *Isthmus*, when fire broke out in the hold. There was enough powder, he thought, in every passenger's baggage to blow up the ship.

The course to the Isthmus was not always the same, but the usual stops were Havana and Kingston. In Cuba many of the travelers had their first glimpse of semitropical vegetation and their first savor of the customs and mores that Spain had implanted in America. At Kingston they were treated to the spectacle of graceful, sturdy Negresses filing up and down the gangplank, sixty-pound tubs balanced on their heads, coaling the ship. The more thoughtful travelers observed with interest the actuality of a free Negro society. For here the blacks were in the majority and, in contrast to the United States, where slavery still prevailed, they had been free since the 'thirties. There were other diversions. Crosby and his friends paid a state call on General-President-Dictator Santa Anna, then enjoying one of his periodic exiles from Mexico. For the Panama-bound forty-niners, however, these exotic experiences were hardly worth the delay.

Arrived at Chagres, the travelers were unceremoniously landed—dumped ashore, some of them said. They took note of the decayed fortress of San Lorenzo, unrepaired since Henry Morgan had despoiled it. The town itself was merely a collection of hovels; muddy, hot, odorous, and hard pressed by the tropical jungle. Of its neighbor Colón, temporarily yclept Aspinwall after the steamship magnate, one Argonaut observed that its particular excellence was in the size and number of its carrion birds. Chagres shared their attention.

The California-bound pilgrims tarried not, but immediately opened negotiation for transportation up the Chagres River. The natives, a motley array often defying classification as Indian, Negro, or Spanish, had dugout canoes, locally called bongos, which they would paddle, pole, and pull up to Gorgona or, properly encouraged, all the way to Cruces. Initially the charges were reasonable; after a few months the boatmen found that there was a veritable gold mine in these passing travelers. The latter, as Bancroft saw them in 1852, were rigged out "in India rubber and oilcloth suits . . . , armed with pistols, guns, knives, umbrellas, and life-preservers, mild-mannered as belted brigands . . . , equipped with drinking-cups, pots, kettles, forks, spoons, and air-beds, with stores of meat, bread, brandy, and pills." Four to ten to a bongo they voyaged along through the tropical rain forest, bright with strange flowers and alive with monkeys and brilliant-plumed birds. The speed was about a mile an hour, which meant two days' travel on the river.

At the head of navigation the bargaining scene was reënacted, this time for riding animals and pack mules, or for native porters, who accepted loads of as much as 250 pounds. Under the canopy of translucent green through which the sun was seldom seen, the trail wound tortuous, rough, narrow, and muddy. It was the ancient highway over which much of the treasure of Peru had been transported to the Spanish silver fleets. In places the old cobblestone surface was still intact; elsewhere it had fallen into sad disrepair, with the trail plunging into gullies worn and eroded as much as thirty feet below the original level. Highwaymen occasionally waylaid travelers on this route. A more common complaint was that carriers, paid in advance, absconded with the baggage. The greatest danger, of course, was from disease. Yet, for the majority, the Isthmian crossing was not a superhuman feat.

Globe trotter Bayard Taylor summed up his journey across the Isthmus as "decidedly more novel, grotesque and adventurous than any trip of similar length in the world." "It was rough enough," he said, "but had nothing that I could exactly call hardship, so much was the fatigue balanced by the enjoyment of unsurpassed scenery and a continual sensation of novelty." When he insisted that there was nothing, even at the worst season, "to deter any one from the journey," he was contradicting the dolorous complaints of many of his fellow travelers, yet the evidence seems to be that he was substantially correct.

At length the trail debouched upon the coastal plain, and glimpses of tiled roofs, bell towers, and the blue waters of the Pacific told the weary travelers that they were approaching Panama. Journey's end quickened the steps of man and beast, and with keen anticipation the gold seekers advanced on the venerable mistress of the Isthmian crossing.

When viewed from middle distance, the city was impressive. Dramatically situated on a rocky promontory jutting out into the placid bay, girt by massive fortifications, and with most of its buildings two stories or more in height, it loomed large. On closer inspection the forty-niners found that the fortifications and many of the buildings were in ruins, that others were abandoned, that the buildings were an odd assortment of stone, adobe, and wood, that vines and creepers were making inroads on many structures, including the cathedral, and that the sanitary arrangements were most casual. Its commercial importance long since decimated, Panama was but a shell of its former grandeur.

The passengers from the *Falcon* and the *John Benson* were less concerned with Panama's esthetic values than with scanning the roadstead for the *California*. Not seeing her, they descended on the office of Zachrisson and Nelson, agents of the Pacific Mail, to find out what the company was doing toward forwarding them to San Francisco. The company, it became clear, was merely waiting for its ship to come in; meanwhile, selling all the tickets it could in New York and New Orleans.

The impatient Argonauts sought out accommodations in Panama or camped at the edge of the city. They did the sights in the cathedral, at the ancient gun emplacements, along the balcony-shaded streets, and among the ruins of the original city of Panama, six miles away. They were intrigued by Panama's variegated architecture and polychrome inhabitants. Yet, in their anxiety to get on to California, these amusements palled. Probably none of these first forty-niners was in a mood to use Bayard Taylor's later phrase, "I saw less of Panama than I could have wished."

A few of the stranded emigrants seized the opportunity to go into business and, by enterprising in liquors, lotteries, games of chance, or merchandise, profited while they waited. Collis P. Huntington, for example, is said to have increased his capital from $1,200 to $4,000. To the majority the stopover at Panama was a drain on their resources that they could ill afford. Worse yet, it was tempting the fates which dispensed disease.

Foreign to the tropics, the forty-niners were ill prepared to cope with its peculiar problems of warding off illness. Furthermore, germs not yet having been invented, the medical profession did not issue impeccable advice. The prudent traveler was cautioned to avoid the sun, to eschew fruits even when ripe, to eat oranges only in moderation, not to touch oysters, to wear flannel next to the skin by day and by night, and above all to avoid the night air. "Bear the heat, bear the mosquitoes," ran the instructions, "do anything rather than expose yourself to the night air, which is the source of every illness in that climate." A morning draught of two to four grams of sulphate of quinine in a glass of wine was also recommended.

Except for the advice against drinking water, which some of the forty-niners are said to have taken to heart for the rest of their lives, these reckless men committed many indiscretions. By intemperate exertion, eating, and drinking, they laid themselves open to "Panama fever" and assorted ailments, including some, like cholera, which they themselves carried to the Isthmus. Anecdotes of distress and tragedy are numerous and graphic. Taylor tells of seeing one cholera victim stretched out by the trail, attended by a friend in mortal terror of contracting the disease himself. He describes another case, a lank Mississippian, a stranger to all, who suffered out the cholera in the saddle rather than risk stopping anywhere short of Panama. For want of any proper remedy, he downed a bottle of claret, then rode on, sprawled over his horse's neck and writhing in an agony of pain. Although statistics on the disease rate and the death rate are not available, the reputation of the Isthmus was unquestionably bad.

From January 17, when the *California* arrived, until a fortnight later when she was ready to sail, the burning question was who would get aboard. By sailing date Panama swarmed with more than 700 prospective passengers. The ship's rated capacity did not exceed 250, and she had aboard some 69 Peruvians who had engaged passage at Callao.

In the emergency, first priority went to holders of through tickets. The other Americans on hand claimed precedence over the Peruvians, which General and Governor-to-be Smith attempted to bolster by proclaiming that none but American citizens might enter upon the (gold-bearing) public lands of the United States. Refusing to be intimidated, the Peruvians held their places and would not even risk setting foot on shore. At length a compromise was worked out whereby they vacated the staterooms and accepted improvised quarters. By a combination of priority, lottery, bribery, trickery, and ticket scalping, prefaced by mass meetings and committees of protest, the Americans on shore were screened and about 300 lucky persons were selected. Some confess to paying $1,000 for steerage passage. High tides and shelving beach forced all ships to anchor well out from Panama. The loading scene, therefore, was of passengers gingerly mounting the backs of brawny porters, who waded, usually without mishap, to waiting small boats, which lightered passengers and baggage to the ship. When the *California* sailed, on January 31, she was jampacked with an estimated 365 passengers, plus the crew of 36.

The *California* stopped at Acapulco, another entrepot much shrunken since the palmier days of Spanish Pacific commerce. On then to San Blas and Mazatlán, San Diego and Monterey. Although the forty-niners showed little awareness of the fact, their voyage was recapitulating the heroic Spanish advance up this coast from Balboa and Cortés in the early sixteenth century to Serra and Lasuén at the close of the eighteenth. Most of the way they were in sight of land, green and mountainous in Central America and Mexico, stark and barren in Lower California, and with occasional glimpses of missions and whitewashed adobes in Upper California.

Four weeks to a day out of Panama, the *California* churned through the Golden Gate, accepted salutes from the ships of war that were in port, exchanged cheers with the jubilant San Franciscans on wharf and hilltop, and came to anchor. Assured that the gold supply was not exhausted, the passengers hurried ashore. Officers and crew followed, or preceded, and soon Captain Cleveland Forbes found no one left except one of the engine-room boys. This wholesale desertion precluded an immediate return to Panama, but with the coal supply exhausted and the collier from England not yet arrived the *California* could not have sailed even if Forbes had been able to hold the crew.

Meanwhile, at Panama, the less fortunate emigrants were straining at the leash. The *Panama* was supposed to follow the *California* into service on the West Coast, but engine trouble forced her back to New York, and the *Oregon* thus was actually the second to take up duty. By February 23, when she reached Panama, there were 1,200 passengers on hand, of whom she could take only 250. The *Panama*, having rounded South America with 81 gold seekers from New York, on May 18 picked up 209 out of 2,000 clamoring for passage from the Isthmus. Even by May and June, when the *Oregon* and the *California* were available for second runs, the regular steamers could by no means keep up with the traffic.

Company and passengers, therefore, resorted to such other means as were available. The company converted the collier *Philadelphia* to passenger service. The brig *Belfast* sailed with 76 passengers in February; the fare, $100. The whaler *Equator* discharged her oil and accepted passengers at $150. In April another whaler, the *Niantic*, after more drastic refitting, sailed with 250 or 300 passengers at $150. Other departures included the *Alexander von Humboldt* with 300, the *Phoenix* with 60, and the *Two Friends* with 164. The route usually followed was out to about the longitude of the Hawaiian Islands, then north and in. The time expectancy was anywhere from three to five months, or not much less than that on the voyage around Cape Horn.

Aside from the inconveniences of travel on collier or whaler, many of the ships pressed into service proved unseaworthy. The small schooner *Dolphin*, for example, was abandoned by one set of passengers at Mazatlán. Refitted by another group, she was sailed across to Lower California, where several passengers elected to proceed on foot. The others sailed on as far as San Diego, there deciding not to press their luck any further.

Other accounts document the land route up the California peninsula, occasionally the resort of disappointed seafarers. W. C. S. Smith, in later years a newspaperman at Napa, was one such traveler. Distrusting the quondam whaler on which he was a passenger, he landed at San José del Cabo at the tip of the peninsula and, with three companions, took two months to make the trip to San Diego. J. W. Venable, later a state assemblyman, likewise hit the trail in Lower California. He claims to have beaten his ship to San Francisco, a feat altogether possible. There is mention also of forty-niners who started from Panama in dugout canoes; no record, however, that any of these craft completed the voyage to California.

Certainly the difficulty of getting away from disease-ridden Panama was the chief drawback of the isthmian route. Cartoonist "X. O. X." in his comic-strip gold-rush narrative published in 1849, exaggerates it only slightly. After following the experiences of two characters on the way to El Dorado and in the diggings, he starts them home again, one rich and happy, the other with no gold and despondent. When they get to Panama, there stands one of their original companions still waiting for passage to California.

In July, 1849, the Pacific Mail took advantage of the heavy demand to increase its rates to $300 cabin and $150 steerage. It also sought additional equipment, chartering the British steamer *Unicorn* and paying $200,000 for the 1,275-ton *Tennessee,* which had been built to ply between New York and Savannah. On her first trip, in March, 1850, she set a record with 551 passengers. Then came the *Carolina,* the *Columbia,* and the *Fremont,* and late in 1851 the *Golden Gate,* a 2,067-ton beauty, especially designed for the California run and affectionately hailed in the San Francisco papers as the "steam clipper." From twelve sailings achieved in 1849, the company advanced to twelve in the first half of 1850 and with fortnightly regularity.

With these improvements the Panama route began to live up to the expectations of rapid passage. Travelers who could pay the price could count with fair certainty on getting through in six to eight weeks. Complaints were still registered that the steamers on the Atlantic run were dirty and the service poor, that the isthmian boatmen and muleteers were not to be trusted, and that the connecting steamers were not always punctual. But in comparison with all other means of getting to and from California the Panama route had a substantial edge. It became the choice of discriminating travelers. Senators, business tycoons, army officers, and gamblers gave it their patronage and made it the white-collar route to El Dorado.

When use of the Panama route began, steamers were hardly past their infancy and much about them was still experimental. Particularly on a track as distant and as undeveloped as that along the Pacific Coast, serious difficulties were to be expected. Coaling depots, machine shops, repair stations, and supply stations would have to be set up at several places along the line and most of the materials needed would have to come by the same route that delivered the steamers, that is, all the way around South America. The sudden rush of passengers meant much more revenue than had been counted on; but it also complicated the problems of establishing the line and necessitated much improving.

From the outset, the Panama route was big business; and it presented many of the usual concomitants of big business—attempts at monopoly, competition, attempts to stifle competition, lobbying, and various maneuvers to control stock issues and directorates. Through the mail contracts two monopolies were set up, one on the Atlantic, one in the Pacific. But competition was soon attracted; in fact, the first "opposition" steamer sailed from New York on December 23, 1848. Others followed in the Pacific as well as in the Atlantic, posing a threat which the Pacific Mail attempted to answer by negotiations that resulted in its gaining control of four of the five rival steamers.

With two of these ships, the Pacific Mail decided to go after the passenger traffic on the Atlantic side, thereby challenging its mail-carrying partner. The latter countered by putting passenger steamers on the Pacific run. By the end of 1851, however, the two major companies had decided to put an end to such foolishness. They entered into an agreement in restraint of competition, sold each other their off-side ships, and settled down to operate with a one-ocean fleet each.

Far from being the end of competition, this was just the beginning. Edward Mills; Cornelius Vanderbilt; the Accessory Transit Company; Charles Morgan; Davis, Brooks, and Company; J. Howard and Son; George Law; the People's Line; the Atlantic and Pacific Ship Canal Company; the People's California Steamship Company; the Merchants and Miners Line; Brown Brothers; the Central American Transit Company; and the North American Transit Company—these are some of the rivals who contended for the business in the 'fifties and 'sixties, or seriously threatened to do so. Most obviously this strenuous competition led to wild fluctuation in the rates charged. Rates shot down or up as competition flourished, was crushed, or was subordinated by collusion among the carriers.

Unbridled competition put too many ships into service —more than were needed for optimum efficiency. The unpredictable rates were also a drawback. On the other hand, rivalry prompted improvements, including the opening of an alternative route through Nicaragua.

There the landmass is considerably wider than at Panama, but a waterway through river and lake penetrates to within seventeen miles of the Pacific, a better accommodation than that afforded by the Chagres River. Further, the over-all distance from New York to San Francisco would be shortened by some 375 miles, that from New Orleans by 525. Through the genius and the drive of Cornelius Vanderbilt this short line to California began to operate in 1851. It proved a trifle faster than the Panama route, but there was much complaint about incivilities, the inadequacy of the river boats, and inferiority of equipment, especially on the Pacific. In the late 'fifties, revolution and filibustering blighted the route, yet for a time it was a significant link.

Another and perhaps more notable improvement in the interoceanic transit was the Panama Railroad. Incorporated in New York, and with a directorate interlocked with that of the Pacific Mail, the railroad company got a concession from New Granada in 1849 and immediately started survey and construction. To lay track on the spongy soil of Manzanilla Island, to cross the swamp toward Gatún, to bridge the Chagres where it had been known to rise forty feet in a single night, to counteract slides in the rough terrain south of Gorgona, to design docks at Panama, to hold a labor force in defiance of the gold excitement, and above all to withstand the ravages of tropical disease—these were formidable obstacles. To do the work the company tried out crews of Panamanians, Americans, Cartagenans, Frenchmen, Irishmen, Chinese coolies, and Jamaican Negroes, in the end depending chiefly on natives of the Isthmus.

Although there is a story, much bruited about, that this railroad cost "a life for every tie," John Kemble unceremoniously demolishes it by pointing out that, since there were 99,264 ties, to meet such a toll every worker would have had to die six deaths.

While still under construction, the road grossed more than a million dollars. Once completed, it began to coin money. Charging $25 for the 47-mile ride, and with no fear that its monopoly would be broken, it enjoyed a remarkable bonanza from 1855 until 1869, when travelers could choose the transcontinental railroad.

Unmindful of the expense, or perhaps reflecting that the bongo-muleback trip used to cost more, Panama travelers seem to have luxuriated in this train ride, wishing, in fact, that the cars went all the way to San Francisco. As one reminisced: "Seated by an open window, the face fanned by the motion of the train, and armed with a pitcher or pail of iced water, the ride is indeed charming."

Fortunately the travelers by Panama were a lighthearted crew. Otherwise, even after the route was completely mechanized, their pleasure would have been dimmed by thoughts of the imminence of disaster, chiefly at sea. Thus the *San Francisco*, in 1853, with 750 persons aboard was caught in a severe storm two days out of New York. Her engines failed, she fell into the trough of the sea, and half her promenade deck was swept away. A week and ten days later, passing ships took off some of the passengers; the rest and the crew abandoned ship soon afterward; only 550 survived. On the *Philadelphia*, headed for Aspinwall in 1852, cholera claimed a third of the 155 passengers. In 1862 the *Ariel*, southbound from New York, was intercepted by the Confederate raider *Alabama*. The ship money was confiscated; 120 United States Marines aboard were disarmed and paroled; Captain Raphael Semmes debated burning his prize, but ended by releasing her on bond payable after recognition of the Confederacy. Three years later, the *Golden Rule* was lost on Roncador Reef in the Caribbean, though all on board were saved. The worst tragedy in the Atlantic befell the *Central America*, northbound in 1857. Caught in a heavy gale, she suffered engine failure, shipped water, and foundered, carrying with her eight millions in treasure and 423 persons.

On the Pacific, the *Union* went aground 200 miles south of San Diego on July 5, 1851. The trouble apparently was too much celebrating of the Fourth, which left the helmsman too drunk to handle the wheel. Vanderbilt lost two steamers in 1852, followed by two more in 1853, the *Independence*, with 125 lives lost, and the *S.S. Lewis*, which miscalculated the Golden Gate. The *Tennessee* similarly missed the entrance to San Francisco Bay, and the *Winfield Scott*, also fog-bound, was lost on Anacapa Island. At Point Arguello, in 1854, the captain of the *Yankee Blade* "cut the corner" and stranded his ship on a reef. Some thirty lives were lost, partly from an orgy of drinking and rioting while the captain was ashore investigating means of landing the passengers. In 1862 the *Golden Gate* caught fire off Manzanillo and 223 were lost before she could be beached.

Often, the mishaps were regarded as routine—owing to circumstances beyond control, or reflecting merely the normal hazard of operating wooden ships in storm-swept seas and along imperfectly charted paths. Others were attributed to lack of precaution, to foolhardiness, or to immoderate haste. Perhaps these disasters were no more than should have been expected. To modern eyes, however, they somewhat tarnish the aura that surrounds this route—the quick way for the forty-niners, the preferred way throughout the next two decades, the line over which practically all the gold shipments went, the route favored by the returning Californians, through most of the period the basic mail line, and, indeed, the essential transportation link attaching California to the States. The early Californians were a sturdier lot. They did not let these occasional mishaps shake their admiration for the Panama route.

CHAPTER 5

Rounding the Horn

OF THE main traveled roads to California in '49 the second in order of adoption was the one around South America via the Strait of Magellan or Cape Horn. It was a long way around, 17,000 or 18,000 nautical miles, and four to eight months in the probable elapsed time.

To the unseaworthy such a voyage was naturally forbidding. A mere landlubber's misgivings would also be heightened by recollection that Magellan and Drake got only a ship apiece through the Strait and that Dana and others who had rounded "Cape Stiff" gave terrifying descriptions of contrary gales, mountainous seas, and frigid cold. There exists, however, and did in '49, another breed of men, who had an experienced respect for the perils of the deep but were confident in their ability to cope with its hazards. Given choice of a land trek or an ocean voyage, they unhesitatingly chose the sea. Among natural-born seafarers the instinct itself is prob-

[77]

ably sufficient explanation. They rationalized, however, that the overland trails were long, traversed mountains and deserts, and passed through the country of hostile Indians; that the trails through Mexico might not be safe for Americans so soon after the Mexican war; and that the Panama route was largely untried. They recalled the laws of mechanics which, ever since rafts started to evolve into ships, had given water transportation an edge in economy. With undue optimism they also reasoned that when they got to California their ship could be their home, their base for mining operations, a storehouse for their belongings, an asset in West Coast or Pacific commerce, and at length the vehicle for the voyage home.

At the commencement of the gold rush the Cape Horn route was also the best-established California connection. It boasted an antiquity almost on a par with Panama's. Magellan, threading the straits between Patagonia and Tierra del Fuego, had emerged on the ocean which he called Pacific just seven years after Balboa's Indian friends took him on the first conducted tour across the Isthmus, thus enabling him to discover this same ocean, to him the South Sea. In the long span between Balboa and the forty-niners Panama was an important gateway southward to Peru but was almost never used as a portage toward California. As a travel route it was, therefore, almost as newfangled as its steamers. In contrast, as expounded by Raymond Rydell, the Cape-Strait route to California was a traffic artery used intermittently since the time of Drake and in substantial volume for several decades prior to 1849.

Tested in the voyages of discovery and piracy, and more recently by the ships of the China trade and the subsidiary fur trade, by the United States Navy, the whalers, and the carriers of hides and tallow, it had become the principal commercial link with California. These many sailings had built up a body of knowledge about the route and its requirements that took most of the gamble out of it. Of the several Argonaut courses it was, in all probability, the most predictable, the one for which the conveniences and the difficulties could most reliably be charted in advance. New England and New York, whence had come most of the earlier sailings, gave the Horn first preference. In England and the European continent, whence the start would have to be by water whatever route was chosen, it was likewise in high favor.

It may seem curious that before there was any general impulse to rush off to California certain businessmen of New York and Boston had recognized the province as a likely market for a speculative cargo. A number of ships were already loading staples and mixed goods for San Francisco when the gold fever struck. The *John W. Coffin* sailed on December 7, 1848. With the onset of the fever still others decided to venture goods by the shipload. All these ships accepted passengers, and before long the demand for such places was so great that additional sailings were announced in which freight hauling would be incidental to the passenger business. Thus, although no lines were operating, the gold seekers who wanted to go by way of the Horn had a fair number of public carriers to choose from. They also had a corresponding number of chances to sign on as crew members filled to its limit of a hundred and fifty members. These included two clergymen, four doctors, eight whaling captains, seventeen professional men, a number of businessmen and farmers, and seventy-six mechanics. The crew of twenty included ten former mates. A constitution and by-laws were adopted, designed to regulate the group during the voyage and in its mining and trading in California. The regulations imposed fines for swearing and gambling and declared against drinking and against unnecessary work on the Sabbath. The company elected officers, headed by Henry Smith as president and captain. It purchased the *Edward Everett* and set about provisioning for two years. The ship also loaded a cargo of picks, shovels, wheelbarrows, wagons, bricks, four steam engines, a steamboat, and two prefabricated houses. It mounted two guns with which to repel pirates.

On the Sunday preceding departure the company marched to church and heard the minister exhort them to take their Bibles in one hand and their New England civilization in the other and conquer all the wickedness that stood in their path. Later the company was addressed by the father of two of its number. Distributing Bibles to the company, he advised that they take the Holy Word in one hand and their New England civilization in the other and implant their principles on the California soil. From President Edward Everett of Harvard also came a present of books, with a letter saying: "You are going to a strange country. Take the Bible in one hand and your New England civilization in the other and make your mark on the people and the country."

Our informant, William H. Thomes, though a member of the company, was in later years an accomplished fictionist and doubtless should not be taken literally. Nevertheless, it is obvious that there was lively community interest in the venture on which New England's young men were setting out, and equally obvious that this interest was tinged with an exalted purpose, a sort of missionary zeal, that only the proper Bostonians would have thought to associate with so sordid a business as gold grubbing. New England writers still like to point out that the flower of their section's manhood was a tremendous gift to California and virtually the making of its civilization.

A few companies were larger than the one on the *Edward Everett*; others were as small as ten or a dozen men. Usually the company assumed the responsibility for sailing the vessel to California, but sometimes. it merely contracted with a ship operator for transporting the group. Some chartered only part of a vessel; for example, the Boston Mechanics Mining and Trading Company, the Neponsett and California Mining Company, the Norfolk and California Company, and the Roxbury and California Company all left Boston on February 9 on the bark *Lanerk*.

By the end of February, 1849, London calculated its total investment in California-bound companies at 1,200,000 pounds sterling. France was sending a number of ships, outfitted and manned by means of lotteries. O. T. Howe lists 124 Massachusetts companies, most of which took the Cape Horn route. Another makes out the total of ships clearing eastern ports in 1849 for California at 775. Such figures are forcible reminders that this was a large-scale migration of much potential significance.

Incidentally, these sailing companies rendered a great service to the American merchant marine. Among the ships available they tended to select the cheapest and therefore usually the oldest and poorest. These were patched up and sailed away to San Francisco, most of them never to return. For the service of regular trade new ships were built, and this was one of the factors that made the 1850's particularly glorious in the annals of American commercial seafaring.

As they sailed away in their second-rate ships, a large number of the Cape Horn forty-niners felt an obligation to perpetuate for friends and posterity some record of their experiences. Some did it in letters which they hoped to post by transfer to passing ships or at ports of call. Others set out to fill notebooks and ledgers with journal entries. Many such documents are preserved, and quite a few have been published. It is an exaggeration, of course, to say that if you have read one you have read them all. Yet the element of common experience was large for the travelers on this route, and the repetitions from diary to diary are striking.

The first days out were a time of seasickness. Almost every diarist mentions it, and the honest ones usually confess to being victims themselves. Then came days when there was better opportunity to inspect the ship, the shipmates, and the fare. Before long, opinions are entered about the captain, his martinet qualities, his mannerisms in profanity, his caution or daring in putting on sail. Oftentimes a reshuffling of cargo was necessary to make amends for careless loading. Soon the ship entered warmer seas, and usually it was becalmed before catching the trade winds. By this time many of the travelers found that their reading matter was running low. By this time also every ship had its interminable card games, though apparently with less gambling than on some of the Panama steamers. The sea diaries are rich in weather notes, on tropical sunsets, on electrical displays, on rains that made possible soft-water baths.

Of course, there were oddities too. From the *La Grange*, ten days out, three hens were blown overboard, but the captain put about and was able to effect a rescue. The *Duxbury* recorded thirty cases of mumps and fifteen of measles. On practically every other ship the health record was excellent, except for touches of scurvy. On every ship troll lines were kept baited, at first just for sport, but soon with the active purpose of supplementing and varying the messes. The fishermen pulled in many strange varieties of fish, and when the larder was low they tried to cook and eat even the kinds that were supposed to be inedible. Near the Horn they also succeeded in hooking gonies, gulls, and albatrosses. These likewise found their way into the experiments of the galley.

At the equator, Neptune was apt to come aboard to supervise the traditional hazing of first travelers, although some ships apparently did not have enough shellbacks to perform the rites. Many of the companies had religious services; on the *Edward Everett* the two ministers alternated in preaching, attendance was not required, and smoking was permitted. Amateur theatricals were staged on several ships, and athletic contests were also common. Occasionally some elaborate hoax was perpetrated. Feast days such as Christmas and state holidays such as the Fourth of July were customarily observed with a more elaborate repast, suitable oratory, and a round of toasts. Still another entertainment feature, though by no means universal, was the ship's paper. On the *Edward Everett* the *Barometer and Gold Hunter's Log* was read aloud to the assembled passengers. The weekly *Petrel* on the *Duxbury* circulated in manuscript. Without benefit of wireless these sheets were strictly shipboard productions. They featured gossip, personal notes, humor—oftentimes rather broad, and creative efforts too often in doggerel verse. George F. Kent's "L. E. G. (Elegy) to a Pig Lost Overboard," though confided only to his journal, is an example of the sort of thing perpetrated.

Almost every company boasted musicians who entertained with violin, guitar, flute, clarinet, and song. On board the *General Worth* traveled a certain James A. Varney, an accomplished singer and violinist, who "for the more permanent enjoyment" of his fellow passengers also practiced tatooing. On another ship a group organized what they called the Sacramento Minstrels, featuring banjo, tambourine, fiddle, and a repertoire of all the popular songs. These included much of Stephen Foster, other older favorites, and a number composed specially for the forty-niners. The theme song of the migration unquestionably was the many-versed

Oh, Susannah, don't you cry for me,
I'm off for California, with my wash bowl on my knee.

Its strains were wafted over the South Atlantic and the Pacific, the overland forty-niners chanted it round their campfires, and Bayard Taylor reports that a Negro bongoman on the Chagres had adapted it as a boating song.

On their southward course the ships customarily worked eastward almost to Africa. Few diarists record sighting that continent, but several mention a film of red desert dust settling on spars and deck. Then the course lay southwestward, oftentimes with the intention of a call at Rio de Janeiro or Santa Catarina. At the capital city in particular the travelers piled ashore to stretch their legs, see the sights, and revel in the delightful foods that the land afforded.

Franklin Buck, for example, mentions a feast of ham, omelette, roast chicken, steak, watercress and lettuce, bananas, oranges, guava jelly, citron, green cheese, claret and Madeira, and coffee such as he had never tasted before. Some visited the emperor's botanical garden on the outskirts of the city. A few attended the theater, where Dom Pedro II was honored guest. Many expressed regret that the custom of the country was to keep the women so cloistered. The impetuousness of some of these gold seekers is said to have given the impression that they had come to seize the country for the United States. On the whole, however, the shore leave was passed with a minimum of incidents, and when the ships sailed, reprovisioned and some of them repaired, the travelers carried happy memories of their Brazilian visit.

Proceeding southward again, the captains had to choose between rounding the Horn or sailing through the Strait of Magellan. For the steamers on the marathon run to West Coast assignments the customary route was through the Strait. Twelve or fifteen of the sailing vessels also elected it, most of them small schooners for which serious difficulty might have been expected off the Horn. The Strait route, of course, was shorter, and with perfect luck it would mean a quicker passage. However, the channel is tortuous and narrow, there are strong currents, the shores are rough and inhospitable, sudden storms are characteristic, the prevailing winds come in gusts and seldom from the east, anchorages are few and unsatisfactory, and gloomy skies, snow squalls, and the persistent head winds made most forty-niners regret having chosen this course.

The pilot schooner *Anonyma* got through fairly easily. The brig *Saltillo* negotiated the passage in 52 days, the *Sea Eagle* was detained a long time, the *Velasco* required 70 days, and the *Acadian* 57. The schooner *John A. Sutter* was driven ashore in a snowstorm and was lost, though crew and passengers and much of the cargo were saved. The bark *Hebe*, with some men ashore to trade, was caught in a sudden wind and tide, dragged her anchors, and could not pick up the men. Fortunately they were rescued by another ship. The *John Allyn* had a somewhat similar experience. Her first mate and a passenger were seized by hostile natives, who accepted ransoms but released only the passenger. On the ninety-seventh day of his captivity the mate managed to escape and swam out to a British ship. From it he transferred to a whaler, and thence to a California-bound ship. The *John Allyn*, meanwhile, had given up

the Strait and was tackling the Horn. It is questionable
that any sailing vessel saved time by the Strait.

The prescription for rounding the Horn, as worked
out by experience and codified in Matthew F. Maury's
Sailing Directions, was to get sufficient southing to beat
around despite the prevailing gales from the west. It
was not always easy to achieve; the clipper *Golden
Eagle,* a few years later, was held up for ninety days, and
some earlier vessels in the China trade gave up and made
for the Pacific by sailing round the world the other way.
Some of the Argonauts had ideal fortune and turned the
corner in less than a week; others required as much as
forty days. All the travelers got a taste of Antarctic cold
and the ships were pitched about so violently that table
meals were a rarity. All who could stayed below decks.
Yet casualties were rare. The *John Allyn* and the *Pauline*
each lost a man overboard. Several vessels shipped
damaging seas. But, as the voice of experience had said,
this was a feasible entrance to the Pacific.

Once fairly upon the Pacific, the customary procedure was to head for a port of call, sometimes Talcahuana or Juan Fernández, but more often Valparaiso
or Callao. The primary purpose was to reprovision by
loading water, flour, potatoes, beef, fruit, and a few head
of sheep or cattle. Some of the ships also stood in need of
repairs after the battering at the Horn. The diaries,
however, contain little detail on these operations, because
the passengers rushed ashore with all possible haste.

Of Spanish American civilization as they saw it at
Talcahuana, port of Concepción, these visitors had few
complimentary remarks. The climate admittedly was

pleasant, and the people reasonably affable, but the adobe buildings did not impress, and the shops most flourishing, and most patronized, seemed to be the liquor stores. Valparaiso was much more of a place. The forty-niners tramped the streets, hired horses for more extensive forays, went to the theater, sampled the local drinks, tried out their Spanish on the citizens, bought fruits and nuts and curios, and visited the stream where laundering was done, the schools, the cemeteries, and even the calaboose. One of the boys from the *Edward Everett* reported of the school, "The children write a good hand and can do sums."

From Callao, "a mean, dirty hole, filled with sailor grog shops and low taverns," as many travelers as possible caught the first stage for Lima. The old viceregal capital was still a walled city, most of its buildings held down to one or two stories, out of respect to earthquakes, but boasting a magnificent cathedral with an altar said to be of solid silver. At least one Yankee was fascinated by the women of Lima, the most beautiful he had ever seen, flashing of eye, trim of ankle, lithe in their walk, and exceedingly graceful in manipulating their cornhusk cigarettes. Although he grumbled at 62½ cents letter postage to Panama, he vowed that once he had made his fortune he was coming to Lima to live.

A more idyllic halo of romance hovered over Juan Fernández, the island made famous by the stranding of Alexander Selkirk, who in real life prepared the way for Defoe's Robinson Crusoe. The forty-niners approached this little island with storybook anticipation, and, strange to say, it did not disappoint. A wooden trough delivered mountain spring water at a most convenient spot for cask filling. The eleven inhabitants stood by tolerantly while the visitors ranged the island, drinking in the scenery, fishing from the rocks, plucking wild fruit, hunting goats, and looking for Friday's footprint. All attest the good fishing; and the *General Worth* sailed away with fifty bushels of peaches.

The rest of the journey seemed a downhill course. True, some of the travelers got increasingly on each other's nerves as the voyage strung out into its sixth or eighth month. The passengers on the *Capitol,* who had sought out the American consul at Valparaiso to protest the incompetence and rascality of their captain, liked him now still less. On most ships the tedium got worse. The diarists have fewer compliments for the melodeon bands, the Sacramento Minstrels, and the Shakespearean readings. Yet, as the long-sought goal got nearer, spirits rose. All began to prepare for going ashore. Some fashioned containers for their expected gold, and one fellow rigged up a scoop on the end of a pole so that he could work river bottoms.

No thrill of the entire trip exceeded that of sailing through the Golden Gate and coming to anchor off San Francisco. The prospects from shipboard varied, of course, according to the season and the weather. Those who arrived in late spring, summer, or fall saw the city nestled against a backdrop of brown hillsides. Later arrivals saw more greenery and also a larger fleet of ships riding at anchor. In general, however, the impression from the bay was favorable and exciting. Not merely would these travelers escape from the ship on which they had been cooped up for weeks, but they would enter into El Dorado. When landed, many were disillusioned by the streets deep in dust or mud, the flimsy tents and shacks that served for buildings, the unkempt appearance of the citizens, the outrageous prices for services in demand, and the glutted market for tobacco, flour, and many of the things brought as cargo. Wrote one passenger on the *Leonore*, "Just arrived—San Francisco be damned! further particulars in my next."

The first steps were usually to hunt up quarters or to make camp, to taste some shore cooking, to inquire at the post office for letters from home, and to start making arrangements to go to the mines. The Cape Horn companies often solved this problem, at least in part, by sailing their ships to Benicia or all the way to Sacramento. Other options were to buy passage on one of the small river boats or to outfit with wagon or pack mules for the trip overland. By any means it was a several-day trip to Sacramento. The river travelers frequently got stuck in the mudflats of Suisun Bay. They had prodigious stories to tell of the mosquitoes—so thick that the only way to eat was to climb into the rigging; so big that if your hat blew off it would remain in midair, buoyed up by the mosquitoes.

Whether it was in San Francisco or Sacramento or at the mines, the Cape Horn forty-niners soon discovered that the company device which had served well on the voyage was not suited to California conditions. The defect is usually stated in antisocialist, anticommunist terms —that too many of the men would not exert themselves for the common good and that the energetic and productive got tired of carrying the drones. Individual ambitions did run counter to the profit-sharing coöperatives, but it was true also that practically all the enterprises that flourished in California in '49 were of a sort most efficiently operated by a crew considerably smaller than the average Cape Horn traveling company. In short order, therefore, these companies dismantled their trading and mining plans, liquidated whatever assets remained, and distributed the proceeds among the shareholders. The forty-niners who had rounded the Horn then mixed in among the others and soon were almost indistinguishable.

The abandoned hulks rocking at anchor were left as a reminder of the magnitude of the migration round the Horn. A few of the ships proved serviceable for bay and river traffic or in coastwise shipping. Others served as warehouses in San Francisco or Sacramento and as prisons. Some were dismantled for their canvas and cordage. The *La Grange* was stripped of copper to make rocker plates. Most of the round-the-Horn fleet simply rotted away or settled into the mud. The cargoes these ships had brought were probably more of a contribution. Unfortunately, they included too little of lumber and bricks, too many patented gold-mining machines, and such a surplus of tobacco, boots, flour, and stoves as to glut the market. Yet it was ship-borne supplies that very largely outfitted the Panama and overland gold miners.

Of the people who came round the Horn there is an easy rationalization that they were so softened by the long period of inaction that they did not make good miners. Perhaps it is so. Yet the route seems to have been the most disease-free of all that were in use. The casualties en route were the fewest, and this is quite an offset to the putative toll in the diggings. Admittedly, the Horn did not deliver as many farmers as the land routes. The company recruiters sometimes worried that they were not drawing enough mechanics, or men accustomed to labor. Yet their route was less patronized by the professions—sometimes ridiculed as nonproductive—than was Panama. In summary, therefore, no particular apology is needed for the several thousand Yankees who took the all-water route in '49.

Other travelers, though not quite so many, followed in the 'fifties: For years to come this was to be the California freight route par excellence, but that is another story.

CHAPTER 6

Highway to the Mines

OF ALL the gold-rush routes the people's choice was the
one that ran overland. It attracted some companies right
out of the land of the cod and the Horn. Others came
from New York and the national capital, which on the
whole inclined toward the sea lanes. And throughout the
American heartland, from the Appalachians to the Missouri, the overland trail was the great favorite.

A generation earlier, Lewis and Clark had dramatized
the feat of crossing the continent. Others adopted their
example. From Missouri a famous caravan route angled
southwestward to Santa Fe; over it, in the recent war,
had traveled the Army of the West, some detachments
pushing all the way to California. Northwestward from
Missouri angled an equally famous artery, the Oregon
Trail, used by missionaries, fur trappers, and pioneer
settlers. Within the decade this highway had acquired a
California spur used by such newsworthy people as

John Bidwell and the Donner party, and further publicized in the writings of John C. Frémont and Lansford W. Hastings. Still another trail, well rutted by
1849 and much noted in the western press, was the path
of Brigham Young and the Latter-day Saints from
Council Bluffs to Great Salt Lake. Much of this earlier
travel had been aimed with only indifferent accuracy
toward the gold fields. Other phases of it fell considerably short of that mark. On the trail the forty-niners
would find pioneering still to do, yet they would have
the benefit of many lessons learned by those who had
preceded them into the "Great American Desert," the
Rocky Mountains, the Great Basin, and the Sierra
Nevada.

Like the girl next door, the overland route appealed
to midwesterners because it was near at hand. River
steamboats offered easy transportation to where the trail
began, and many prospective gold seekers were only a
short distance across country from the customary starting places at Independence, St. Joseph, or Council Bluffs.
Furthermore, whereas the ocean routes usually required
a cash outlay, the standard equipment on every farm
could easily be converted into a trail outfit: a farm team,
a wagon, ax and gun, and the home-grown staples such
as flour, meal, and bacon. A farmer's work clothes were
ideal garb for the trail. As a home on wheels the covered
wagon might be expected to have many of the advantages advertised for today's trailers. At the other end of
the line, too, it seemed logical to expect that wagon,
team, and tools could be reconverted to the uses of
California life.

In the light of all the circumstances it is quite natural that gold seekers by the tens of thousands rallied along the Missouri to join the overland trek. In numbers they exceeded the forty-niners by sea. They also made a greater show, because they ganged up for departure in April or May, late enough to find grass on the prairie and early enough to cross the Sierra before winter snows closed the passes. Encamped near the river towns they looked like an army in bivouac.

With the gold fever rampant as early as December, and nature's ordained starting time some months later, the overland forty-niners had time to get ready. In Washington, J. Goldsborough Bruff joined with other young men in forming a company, adopting regulations, choosing a uniform, and holding meetings to discuss the problems of the intended journey. He consulted the standard literature, such as Frémont, Palmer, and Bryant, and from government records traced maps that he hoped would be useful. Out in Iowa young Jacob Stover got busy trapping wolves for the bounty of one dollar each and twenty-five cents for the pelt. When they got scarce, he split rails at sixty-two and one-half cents a hundred. By spring he could buy a yoke of oxen, the necessary grub, and had five dollars to spare. W. L. Manly bought an Indian pony as his mount for the journey, tanned some buckskin, and cut and sewed himself a frontier suit.

The commoner practice was for three or four men to band together in rigging a farm wagon with bows and canvas top, and in lining up the team, three or four yoke of oxen or as many span of horses or mules. Into the wagon they loaded several barrels of flour or meal, often with butter or eggs laid down in the meal. Bacon or salt pork, coffee, salt, and saleratus were universals, along with matches, frying pan, water bucket, and firearms. Blankets and extra clothing, a few lengths of rope, and an ax were in every wagon. The things that might be added are almost without number: dried apples, a lantern, painkiller, assorted pills, seeds, farming implements, furniture, musical instruments, a small library, gold-washing machines. If the whole family was going, the amount of incidental baggage was considerably increased. Often, too, something was taken for sale in the inflated California market—a crate of chickens, a demijohn of whisky, or an extra quantity of bacon.

Eventually the time came round to head for the frontier. Often it was no idle matter to say goodbye to home and friends. The vast majority of the forty-niners intended merely to go west and make their pile and then hustle back home. The journey, however, would be long and full of the unknown; the adventurers might not get back; the farewells, especially by the dear ones left behind, were often said as though they were to be final. The travelers started off more jauntily, but their diaries almost immediately reflect homesickness, they brood over separation from parents and, some of them, from wives and children, or they worry that a certain girl, after all, will not be content to wait.

En route to the assembly points, the wagon travelers found the going cold and muddy. Although they had more team than was customary in farm hauling, they frequently got stuck and had to unload, pull out, and load again. They had accidents, too, breaking harness, tongues, wheels, and axles, though since they were still passing through a settled area it was easy to get repairs. The driver of one of the Washington City wagons managed to spill his wagon off a log bridge into a creek. John Steele, on the second night out in 1850, was equally unfortunate, but because his partner's share in their rig was attached by the sheriff, which sent him on without much more than a gun and a knapsack.

Together with the river-boat travelers, the wagon men converged on Independence, St. Joseph, and the other Missouri towns famous as the last outposts of civilization and the places where the West really began. In the matter of western color, these towns were all that anyone could ask. They featured frontier garb, talk of the trails, shops and stores attuned to the emigrant needs, and wide-open gambling halls and saloons. As outfitting points, however, they came in for some bitter criticism. The background of experience was there all right, built up through many years of business with Santa Fe traders, Rocky Mountain trappers, Oregon emigrants, and Mexican War caravans. But the forty-niners descended in such a flood that demand outran supply. Oxen advanced in price to $60 or $70 a yoke, and mules to $70 or $100, with other things in proportion. Even a year later Eleazer Ingalls could complain of St. Joe: "Every little thing costs three or four times as much here as at home. . . . It is the greatest place for gambling and all other rascality that I ever was in."

A few of the forty-niners put up at such hotels as the Edgar House at St. Joe. The more frugal practice, commoner and at least as comfortable, was to make camp somewhere on the outskirts, or, from Independence, to go out a few miles on the trail and camp. Meanwhile, there was much scurrying around as new arrivals sought out the friends or even the relatives with whom they intended to travel. Others got themselves accepted into one of the companies or recruited a group to go together.

The necessary delay about setting out was compensated for in various ways. Some concentrated on inquiring of the local celebrities, who were supposed to know how to go, what landmarks to watch for, what hazards to avoid. Others were more intent on a last fling at the comforts of civilization at bar or card table. Still others seized the opportunity to repack or even to refit, and numbers were engaged in the strenuous task of breaking to harness their newly purchased mules. According to Isaac Wistar, the method was to lasso, throw, harness, and drag these reluctant animals into place, after which the most ambitious man mounted the wheel mule, and "the circus began." Each animal was restrained by a choke rope, "at the other end of which was a mad and excited individual who walked, ran, jumped, fell, swore, and was dragged alongside," as the procession moved. This was the traditional way of breaking mules for Santa Fe freighting. Perhaps it helps to explain why oxen were much more highly recommended.

Since St. Joe was on the east bank of the wide Missouri, the immediate requirement for those who elected this starting point was to get ferried across—no mean task, with thousands of wagons waiting their turn and only two old scows in operation. One forty-niner likened the mass of waiting wagons to a giant flatiron pointed toward the landing. Bruff reports that fighting for places in line was a common occurrence and that two teamsters, in one of these disputes, killed each other with pistols. Estimating that it would take a fortnight to get his wagons across, he himself decided to try another ferry farther north. There they had the misfortune of seeing the ferry strike a sawyer, capsize and sink, spilling wagon, cattle, and passengers into deep water, and drowning the ferryman. On up opposite Old Fort Kearney, they finally got across, one wagon at a time, two men with poles being assigned to ward off floating logs and trees. Across the river they bivouacked again, until the entire company was reassembled and it was time to take the trail.

Impatience to be off was the ruling characteristic of these encamped gold seekers. The trail-wise cautioned against going before the grass was up enough to nourish the teams. An earlier start, they said, would only wear out the stock and not get one to California any sooner. On the other hand, no one wanted to risk having the teams ahead eat up all the grass, and no one wanted the rest of the forty-niners to get to the diggings ahead of him. Consequently, even the conservative tended to start a bit too soon.

Novelty, of course, attached to the first day's travel— the management of a strange team, concern whether something had been forgotten, the question of how far to go in a day, the choice of a camp site. Except when rain turned the trail into a quagmire and raised the streams above fording level, this first stretch was plain sailing. The road and the major variations on it were clearly marked by previous travel, so that it was almost impossible to go wrong. There was wood at every camp and water near by. Unless the start had been made much too soon, there was adequate pasturage; and many of the emigrants carried a few feedings of grain. Some were greenhorns at camping out, but all were bountifully supplied, and they had not yet reached the region where Indian danger was cause for concern. The only serious problems were at the stream crossings.

The crossings were by ford, bridge, or ferry, and sometimes it was hard to tell which was worst. At the fords one had to drive down the bank, sometimes too steep for comfort, force the reluctant or fractious team into the water, hope for solid bottom, and push on across. If the far bank was steep, it would be necessary to double-team to get up to the plain again. Broken axles, snapped tongues, and mired wagons were the most frequent casualties at the fords.

Where a bridge existed it was certain to be a primitive one. Bruff describes the log bridge floated across Salt Creek, narrow, tilted, sagged, twisted, and oscillating. Rather than risk driving across it, he had the mules led over, each wagon lowered by hand and rope, hand-drawn across, and double-teamed up the opposite bank, after which he rewarded each of his bridgemen, that is all members of the company, with a horn of whisky.

On this first lap of the journey the travelers made valiant efforts as hunters, but without much success. Delano waxes lyrical over a breakfast at which a savory raccoon was added to their customary bill of fare. Most of the travelers mention wild onions and prairie peas, and several comment on the spring wildflowers. From the first camps it frequently happened that horses or oxen strayed away, usually on the backtrack toward the Missouri. Usually they were overtaken and recovered, but sometimes they were not, and this of course could spell disaster. The forty-niners themselves had a tendency to stray. Almost every company could record at least one occasion when hunters got lost or unofficial scouts walked off in the wrong direction. Occasionally it was a child who wandered away. Search parties, bonfires, and signal shots usually guided the errant member back.

The record for the first days on the trail is marred, furthermore, by an appalling number of accidents. Too many of them roughing it for the first time, these travelers were careless with their axes and equally careless with their firearms. Almost everyone had a pistol strapped on, and the wagons were rolling arsenals. At the merest hint of game or Indians they reached for their weapons and prepared to blaze away. Perhaps the most frequent error in this category was to try to pull a loaded rifle out of the wagon, muzzle first. The wagons themselves were almost as deadly. Usually it was a pedestrian or a bystander who miscalculated; occasionally, someone in a wagon who fell out. A few times, where the ground was soft, men were run over without being hurt, but usually the heavy wheels meant broken bones or even fatal injury.

Of course, there were mishaps that were merely ludicrous. As old Mr. Greene was testing a ford, the cinch on his mule loosened and he was catapulted over his mount's head into the cold waters of Wyeth's Run. Mounted again, he rode in to lead the wagons across, and got a second ducking. At the Platte, Willy Webster borrowed a gig and waded out after some fish. The current betrayed him and rolled him into deep water, meanwhile weighting his clothes with sand so that he would have drowned if two companions had not stripped, plunged in, and pulled him out.

Somewhere in this stretch the forty-niners usually saw their first Indians—not counting, of course, the tame ones on the streets of Independence or St. Joe. For one train, it was a band of eighty Sioux on the warpath, but out for Pawnees rather than white men. Another company met a wounded Pawnee, victim of these same warriors, and administered first aid. Others got merely a glimpse of a brave or two, watching at a distance, or silhouetted on a hilltop. More often it was a small group accosting the emigrants for a toll for crossing a creek (Stover's party met such a demand at the Elkhorn River), or simply begging. It was a pitiful and disillusioning spectacle. "Alas!" observed Bruff, "the great warriors, arabs, and terror of the plains, turned out to be a sadly reduced, starving, contemptible race! They begg'd me for bread, opened their dingy robes, and exhibited their prominent ribs and breastbones."

But the real scourge of the trail in 1849 was neither accidents nor Indians, but illness. Travelers were laid low by chills and fevers and by various other complaints, and as the journals richly attest, they paid little heed to guidebook-writer Ware's sage counsel against over-doctoring, but on the contrary prescribed themselves prodigious doses of physic, blue pill, quinine, calomel, and laudanum.

Their most baffling affliction, and by all odds the deadliest, was Asiatic cholera. Science, of course, was at the time none too explicit about what caused the cholera or how to treat it. It reached the gold seekers by way of New Orleans, was transmitted north on the riverboats, plagued the crowded boats and the congested and often unsanitary camps, and pursued the forty-niners out on the trail, claiming victims all the way to the continental divide.

Cholera struck hard and mercilessly. Many of its victims died within a few hours; most by the second day. Those who could resist longer were apt to recover, but the malady was so deadly and the suffering of its victims so intense that the forty-niners were thrown into panic. Some with quiet heroism ministered to the afflicted, even to strangers. Wistar, for example, acknowledges such help from an unnamed fellow passenger on one of the boats. Others deserted the stricken as though they were pariahs.

Quick burial was naturally the rule. Wistar's boat halted to inter eighteen or twenty victims. The *Embassy* stopped just above St. Louis to bury a young man of the Charleston Company. Some of the burials were without ceremony. More often, someone read the burial service, recited a passage from the Bible, or extemporized a prayer. The Washington City Company turned out in uniform for a procession to the grave of its one victim, the dirge was rendered with the instruments available (key bugle, flute, violin, and accordion), the Stars and

Stripes were draped over the body, and a salute was fired as it was lowered by bridle reins into the grave. A headstone had been sculptured, and in his journal Bruff composed a poem to commemorate the event. A pile of rocks to discourage the wolves, and a simple marker mentioning name, age, home, and date, were about all that the best-intentioned company could achieve. Some of the graves are still identifiable; the forty-niner diarists record them by the hundreds. They recognized the pathos, too, as for example Delano in his remark, "Instead of turning up the golden sands of the Sacramento, the spade of the adventurer was first used to bury the remains of a companion."

It is small wonder that with all these discouragements of accidents, Indian scares, loss of stock, and the toll of disease, quite a number of the emigrants changed their minds about going to California, turned round, and began a retreat to the States. Some had provisions enough to see them home again; others depended on charity from the outbound companies.

In the earlier migration across the continent the custom had been to postpone choosing officers until the company had been a few days on the trail. Most of the forty-niners organized before leaving home. They were much more military about it, too, often with elaborate rules and regulations, uniforms, and even a bugler. But they did show full respect for another tradition of the trail, the propensity to amend rules, depose leaders, and reshuffle companies en route. Sometimes they recognized incompetence. At other times they disliked the division of the watches, the choice of camping places, or, more vital, the decision which fork of the trail to follow. Those who dissented could demand a referendum, an amendment of the rules, a new election, a dissolution of the company, or a split-up of its members and property, or they could simply resign their own membership. All these things happened, and others as well, so that some regard the migration of 1849 as a marching laboratory of political experiment. Another possible interpretation is that the bonds of company organization were fragile when challenged by the tensions of life on the trail. There was, at any rate, much instability in the company organizations.

There were times along the trail when a company seemed to have the prairie all to itself, as had been true of earlier emigrants. At other times, from a vantage point such as the crest where the Platte first came into view, there was a forcible reminder that a great concourse of people was on the move. Of this vista, commanding the junction of the roads from St. Joseph and from Old Fort Kearney, Delano writes: "For the whole distance in view, up and down the river, before and behind us, long trains were in motion or encamped on the grassy bottom, and we could scarcely realize that we were in an Indian country, from the scene of civilized life before us, and this was all caused by the magic talisman of gold."

Of the sight from another eminence he offers this picture: "For miles, to the extent of vision, an animated mass of beings broke upon our view. Long trains of wagons with their white covers were moving slowly along, a multitude of horsemen were prancing on the road, companies of men were traveling on foot, and although the scene was not a gorgeous one, yet the display of banners from many wagons, and the multitude of armed men, looked as if a mighty army was on its march."

In the valley of the Platte the emigrants became increasingly conscious of the wonders of nature. The Platte itself, a mile or more in width and with ever-shifting channels, seemed to them a most illogical stream. Accustomed as they were to the deep and stable rivers of the East, they would have agreed with the later comment, "Stood on edge, it would make a good river." Fording the Platte was quite an adventure, costing some emigrants their wagons, and occasioning others several days' delay. They marveled at the strange formations of Castle Rock, Courthouse Rock, Chimney Rock, and Scotts Bluff. Farther on, they clambered over Independence Rock, for the view, for the climb, and to inscribe their names on this "great register of the desert." Still farther on they were somewhat prepared by Frémont for such wonders as Devil's Gate, the deceptive flatness of South Pass, and the snorting of Steamboat Springs.

They showed equal interest in the fauna of the plains. The prairie dog fascinated as an underground town dweller and as a target. A few emigrants tasted the flesh, well roasted, and pronounced it as good as squirrel meat, as no doubt it is. Other game such as antelope, sagehens, and hares was taken where available. However, as the trail became crowded with thousands of wagons, tens of thousands of persons, and an even larger number of head of stock, much of the wild life was frightened away and the hunting was not nearly so good as had been the norm.

For days the travelers strained their eyes for buffalo, and when the herds at last were sighted nothing would do but that some of the boys should ride out to hunt. The dashing way to do it, of course, was to try to ride close enough to put a heavy ball, or several of them, into a vital spot, but this was a method requiring a good deal of skill, a good mount, and a favorable opportunity. Another way was to try to get close enough for a set shot. The journals doubtless contain only a partial reckoning of the casualties of buffalo hunting, but they record all sorts of accidents: riders unhorsed and trampled or gored, horses broken down by the hard run, rifles and pistols strewn over the plain, and horses getting away and stampeding off with the herd.

Even a successful hunt might pose a problem. Stover tells of a big bull killed half a mile off the road. The party took out three yoke of oxen to drag the carcass to camp, but found they had to hook on two more yoke. Buffalo hunting, nevertheless, was a zestful activity that the forty-niners could not have been expected to forego; it also provided a welcome supplement and change in their regular diet of bread, bacon, and coffee.

After the Pawnees the travelers encountered more stalwart specimens of Plains Indians. The more reflective took note of evidences of partial accommodation to the ways of the whites. Near Bear River, for example, Bruff came upon three Indians, one in native garb, one in a shabby frock coat, blue-striped cotton shirt, nankeen trousers, white yarn suspenders, and black fur hat, and the third in deerskin leggings and moccasins, ragged marseilles vest, and large straw hat. Here and there, too, they came across fur-trapper squawmen with a bevy of halfbreed children and living in circumstances at least half Indian.

Most of the forty-niners, it must be admitted, gave little thought to such matters. They had plenty to do in working their wagons westward. Viewed in the large, the trail ran without obstruction alongside the Platte and then the Sweetwater until it crossed the divide at South Pass. It was a long pull. Some camp sites were lacking in grass, others in good water, and for a long time the only fuel available had been the well-dried buffalo chips. If the night herders were careless, the locomotive power of a whole train might stray away. Careless descent into a gully could mean a breakdown, and a single smashed wheel, a cracked axle, a splintered tongue, or a lost coupling pin could put a wagon out of commission.

Along the Platte these emigrants made forced reappraisal of their baggage, and began to discard what they found nonessential. Oddments of clothing, stoves, barrels of flour, salt pork, and pieces of furniture were cast aside; so much, indeed, that the impression came to be that of a people in flight. By an unadmirable quirk of human nature, aggravated no doubt by the competition to win the race to the gold fields, many of the forty-niners in lightening their loads took care to spoil whatever they threw away, setting fire to abandoned wagons, tearing blankets and clothing, and dirtying flour and meal. Another example of wanton destruction was grass burning by a man who had gotten into the vanguard of the march. A posse rode ahead and put an end to this practice and to the culprit as well.

The lower Platte crossings had been by fords across a broad and sandy river, so turgid, it is said, that where it was as much as an inch deep the bottom could not be seen. Barring quicksand, it was usually possible to get across safely without floating the wagons or swimming the stock. The upper Platte, narrower and freshly fed by melted snow, was too deep to be forded. At Deer Creek and a few miles above, near modern Casper, rude ferries were in operation by 1849 on which wagons and people could be rafted to the other side, for a price. Travelers who could not or did not want to afford the fee might caulk their wagons and try to float them across. The stock, in any event, would have to swim and some of the men would have to cross with them, in the saddle or clutching a horse's tail. At Deer Creek, when Charles A. Kirkpatrick crossed, early in the 1849 season, twelve men had been drowned. Another unfortunate emigrant, neglecting the precaution of removing his wagon cover, saw the wind get under it, tilt the raft, and blow his wagon off into the stream.

Its course shaped by the Sweetwater, the trail swept on to the westward past Devil's Gate and Independence Rock and then, by a very gradual climb, ascended to South Pass. The guidebook readers were prepared for open flatness, which made it almost impossible to tell where the divide really was, and the beginning of the (theoretically) downhill run to California.

A short distance ahead, at the Little Sandy, the emigrants had to make a momentous choice. The old trail swung south toward Fort Bridger, another outpost of the fur trade, then northwest again toward Fort Hall, or, by a southwestward course to Salt Lake City. From the Little Sandy, however, an alternative route known as Sublette's Cut-off led across the Green River desert to the river of the same name. The road was direct and hard-packed, but it stretched an estimated thirty-five waterless miles and ended in several miles of sandy going and an abrupt drop to the river. The more conservative travelers took the Fort Bridger road.

At the fort this minority divided again, some working northwestward to Bear Valley and others choosing the rough Mormon Trail through the mountains to Salt Lake City.

Though visited by only a few thousand of the overland forty-niners, perhaps a tenth, the Mormon capital was viewed with much interest. Founded only two years earlier, it had shown lusty growth. Modest homes and stores and several larger public buildings lined streets laid out in magnificent width. The Mormons had diverted the waters of Jordan Creek to irrigate fields and gardens and had prospects of good crops. After their persecution in the Midwest they had no reason to be cordial toward the Gentiles, but they did extend hospitality. Also they did several sorts of business with the gold seekers, operating ferries at several of the crossings, buying surplus goods from some emigrants, selling needed supplies to others, and trading sound animals for worn-down ones (with consideration added) which then could be reconditioned and traded to some later emigrants. Rumor took root that the Saints misused the forty-niners, but evidence to support the charge seems not to exist; on the contrary, various diarists gratefully acknowledge assistance received.

From Salt Lake City the most direct route to the diggings was westward over the salt flats on what was known as Hastings' Cut-off. Again, in remembrance of the Donner tragedy, this path was deservedly shunned. Some of the forty-niners decided to winter among the Mormons. Others, as we shall see, were persuaded to tarry a few weeks and then take a southwestward course toward Los Angeles. The more common practice, however, was to swing north around the lake on a path that would intersect the main trail near the headwaters of the Humboldt.

Notwithstanding the advice of a travel agent maintained by Bridger on the Little Sandy, the majority of the emigrants took Sublette's Cut-off. Perhaps they had heard of the troubles of the Donner party on the other route; more probably it was the attraction of the shorter way. With water kegs filled, and often with more water in an emptied flour barrel, they set off at dusk, so as to cover part of the distance in the cool of the night. The worst going was reached the next afternoon. Usually some of the oxen gave out, had to be driven ahead to water, and then back to bring in the remaining wagons. The end of the march was also complicated by a three-hundred-foot bank that had to be descended with caution, and, with the animals sniffing the water just ahead, caution was indeed difficult. Though they berated the guidebooks for underestimating the distance, most forty-niners were convinced that the cut-off was the way to go.

Green River had to be ferried, with hazards analogous to those on the upper Platte. The next stop was famous Bear Valley, extolled by Frémont as an ideal place for recruiting. The forty-niners found it so, lush with grass, with plenty of wood for cookfires and campfires, the hills abounding in berries and wild onions and teeming with elk and antelope. Most companies lay over for a day or two, to let their stock rest and have a good feed, to rest themselves, and have a washday. With garments spread out to dry, kettles boiling, wagons drawn up in a circle, horses nibbling the grass, oxen chewing the cud, and with the emigrants lolling about, reading, smoking, or fishing, the Bear River bottoms presented a thoroughly domestic appearance. It was the most homelike place the pioneers had found in a thousand miles of travel. It was a fit spot, as one emigrant wrote, "for instrumental and vocal music."

As a counterbalance to this idyllic picture, the diaries offer a great assortment of realistic passages; for example, Charles A. Kirkpatrick's self-inspection: "First my clothing. It consists of an old pair of boots run down at the heels and an old pair of striped pantaloons, a hickory shirt which I have worn for ten days and which was as dirty as it could well be, and my hat—well I wont say anything against it for apart from my team it is the best friend on the road to me; protecting me from the sun, serving for a pillow as well as a drinking cup, for the rim forms a cup from which I have often drank. Whiskers three inches long, hair seven inches long, and all covered with dust, dirty face, hands the same. My hands being sun burnt I had put on sweet oil to heal them and to this oil the dust stuck. In this plight I might have been seen with three others sitting around an old greasy board (which had served for a dining table), playing Euchre."

Resuming the march, the emigrants went on to Soda Springs, or, as sometimes called, Beer Springs. A few miles beyond, they had a choice of the old Oregon trail to Fort Hall on the Snake or a new route variously known as Hudspeth's, Myers', or Bear River Cut-off. Actually there was not a great deal to choose between the two routes, the one favored by tradition, the other by being called a cut-off. Gradually the new road gained the preference. After several days of rough going, both led to Raft River, a junction with the trail from Salt Lake, and the headwaters of the Humboldt.

Perhaps the best description of the Humboldt is to say that it is an inferior western counterpart of the Platte. Considerably less of a river, it starts out with a fair flow, gets shallower as it proceeds, and at length loses itself in the desert just short of the modern California state line. Its one virtue, like the Platte's, was that it pointed in the proper direction. Though useless for navigation, it was a proper channel by which prairie schooners could steer their course for the diggings. To-day it performs a similar service to railroad and automobile highway.

According to Frémont, Bryant, and the guidebooks, the course of the Humboldt was marked by a line of cottonwoods and willows, its valley was "rich and beautifully clothed in blue grass, herds grass, clover, and other nutritious grasses," and for three hundred miles it offered everything "requisite for the emigrants' comfort, in abundance." Many of the forty-niners had difficulty seeing the line of timber and still more trouble finding the luxurious grasses. As one remarked, "We all began to be greatly disappointed." Others waxed much more strident in their complaints against "the learned & descriptive Mr. Frémont," "the elegant & imaginative Mr. Bryant," and all the "scribbling asses" who told of "nutricious grasses." One preferred to call the river the "Hellboldt"; another inscribed verses to it as the "Humbug"; and in 1850 still another addressed the poor river in verse beginning,

> Meanest and muddiest, filthiest stream,
> most cordially I hate you.

The truth about camping facilities of course is relative —relative to the number of persons involved, to their expectations, and to the alternatives available. For the smaller parties of the years before the gold rush the valley had wood and grass enough to take care of them very comfortably. Perhaps Frémont and Bryant also had a better awareness of what it would have been like to cross the wasteland from Salt Lake to the Sierra without the assistance of this humble watercourse. The forty-niners, at any rate, represented more traffic than the valley could bear. They soon exhausted the meager supply of wood. Their stock ate all the grass along the south bank, and they had to go "haying" on the other side, which was a nuisance and an extra chore. Also— and here the travel mentors had sounded a warning,— the Indians along the Humboldt were the most thievish to be met with anywhere on the route. They specialized in small pilfering, which was merely an annoyance, in raiding the cattle herds, and in putting an occasional arrow into an animal in the hope that it would have to be abandoned. Lulled into undue complacency by the absence of genuine Indian trouble on earlier marches, the forty-niners were not as much on their guard as they might have been and therefore suffered avoidable losses at the hands of the lowly Utes and Diggers. These experiences tended to lower still further their appreciation of the attenuated oasis that was helping them westward.

At approximately the point where it comes in sight of the massive rampart of the Sierra Nevada, the Humboldt succumbs in discouragement and sinks into the sand. Herein is nothing unique; the intermountain basin and California abound in streams that perform this trick more or less thoroughly: the Sevier, the Mojave, the Los Angeles, and the Salinas, to mention just a few. The first traveler along the Humboldt presumably was disappointed to have the river disappear. The forty-niners were forewarned. Short of the actual sink they began to prepare to cross the forty miles of desert separating them from their promised land.

In width, contour, and mechanical difficulties this desert was a reasonable facsimile of Sublette's Cut-off. It exacted, however, a far heavier toll. It was a hotter crossing, which made it harder, but the telling differences were that it was almost a thousand miles farther along the trail, which meant that men and animals were appreciably more fatigued, and that it came after a long stretch of poor hunting and poor feed, which meant lowered reserves of strength.

Again there was a choice, but between almost identical evils. Impartially the desert stretched forty miles westward to the Truckee and about the same distance southward to the Carson. Halfway on the westward route there was a place called Boiling Springs, with waters almost too bitter to drink even when cooled. The Carson route offered no such solace. Most forty-niners chose according to the Sierra crossing they preferred, by Donner Pass into the northern diggings or from the Carson into the southern. And again, except for the blight of the Donner tragedy, the Truckee–Donner Lake route would have drawn a still larger majority.

Crossing the desert was the most concentrated ordeal of the whole journey. Hardly a team got through intact. Emigrant after emigrant had to carry water back to played-out animals and persons. It was common practice, too, to leave someone huddled in or under a wagon while the team was taken to water and refreshed.

At Fort Laramie cne emigrant had estimated that he saw 30,000 pounds of provisions thrown away, along with much miscellaneous property. The trail the length of the Humboldt was littered with the lares and penates of the emigrants, the rotting carcasses of their cattle, and, too often, with their own corpses. All this, however, was as nothing compared to the scene on the desert. "Such destruction of property as I saw across the Desert I have never seen," wrote Milus Gay; "I should think I passed the carcases of 1200 head of cattle and horses and a great many waggons—Harneses—cooking utensils—tools water casks &c. &c. . . . We also see many men on the point of starvation beging for bread."

Out of this valley of destruction the surviving travelers straggled into the shade of the giant cottonwoods at Ragtown on the Carson or to the clear, cold waters of the Truckee on its way to Pyramid Lake. As at Green River, the stock plunged at once into the stream, and many a forty-niner nudged his cattle over so that he could cool his own body and slake his thirst. While the cattle luxuriated in the grass on the banks of the river, the men washed off the accumulated dust and grime of the trail or even turned out some laundry. A few ventured back into the desert to rescue stranded companions or animals needed for the last leg of the journey. Hardly anyone went back to salvage material possessions; the threat of the desert was too great, and the greater riches of the gold fields seemed now almost within grasp.

From the desert's edge the emigrants turned toward the mountains, sure that the worst was behind them. Henceforth there would be water in abundance and wood at every camp. Also, the grass, at least to begin with, was of the best, and though there seemed to be little game, the streams abounded in trout. Better days did lie ahead, but also another round of hard work and hardships.

The first disconcerting discovery was that, whether they were on the Carson or the Truckee, the trail not only forded various tributaries but also wound back and forth across the main stream in an endless succession of ice-cold fords, often rendered difficult and dangerous by the stones and boulders with which they were lined and obstructed. They discovered also that it was a big climb to surmount the Sierra, most of the passes being 2,000 or 3,000 feet higher than South Pass. Struggling on with jaded teams, all but the most fortunate companies found it a hard scramble. Others had to abandon wagons and sacrifice more possessions.

By this stage of the journey, also, many of the forty-niners were on exceedingly short rations. There was a certain amount of sharing, but the tail end of the migration represented mostly the weaker and most poorly provisioned. A tragedy of starvation might well have developed in the Sierra, except that generous Californians, headed by Sutter, subscribed for the relief of these belated forty-niners, sent wagonloads of provisions across the divide, and succored the unfortunates. Similar relief was provided to the stragglers of the migration of 1850.

After herculean feats of climbing, pushing, lifting, and bracing, the forty-niners got a few of their wagons to the passes above timberline. The majority had left only what could be packed on a weak horse or ox or on their own backs. From the crest the trail plunged down more abruptly. Successful navigation of the rest of the journey would be mostly a question of adequate brake power, supplied as usual by locking the wheels or by snubbing a rope around a convenient tree or stump. On this wise did the overlanders descend upon the diggings, gaunt, weathered, ragged, and unkempt, almost all of them ravenously hungry, and many of them empty-handed.

That many arrived without store of property is not necessarily a condemnation of the route, which after all was designed to deliver men rather than goods. That hundreds or even thousands died on the way is a much worse item on the record, most of it attributable to the cholera. That many of the emigrants, especially among those longest on the trail, suffered grievously and were impaired in health and vigor, also detracts from this route's standing. These defects are not to be idly dismissed; yet there is another side to the picture, represented in force by the companies that got through in July or August or September, and by a host of young men who found that the overland jaunt put them in trim for the strenuous life in the diggings.

Very probably these men remembered longest such things as the vista of innumerable wagontops strung out along the Platte or seen from Independence Rock, the majestic thunder of the buffalo herd, the savor of game roasted over the coals, the Eden-like beauty of Bear Valley, an oddity like having one's hair freeze to the ground on a cold night, or the thrill of successfully completing the adventure of a lifetime. Nor did they need to be reminded that they had helped to pioneer the avenue that was to prove most significant in the subsequent development of the Far West.

In 1850 and succeeding years this path was traveled almost as heavily as in 1849. Installation of ferries at most of the river crossings, establishment of supply depots on a commercial basis at many points along the way, and the subsidence of the cholera epidemic made travel much safer. Some years the grass was poorer, and in 1850 unusual rainfall along the Humboldt drowned the river road and forced the wagons to a rougher paral-

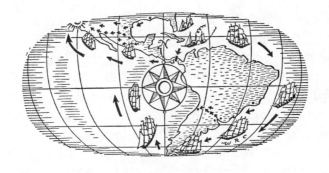

CHAPTER 7

The Byways

ALTHOUGH experience and the logic of geography pointed emphatically to Panama, Cape Horn, and the Platte-Humboldt trail as the best courses for the California-bound, a fifth or a sixth of the forty-niners chose other routes.

Sometimes necessity was the mother of their experiments, as when the press of numbers on the main arteries forced part of the traffic onto secondary roads. At other times sheer and exuberant optimism led them to attempt to find something better than the conventional path. On still other occasions it was a combination of need and hope that prompted their efforts. On these almost innumerable trails, scattered from the Strait of Magellan on the south to Lassen's Cut-off on the north, the luck of the forty-niners ranged from fair to very bad. In the end, however, practically all these attempted supplementary routes remained mere byways.

[123]

As an age-old variant and, in fact, the antecedent of the Cape Horn route, the Strait of Magellan perhaps should not be classified as an experiment or a byway. The Strait figures in one incident which illustrates the susceptibility of the forty-niners to the temptation of a possible short cut. As the *Edward Everett* approached the Horn, Captain Smith spoke of the discomforts of this cold sailing and asked if any would prefer to walk across to the Pacific. Pretending that the volunteers would need to defend themselves against hostile Indians, he put them to drilling on deck. Only gradually did the drill squad catch on that it was the victim of a hoax.

A little farther to the north Friedrich Gerstäcker and his party broke their voyage, though not by free choice, and headed overland for the Pacific. They had been able to arrange passage only as far as the mouth of the Plata. Landing, they trekked across the pampas and the Andes and went on to Valparaiso, hoping to find a ship for San Francisco. They got through, but had no illusions that their route was better than Cape Horn. Similarly, the forty-niners who journeyed from Panama to San Francisco via Callao would greatly have preferred a direct sailing up the coast. Likewise, the footsore pilgrims who walked the length of the Lower California peninsula were fully aware that, given a good ship, the sea lane on their left would have had every advantage. All these were forced detours.

Use of Mexico as a stepping stone was a voluntary choice. There the continent was invitingly narrow. It was a populated country, presumably with accommodations and supplies which travelers could buy. Furthermore, it offered two options for getting on to California: the sea route from a Pacific port such as San Blas or Mazatlán, or an itinerary by land through the northern provinces of Chihuahua and Sonora. The record does not tell explicitly whether the veterans of recent Mexican campaigning inclined toward the routes through Mexico or shunned them. Certainly the wartime publicity had drawn the entire nation's attention to the land below the Rio Grande as one way to the diggings.

The company known as the New England Pioneers, led by Charles A. Paul, allotted nine days for the 280 miles from Vera Cruz, twenty days for the 900 miles to Mazatlán, and thirty-five days for the voyage to San Francisco. The actuality they found to be appreciably different. Four horses were all they were able to buy at Vera Cruz, and so most of them had to walk as far as Jalapa. They complain about poor facilities for travelers and about discomforts. Also, though armed to the teeth like all the forty-niners, they thought Mexico too turbulent for safety. And their fears were realized. At a bath in the capital city some of their number were robbed of a hundred dollars.

After further misadventures they reached San Blas, where it appeared they would have to wait indefinitely for a ship. Improving their time by attending a dance, they got into trouble with the townspeople, presumably through their own overbearing attitude. The affair quickly reached the shooting stage, ending with several men wounded and one of the townsmen killed. The Americans moved on to Mazatlán, chartered a schooner on which they risked themselves only as far as Lower California, and thence continued their disconsolate way by land. Although the southern Mexican crossing sometimes worked out more satisfactorily, it is probably just as well that relatively few chose this route.

Trails across northern Mexico attracted a larger number. From New Orleans and its vicinity, in particular, unless the journey was to be by Panama, it seemed most natural to head for the Rio Grande and follow the military roads of Taylor or Wool. As an all-year route the trail was open immediately, without need to wait for the setting-out time as was true on the northern plains. For at least half the distance, too, the traveler would be passing villages and ranches where he could buy corn and hay for his animals and provender for himself. Consequently he should be able to travel light and fast.

In the first months of 1849, gold seekers in some force arrived at the Texas ports, Galveston, Indianola, Port Lavaca, Corpus Christi, and Brownsville, or gathered at San Antonio to outfit for the trails through Mexico. Wherever the forty-niners went, it seemed to be their lot to be disappointed in the supplies and services available to them and in the prices asked. These Texas towns, notwithstanding their experience as bases for the army in the recent war, were no exception. Sprinkled through the letters and diaries of the travelers are such phrases as: "Climate [at Corpus Christi] delightful. Morals bad. Every one carries a knife and the way they drink is not slow"; "Brownsville is full of blacklegs and gamblers"; "This is the most Godforsaken country I ever heard of." Others were rhapsodic about the beauty of the landscape, the future of the state, and the hospitality of the Texans, and even took in stride the experience of being caught in a norther and having the whole camp thoroughly drenched.

No one could jest, however, about the smallpox and the more deadly cholera which plagued this sector of the gold rush. Cholera infested the ships from New Orleans, visited sudden death on the miners encamped at the Texas towns, and followed them out on the trail. It appears to have been even more virulent than in Missouri and along the Platte. On the *Palmetto*, off Galveston, George Evans reported a Negro stricken, dead, and buried by ten o'clock one morning, and a passenger gone by five that afternoon.

Brownsville had one hundred fatalities, Camargo two hundred and fifty, and San Antonio such a mortality rate that the tolling of church bells for the dead was forbidden. The Essex Overland Mining and Trading Company lost four men in as many days near Laredo. Two others recovered but could not continue the journey, and beyond the Rio Grande three others died. A group known as the Mississippi Company lost three; one from Ohio lost five. Another company was visited by the cholera on the second day's travel beyond Matamoras. After several members had expired, all the rest except one turned back.

Heading southwest and west from the Texas coast, the travelers through Mexico had many ways open to them. They might cross the Rio Grande at Matamoras, Roma, or Laredo and take the road toward Monterrey. They might cross at Eagle Pass toward Monclova and

Parras, or more directly toward Chihuahua. Some crossed as far west as Presidio del Norte or even El Paso del Norte. Those who went through Parras could continue on a southwestward course to Durango and Mazatlán on the Pacific. Another trail led to Parral, Trinidad, Ures, Altar, Tubac, the Gila, and the Yuma crossing of the Colorado. The one more commonly chosen was by Chihuahua, Corralitos, Janos, Guadalupe Pass, and so to the Gila.

On any of these courses, wagons, though sometimes employed, were pretty much of an encumbrance. The custom of the country favored saddle animals and pack mules. In an inventory of the effects left by one of his companions, a cholera victim, Evans itemizes what was probably a characteristic rig. It consisted of a bay mare and a white mule, bridle, saddle, pack saddle, blanket, rope, shotgun, six-shooter, belt and knife, powder and shot, three cotton shirts and one flannel, two caps, a pair of boots and a pair of socks, pantaloons, a frock coat, a panama hat, handkerchiefs and a satin vest, a pair of kiacks, a mirror, combs, a compass, and a pocket flask. Except for a cannister of tea there is no mention of provisions; this forty-niner depended partly on the company stores and partly on what was purchasable en route.

Both in physical appearance and in cultural landscape northern Mexico was a contrast to what most of these travelers were familiar with. Some of them were interested to observe the strange plants that dominated this semiarid land. Some took notice of the methods of conserving water, of building in a country for the most part treeless, and of other adjustments to a none too hospitable environment. More commonly the tendency was to dismiss the land as relatively worthless and the people as obviously inferior. The feature of their society least appreciated was doubtless the prevailing religion. In their sightseeing the travelers visited many churches and seldom with reverence. In one they dubbed a sacred painting the "Ace of Clubs"; they recoiled also from the "domineering clergy" and the "revolting images."

All these travelers through northern Mexico seem to have heard about the Comanches and the Apaches and their habit of raiding beyond the Rio Grande. They kept a constant alert for these scourges of the frontier, but so far as the record goes seem not to have been molested by them. All along the way, however, they were victimized by sneakthieves and pilferers. Evans, for example, reports that on three successive days at Chihuahua a pistol was stolen from a man named Vaughn, Colonel Watson's camp was relieved of several guns and pistols, and George McKnight, "absent from his pack but a few moments," lost his pistols, belt, and knife. Near Saltillo, John E. Durivage caught a peon trying to steal a blanket and gave him a flogging; but at El Molino he was less alert and *ladrones* got off with guns and other articles worth more than $300. Seldom, however, did thievery become worse than a nuisance.

The major fact about the route as far as Chihuahua was that it was well supplied with way stations separated no more than a day's journey, where travelers could count on the basic necessities. Travel in small parties was recommended, so as not to overtax the facilities.

There was grumbling about Spartan fare, about comforts that were lacking, about the superabundance of fleas, and some complaint about prices. Evans remarked, "I am well convinced that cheaper routes to California exist than this." Yet Durivage made the 700 miles from Mier to Chihuahua in a month, a rapid pace made feasible by the Mexican granaries along the way.

At Chihuahua the emigrants laid in supplies to last them through the remainder of the journey. In general this meant pinole (parched corn, powdered and sweetened), higote (dried beef, well pounded and mixed with onions and pepper, or chile), hard bread, and coffee. Many purchased leather canteens and, if they had not done so already, discarded their American pack saddles for those of the Spanish model.

Northwestward from Chihuahua the Mexican settlements became more and more straggling and the menace of the Apaches increasingly evident. Nevertheless, travel was reasonably easy, with water and grass somewhat more plentiful than east of Chihuahua. At approximately the present international boundary the trail reached Guadalupe Pass. Here travelers on the Mexican gold trail fell in with California-bound emigrants from the States by way of El Paso or Santa Fe. The rest of the trip, therefore, may be regarded as an extension of this more familiar travel through the American Southwest.

In the first flurry of gold excitement Texas and Arkansas boosters spoke up for their towns as the best of all gateways to California. Postmaster S. G. Haymie of Austin issued a circular proclaiming that the "best and

cheapest way to California is, beyond question, the overland route through this state." The editor of the Hous-
ton *Democratic Telegraph* charted a course from Hous-
ton to Fredericksburg, El Paso, and San Diego, which,
he said, "is emphatically the emigrant's route to California." The *Arkansas State Democrat* extolled the
southern route as "the most direct, the best, and the
cheapest route." Characterizing the northern plains and
Panama as the Scylla and Charybdis of '49, the editor
of this paper came out squarely for the direct route in
Arkansas' latitude, passing "through a country among
whose hills is heard continually reverberating the joyous
laugh of spring, and whose valleys wear the warm smile
of an eternal summer."

So far as Texas was concerned, the routes west were
mostly theoretical. The Texan Santa Fe expedition of
1841, for example, had encountered so many dry
marches and had straggled into New Mexico in such
exhaustion as to be bad publicity for the route. In the
summer of 1848, however, San Antonio merchants had
sponsored a Texas Ranger exploration to open a wagon
road to El Paso and Chihuahua. The leader of this expedition, Colonel Jack Hays, got only as far as Presidio
del Norte. He came back with the opinion that the
best way to go was by San Saba and the Pecos. The
national government next entered the picture, assign-
ing Lieutenants W. H. C. Whiting and W. F. Smith
to search out a practicable military road from San Antonio or Austin to El Paso. Leaving San Antonio on
February 12, 1849, they followed the San Saba route to
El Paso and by May 21 had returned by a more south-

erly course which they pronounced better. Indian agent Robert S. Neighbors and Dr. John S. Ford of Austin made a quick trip west by Brady's Creek and the Concho, returning by the Guadalupe Mountains and Horsehead Crossing. By June, therefore, the advocates of travel through Texas could point to the Whiting-Smith "lower road" and the Neighbors-Ford "upper road" as tested routes to El Paso. The Texas editors had already been plugging this general route enthusiastically and a fair number of forty-niners had already set out.

The journal of a typical forty-niner through Texas reports no particular trouble in the hill country west of Austin, "scenery grand," plenty of water, sometimes too much, "grass luxuriant," the hills themselves poor and rocky, but the valleys of the Pedernales, Llano, San Saba, and Concho affording "delightful locations" for camp or settlement. There was some hunting, better fishing, and at one camp site the corpse of an Indian who they supposed had been killed by "Californians" ahead of them. On the plains the diarist found the aspect "very dreary," the country flat and poor, and great scarcity of timber. There were marches of as much as forty miles without water. Ferrying themselves across the Pecos, this particular party encountered more arid stretches, had trouble locating a pass through the mountains, noted sublime scenery but very difficult traveling, took some wrong trails, but came at length to the Rio Grande, got their baggage ferried across by canoe to El Paso (modern Ciudad Juárez), and with no difficulty swam their horses and mules across. Elapsed time from Austin, eight weeks, which approximates the average.

Beyond El Paso the trail divided. One branch ran southwest through barren country to Corralitos and the Mexican trail to Guadalupe Pass. The other went up to Doña Ana, west through the Mesilla Valley, and thus to the Gila. These were long-established trade routes, additionally tested by American soldiers in the course of the recent war. The rest of the way the Texans found themselves mingled with other gold seekers.

North of Texas, the next eligible starting points were Van Buren and Fort Smith, Arkansas. In several respects they were more favored by nature, and also by the forty-niners. River boats made it easy to get to them. As business offered, a number of steamboats plied the Arkansas. The owners of the *Alert No. 2* went further, advertising their boat as a packet between Cincinnati and Fort Smith on which California-bound travelers could make "half the trip across the continent," so the advertisement said. Passengers on some of these boats had just cause for complaint about crowding, poor food, and poor service. There were accidents, as when passenger P. A. Taylor fell off the *Kate Kirkwood* and, weighted down by his money belt, sank and drowned. There was cholera, though apparently somewhat less than in Texas or Missouri. There were complaints also about high charges for mules, wagons, and other necessities. But the emigrants on this route had the backing of the state of Arkansas, which importuned the federal government to open a road from Fort Smith to California and got an assignment of troops for escort and road building.

Westward from Arkansas the forty-niners thought of themselves as following the route of Josiah Gregg, the

famous chronicler of the commerce of the prairies. Gregg
had made several trips to Santa Fe; one in 1839 over
the more southerly course from Arkansas, along the
Canadian to the upper Pecos and the Rio Grande. Army
detachments engaged in topographical surveying had
also traveled this way. But the route was much older
than Gregg. American fur trappers used it in the 1820's
and 1830's, and long before them it had been the path
of French fur traders, as the name Canadian was in
fact a reminder.

As they moved out along this route, the forty-niners
saw surprising little to recall this earlier traffic. Ab-
normal rainfall made the first hundred and fifty miles
of the trail a quagmire, the wagons were constantly
getting stuck, and there was so much trouble that some
parties switched over to packing. West of Chouteau's
trading post, the sun came out, the road got better, the
health and good spirits of the travelers improved correspondingly, and they forged ahead rapidly. Hunters
bagged plenty of game, the captain of the military escort
had a talk with the Comanche and Kiowa Indians, who
agreed not to interfere with the migration, and when
twin boys were born at one of the camps, they were
named Dillard and Marcy after the civilian and military
captains of this migration.

Beyond the Cross Timbers the emigrants came out
upon the Llano Estacado ("Staked Plain"), so named
from the stone-pillared or stockaded bluffs that seemed
to guard its edge. Here they pondered the life of the
prairie dog, mounted to the higher tablelands, and
looked out upon the plains "boundless as the ocean."

Past Cerro Tucumcari, a hill that in the distance reminded Marcy of the dome of the Capitol at Washington, they moved on to the Pecos, beyond which they began to encounter signs of New Mexico settlements: a
flock of 2,000 sheep, the town of Anton Chico, the cultivated valley at Questa, and finally Santa Fe itself. In
Marcy's opinion this was the easiest route to Santa Fe,
and an ideal course for a railroad.

Still another avenue to the gold fields was chosen by
a group of Cherokees from Tahlequah in present Okla-
homa, joined at the start by a number of Arkansans from
Fayetteville. They drew up an elaborate plan of organization, chose officers, and started by way of the
Neosho and the Verdigris to the Arkansas, which they
followed past Bent's Fort to Pueblo. Like other emigrant parties, they were devastated by cholera; like
others, they allowed part of their stock to stray away. In
the customary pattern they disagreed over how to go.
Some turned off before Pueblo, and there the company
broke into several parts. One group turned south toward
Santa Fe. A few packed over the mountains. Others
moved north along the base of the Rockies to Cherry
Creek, the South Platte, and round the Medicine Bow
Mountains to Fort Bridger, a route that came to be
known as the Cherokee Trail. Some of them were at
Salt Lake City in time to witness the Mormon celebration of their second anniversary in the West.

The most thoroughly tested of all the southwestern
routes was, of course, the one that began in Missouri.
Though projected earlier in the travels of Pedro Vial
and Zebulon M. Pike, it had come into its own when

independent Mexico discarded the restrictive system of imperial Spain. Missouri merchants thereupon discovered the New Mexican market, and caravans began to roll over the Santa Fe Trail. By way of the Kaw, Council Grove, and the Arkansas the trail ran southwestward. One arm continued along the Arkansas and entered New Mexico by way of Raton Pass. Another arm cut across to the Cimarron. There were still other variants, for example, Gregg's Canadian River route of 1839.

There were extensions, too, on which American goods were carried down to El Paso and Chihuahua, over into Sonora, and somewhat later on a pack route on an arc north of the Grand Canyon to Los Angeles. Over these trails a variety of goods was channeled to Missouri: silver from Sonora and New Mexico, horses and mules from California, blankets from Santa Fe, and furs from the entire Southwest.

A limited number of settlers entered California by this general route prior to the gold rush. The War with Mexico had a more profound effect in smoothing and widening the road to Santa Fe and its California extensions, notably in the march of Kearny and his dragoons, the Mormon Battalion under Cooke, and Graham and his soldiers. By 1849, therefore, it was a well-known fact that California could be reached by a swing through the Southwest.

That only a few thousand chose this route is not easy to explain—Ralph P. Bieber estimates 2,500, against 3,000 by Texas and northern Mexico, and 3,000 by Arkansas. The military detachments, to be sure, had found travel increasingly difficult beyond the Rio

Grande and beyond the Colorado. Furthermore, the route seemed a long way round to the gold fields in northern California, and at the Missouri towns the southwestern route had to compete with the more direct and expeditious central route.

In the annals of the Santa Fe Trail the forty-niners are usually treated as incidental to the military of earlier years and to the traders who had pioneered it. Nevertheless, at 2,500 they were the largest congregation the route had carried. Beset by cholera only as far as Council Grove, and unmolested by Indians, though plenty of them were seen, the gold seekers journeyed to Santa Fe with only the normal plains incidents of a few dry camps, minor breakage of wagons, a few horses lost in chase of the buffalo, and a few head of stock strayed from their camps.

Santa Fe took them pretty much by surprise. They had some awareness of its Spanish, commercial, and military backgrounds, but they were not quite prepared for its boisterous character. Some diarists were critical of its dissipations—"the hardest place I was ever in," said one; but most of the travelers did not hesitate to dance with the señoritas and patronize the cantinas. A number went broke at the gambling tables and thereby forfeited their chance to go on to California.

A prevalent practice was to refit at Santa Fe, many deciding to switch from wagons to packing. Since the town was swarming with Arkansas travelers as well as those who had come from Missouri, the price of mules and pack equipment soared out of all reason, and, as at Independence, St. Joe, Van Buren, San Antonio,

Corpus Christi, Chihuahua, and Vera Cruz, the forty-niners' lament at overcharging was voiced here.

Most of the emigrants decided to go on by way of the Gila and the Yuma crossing. A few left the Rio Grande at Albuquerque and traveled west to Zuñi and then southwest to Salt River and the Gila. A larger number took the Kit Carson–Kearny trail that left the Rio Grande some distance below Socorro and threaded its way across to the upper Gila. At least one party seems to have taken a course west of Doña Ana approximating the present road through Benson. The most-favored route to the Gila, and the only one over which wagons had gone, lay still farther south. It swung well down into Mexico, one branch passing through Janos and Corralitos, and led to Guadalupe Pass, where travelers from Mexico and Texas joined those from Missouri and Arkansas.

The land west of the Rio Grande is rougher and more desolate than that along the Santa Fe Trail. The shift from wagons to packing was of course one concession to this more difficult terrain yet too many of the forty-niners did not approach this division of the journey with adequate respect. They overtaxed their animals, which at best would have to suffer from poor feed, dry camps, and bad water, and oftentimes they neglected what must be regarded as elementary precautions. Forced stops to recruit the teams, to cut and shrink tires on wheels contracted in the extreme dryness, to cut down the wagons to carts, or to shift from wagons to packing were the common lot of these travelers. They also followed the pattern of the earlier military travelers in trying to induce the Apaches to bring in fresh animals to sell or trade, but without much success.

Experienced mountaineers would not have been fazed by Guadalupe Pass. The trail climbed a bit to reach it— after all, it was a crossing of the continental divide. Then it followed a ledge around a moderately steep cliff and descended abruptly to the valley of the Santa Cruz. Most of the forty-niners on the southern route had seen mountains only at a distance. They had an eerie feeling on the ledge, and in varying phraseology they expressed apprehensions about this sort of travel and about the descent with locked wheels and ropes attached to hold back the wagons. "The worst place for wagons to travel over I ever saw," said one, the road "almost perpendicular for 2 miles." Others reduced the descent to 1,000 or 1,500 feet, hard work and dangerous, yet, as one observed, "by this time . . . we had become inured to hardship, and as to danger we had nearly become reckless."

Next stops were the Mexican towns of Santa Cruz and Tucson. They appeared to be feeble outposts against the Apaches and had very little surplus of provision for this unusually large army of travelers.

Beyond Tucson stretched a jornada of seventy-five or eighty miles concerning which the reports are at variance. It was advertised as waterless, but some of the travelers had the good fortune of being rained on, and others found mudholes from which they could drink, though it was wise to "set their teeth close and keep out the polliwogs." Evans supposed there would always be water at one camp. Others thought this jornada the worst of the entire trip. Durivage, for example, is graphic in description of the parched landscape, the clouds of dust, the withering heat, and the agonies of thirst and exhaustion. He credited his arrival at the Gila to the accident of finding a mule in the desert just when his mount gave out. "The dust in this road," said John W. Audubon, "is over the shoe tops, and rises in clouds, filling the eyes and almost choking us as we trudge along, sore and jaded." Horses and mules gave out, and at least one emigrant, William Fagan of Arkansas, was buried here.

On the Gila the travelers through Mexico were heartened by the sight of American soil, though few crossed to set foot on it. Of more immediate interest, after all had drunk of the water of the river, was trade with the Indians who cultivated this oasis. They were Pimas, the same tribe that had responded with such enthusiasm to the efforts of the great seventeenth-century missionary, Francisco Eusebio Kino. Cooke and Emory had also given them a good character as honest, affable traders. Most of the forty-niners found them so, though inclined to ask high prices for their corn and beans and melons. Bright shirts were the preferred medium of exchange. They had few animals to sell, and one party, waking up minus a lead line and other harness, conceded that these Pimas might have been honest in an earlier day but had "learnt bad manners."

From the Pima Villages the usual trail struck out into the sand again to cut off a bend of the Gila. Some companies took this march in stride, and with no complaints entered in the journals. Others found it heavy going; "*such travel*," said Audubon, "as please God, I trust we may none of us ever see again." "Our road is garnished," he said, "almost every league, with dead cattle, horses or oxen; wagons, log chains, and many valuable things are left at almost every camping ground." Their jaded mules could carry only about a hundred pounds.

An incident in a company from Clarksville, Arkansas, illustrates the strain of the journey. Two young men, Davis and Hickey, got into a quarrel and a fight. Davis got the better of it, but when bystanders pulled him off, Hickey drew a knife and stabbed his victorious foe to the heart. Convening as a court, the company found Hickey guilty of murder and sentenced him to face a firing squad. He was buried on the bank of the Gila.

A minority of the gold seekers elected to navigate the river. One is said to have brought a sixteen-foot flatboat all the way from Lake Michigan for such an exigency. Others collected driftwood and built rafts or boats—the accounts differ. On the voyage, made difficult by shallows and sandbars, a Mrs. Howard presented to her husband an addition to the family, the accounts again differing on the vital question of whether the baby was a boy or a girl, but all agreeing that the newcomer was named Gila.

Along the lower Gila, Durivage reports meeting a Mexican company from Mazatlán which included half a dozen New Yorkers who had despaired of getting passage from Mexico's west coast. Companies of Sonorans were on their way to the diggings, and the late-season forty-niners met other groups going back home.

Another to journey eastward was Lieutenant Cave Couts, sent from San Diego in September with an escort for the boundary surveyors. All across California, Couts found himself besieged by the emigrants for information on the road to the coast and the mines. He complains of being "troubled nearly to death" by them and of having to write out a hundred waybills charting different companies a course to follow. At the Colorado more emigrants besieged Couts for advice and for donations of flour, beef, coffee, etc.

Not least among the contradictions of the southern route was that its driest part, the arid belt at the California boundary, was intersected by the mightiest river southwest of the Missouri, the turbulent Colorado, architect of the Grand Canyon. At its lowest stage the Colorado could be forded. So crossed the Spanish pioneers under Juan Bautista de Anza in the 1770's. By summer, however, the river had a depth of as much as twenty feet and some sort of ferrying was necessary.

The Lake Michigan flatboat and the Gila River craft were put in service. Other emigrants caulked wagon boxes or fashioned smaller cockleshells with willow poles and oilcloth, canvas, or hides. A few tended to their own ferrying, but the main reliance, as in Anza's time, was on the Indians of the vicinity. In camp the Yuma six-footers were recognized as magnificent physical specimens, but it was in the water that they displayed the most remarkable prowess. Swimming with a strong overhand stroke, they performed unbelievable feats. Men, women, and children seemed perfectly at home in the water. Paid a shirt or a blanket, they swam the mules across and pushed small raft loads of belongings and forty-niners to the opposite bank.

To the misfortune of the travelers, however, as history might have testified from the record of a Spanish emigrant group massacred in 1781, the Yumas were both thievish and treacherous. They pilfered a few articles from the forty-niners in camp. Every now and then they swam a mule or a raft downstream and away instead of across. Growing bolder, they threatened open attack upon the wayfarers. As the season progressed the journals of these travelers came to have more and more entries complaining against the Yumas. The record book which Isaac Williams opened at Rancho del Chino also abounds in such charges, to which of course must be added the accident toll that the river itself collected. Just before Durivage arrived at the crossing three Missourians were lost from a capsized raft. Later, a double-canoe raft overturned and four men were drowned.

Despite this double hazard most of the forty-niners got safely across. Technically, they were now on California soil; but few rejoiced, because they still faced a weighty problem—ninety miles of desert sand and heat before they could enter the friendly mountains beyond. Seventy-five years earlier, Anza's pathbreakers had found the battle with sand dunes and desert more of an ordeal than the Colorado crossing or earlier jornadas. Too many of the forty-niners got to it in a state of progressive exhaustion, their animals jaded, their provisions drained by ferry charges, thievery, and forced abandonment, to less than the minimum for safety.

As best they could they readied for the ordeal. Some gathered twists of grass or mesquite leaves and beans to carry along as a bait for their mules. Evans' company bought pumpkins from the Yumas to use for mule feed. Traveling by night as much as was possible, the emigrants made what haste they could across the desert. The trail was well marked by the tracks of Kearny, Cooke, and Graham, as well as the forty-eighters from Sonora, and by all accounts it was liberally strewn with the shriveled carcasses of horses and mules.

To this holocaust the forty-niners made a substantial addition of played-out animals, packs, harness, and assorted belongings. Bayard Taylor interviewed one traveler who said he had counted 300 dead animals at one camp and, more appalling, the bodies of three emigrants left unburied by the trail. Another asserted that "the whole road on the desert seemed almost covered with the carcasses of dead animals, the stench of which was terrible." Durivage reported the trail "plainly marked by scores of dead mules, saddles, bridles, blankets, broken trunks, bags, and canteens, until on all sides misery and death seemed to prevail." According to Audubon, "broken wagons, dead shrivelled-up cattle, horses and mules as well, lay baking in the sun."

In June, 1849, the desert crossing was improved by the discovery of New River, actually not more than a lagoon, where, as one traveler described it, there was "plenty of good water for emigrants (but bad to those of more fastidious tastes)." Had it not been for this oasis, the tragedy of the desert might have been even greater. There was a great sacrifice of property, and there were deaths, though exactly how many is not on record.

From New River the emigrants plodded on, encouraged after some hours to find that the trail was rising, and at length rewarded by coming to the base of the mountains and a spring of sulphur water which man and beast pronounced good. In the words of one of the travelers, "entering the mountains . . . was like coming into Paradise." Carrizo Creek was followed by San Felipe and Warner's Ranch at Aguas Calientes. At one of these spas it was customary to stop and rest. Shortage of grass, however, forced them to move on, the trail winding through the mountains and passing a number of Indian villages where some of the diarists speak rapturously of corn in the ear, peaches, and grapes. Another describes his last meal before entering San Diego— boiled bacon, the last hard biscuit in the haversack, and a watermelon given his young companion by a señorita they met on the trail. Durivage, arriving at San Diego empty-handed, wangled an invitation to the army mess hall and says that the food there was delectable. The plain fact, of course, is that at the end of the trail almost anything would taste good.

Undoubtedly, many companies got in from the Gila in good condition. The ones described in writing, however, appeared badly used up, walking "with a kind of dead march step," ragged, dirty, starved, worn down, and exhausted. Bayard Taylor saw some of them come aboard the *Panama* when it stopped at San Diego. He noted, of course, that they were lank and brown, their clothes in tatters, their boots run down or replaced by moccasins, and their possessions reduced to their rifles and little else. From their faces, it seemed to him, "the rigid expression of suffering was scarcely relaxed." A self-description by one of the travelers confirms the outward appearance. Except for an extra pair of socks this forty-niner had only what he was wearing—a thin calico coat, a worn-out vest, duck trousers, a worn-out overcoat, and a beat-up hat.

At San Diego these people were still a long way from the diggings, though if there was room on the steamer the rest of the journey would be easy. Many chose to continue with pack or wagon, in which case they by-passed San Diego, took a northerly course from Warner's Ranch to El Chino and Los Angeles, and by the coastal valleys or the San Joaquin went on to the mines. This was a journey of five or six hundred miles, but through a land of abundant forage and with beef, grain, fruit, and game for the traveler. By the time they reached northern California most of these pilgrims from the Gila were fairly well recuperated. Taylor met several such companies near San Jose. He describes them as "wild, sunburned, dilapidated men, but with strong and hardy frames," and he thought them "little affected by the toils of the journey." Travelers fresh from the desert were seldom given such compliments.

On the whole, history has dealt in unkind terms with the southern gold trails. Doubtless this is in part because of the extraordinary vigor with which some of the contemporary chroniclers complained about the hardships. The desert crossing was a nightmare, and some of the jornadas south of the Gila were almost as bad. The Colorado was a formidable obstacle, rendered worse in the fall of 1849 by Yuma hostility, and then still worse by John Glanton and his gang of assassins who took over the business of ferrying.

Whichever variant was followed, the southern route was less well watered than the Platte-Humboldt trail. Furthermore, it led to California but not to the diggings, which made it actually several hundred miles longer and slower. Yet this route avoided the worst mountains, was dotted with supply stations, and instead of being closed in the winter was in some respects then at its best. Over it came eight or nine thousand forty-niners, a considerable element in the grand total.

To round out the tracery of the southern trails, which resembles a snarl of tangled yarn with many loose ends, some notice needs to be given of the attempted use of the Old Spanish Trail circling north of the Grand Canyon and of its tie-in with another byway reaching southwest from Salt Lake. Though not as ancient as its name implies, the Old Spanish Trail had been thrust into southern Utah by Fathers Escalante and Domínguez in the 1770's and extended to Los Angeles in the Mexican epoch. Occasional companies of traders had followed it since 1829 and with them at times came a few Americans to settle in California. The route, therefore, was known to be negotiable, and some of the forty-niners decided to strike out upon it from Santa Fe.

One such company, progressing about two hundred miles, came to a river, the Chamas, which they could not cross. They retraced their steps to Santa Fe and made for the Gila. Others persevered. It was not a route for wagons. The first leg of the journey was over rough terrain. The two rivers that make the Colorado, the Grand and the Green, had to be crossed. Then followed more rough country, and a succession of long marches between scant and uncertain watering places on the desert that ended at Cajon Pass. Only fragmentary evidence of travel over the route has been preserved. There are a few entries in the register which Isaac Williams opened at Rancho del Chino. In the Santa Clara Valley in what is now southern Utah, we are also told a party from Salt Lake found a written notice, "Look out, for we have killed two Indians here." The probability seems to be that it was written by packers from Santa Fe. Yet the lack of a circumstantial journal by a forty-niner on the Old Spanish Trail is itself a hint that few came this way.

The southwestward course from Salt Lake drew a larger clientele. Mostly it was of interest to the laggards in the vast multitude swarming over the Platte-Humboldt trail. At the Mormon capital these people heard gloomy reports of the route to the westward, the forbidding salt desert beyond the lake, and the grass burned up and consumed by earlier companies. Also, they were reminded that they would have to hurry to get across the Sierra before snow began to fall, and so soon after the Donner tragedy this indeed was something to think about.

At Salt Lake City there was active propaganda for the Los Angeles route, which winter would not close, and over which a few outfits had traveled in preceding years. A certain Barney Ward issued a guidebook, presumably in manuscript. And Jefferson Hunt, a former member of the Mormon Battalion, offered his services as guide at ten dollars a wagon, provided one hundred wagons could be lined up for the trip. The number was easily made up. It included some smaller companies more or less intact, plus a miscellaneous assortment of persons who had got to Salt Lake with trains that kept on toward the Humboldt. The majority had come in by way of Fort Bridger and Echo Canyon.

One small group headed by W. L. Manly came on a detour all its own. At the Green River crossing these men found a crude boat, abandoned by earlier ferriers. Alarmed by rumors of Mormon hostility, and excited by the knowledge that the waters of the Green flowed to the Pacific, they decided to quit their jobs as ox drivers and turn boatmen. For a few days the river carried them forward at an agreeable speed. Then it entered canyons; they had trouble at cataracts and rapids and at length lost their boat while trying to work it around a huge boulder. In hollowed logs they went on, finally meeting a band of Indians whose chief drew them a map in the sand and by signs warned them of the still more dangerous stretches of white water that lay ahead. Five of the seven therefore quit the river and trudged overland toward the Mormon settlements. Having lost all their equipment, these young men were delighted at the chance of hiring on as teamsters with the emigrants waiting for a cooler season on the Los Angeles trail.

Early in October Hunt was ready to go. At his suggestion they all moved down to the Spanish Fork, south of Provo, and there organized as the Sand Walking Company, consisting of seven divisions, each with a captain, and with Hunt as commander and guide. Wagons numbered 106; personnel was estimated at 500. For several days things went smoothly. They tarried a day at the Sevier because two men were sick. They came across broken pottery of superior workmanship and concluded that the land had once been inhabited by better Indians than the Paiutes. At a mountain valley teeming with rabbits they staged a big hunt and bagged one for each member of the company.

For many of these travelers, however, the pleasures of the trail were alloyed by a hankering to go westward toward the diggings rather than south. Finally some of the men pressured Hunt to try to find a short-cut. Reluctantly he rode out to explore, the whole train following to a dry camp. After thirty-six hours Hunt was back, gasping for water, his tongue so swollen that he could not speak. They all got back on the trail.

A few days later the train was overtaken by a small group of packers led by O. K. Smith. He claimed to know a direct route via Walker's Pass that would save five hundred miles and bring them to the diggings in twenty days. The Smith short cut was debated over the campfires. Its first converts were the Flake-Cannon company, another small group that had caught up with the Hunt train. The men of this group began to make pack saddles so that they could turn off with Smith. Finally a general meeting was called. Hunt spoke strongly for the route he knew, roundabout though it was. He predicted that those who turned off would "get into the jaws of hell." Yet the opposition had the pleasanter argument. Eighty wagons voted for the cut-off, and the hilarious Smithites celebrated the break-up of the party by boring holes in trees, filling them with powder, and setting off the charges. At the actual forking of the trails only seven wagons followed Hunt; eleven men, two women, and three children, Mormons all.

Although this group was too small for safety from Indian attack, it had a pilot who knew the way. Furthermore, since it was now on the Old Spanish Trail, it picked up various signs of recent use by travelers from Santa Fe. At the Muddy the group was reinforced by a handful of Mormons under Brother C. C. Rich who were disillusioned about the cut-off and had turned south hoping to intercept Hunt's trail. The road was not entirely pleasant, passing over an alkali desert to Salt Springs, over a snow-covered pass, and through heavy sand where all had to put shoulders to the wheel to help the teams through. Nevertheless, soon before Christmas the Rich and Hunt parties had got through to southern California, where they joined in a Christmas dinner. Empty-handed though they were, this was a happy ending for their overland trek.

Meanwhile, the emigrants who had turned off on the Smith route had had a great variety of unpleasant experience. Two or three days after the split-up, they came to a precipice which the wagons could not descend. Smith found a trail down which his mules could scramble. He went down, turned south with the canyon, and disappeared. Other packers followed. The wagon people of necessity made camp on the mesa and sent out scouts to find a place to get the wagons down. In token of their discouragement they named the spot Mount Misery. Here also an emigrant died and was buried "in as good style as the circumstances would allow."

From their impasse at the jumping-off place a part of
the travelers decided to retrace their steps and follow
Hunt's trail. An estimated three hundred did so, and
others would have joined them except that they had to
wait for their scouts to return. These three hundred did
not catch up with Hunt, who had a week's head start,
but they followed the road with only the routine priva-
tions and in due course arrived safely in southern California.

Of those remaining at Mount Misery, the horse and
mule faction made packs and followed Smith's trail into
the canyon. They split again, with Rich and his fellow
Mormons working south and finding Hunt, as already
related. Another group, including Jacob Y. Stover, who
later wrote a narrative of these experiences, turned
westward in Smith's path and caught up with him. After
twenty days, the time span that was supposed to have
brought them to the diggings, they found themselves
camped at the eastern base of a big mountain covered
with snow. Smith had had enough. He saddled up to go
back to Salt Lake, though one account has it that when
he got to Hunt's trail he turned and came on to California.

Stover and his companions named their camp Dead
Horse Spring, because they had to resort to killing a
horse for food. One of the boys had additional reason
to remember the camp; in the night a coyote stole one
of his boots, and to replace it he "skinned the old gray
horse's hind leg and stretched it on his foot and leg."

Among the three dozen men still left at Dead Horse
Spring, opinion was divided on how to proceed. One

group, nine or eleven in number, was for persisting toward Walker's Pass, even though it would have to be on foot. Concerning their experiences a great many contradictory statements have been made, along with some others that are probably ill founded. In the middle of a "big desert" they are said to have considered drawing lots to see who should be killed and eaten. Rather than participate in the lottery, two men, Pinney and Savage, stole away by night, got to Owens Lake in sad shape, were rescued by the Indians, and assisted across Walker's Pass and to the diggings. Nine skeletons found a decade later behind a brush windbreak on the Slate Mountains were taken to be the remains of the rest of this party, but the identification is conjectural and some at least may have reached the mines.

Stover and his group backtracked for one day, then worked southward, and struck Hunt's trail. They subsisted on horse meat and on mule meat, which Stover insisted was much better, and at one camp found a steer that had been abandoned. Along the lower Mojave they at last caught "the tail of Hunt's train," from which they received a dole of beans and meal. Hurrying on to Cajon Pass, they were met by a man who had come out with fresh beef for the relief of the emigrants. Stover says that he and a companion began with a thick slice of cold tallow and followed it with chunks of beef broiled on the coals and meal that was "wet up" and cooked on flat rocks. At sundown they came to where the canyon opens out on the San Bernardino Valley, which he describes as "the loveliest place I ever saw; everything looked so nice and warm; the frogs were singing and the birds too; it seemed like we had passed into a new world." On Christmas Day they were guests at Cucamonga Rancho.

These arrivals left one faction still unaccounted for, the ox-team people at Mount Misery, whose scouts had gone off to search for a way to get down from the mesa. One was found to the northward, and toward it they set their course. Most numerous in this group were the Jayhawkers, a company of young men who wanted no encumbrance of women and children as they tried the untested short cut. The Rev. J. W. Brier, with his wife and their three young sons, tagged along with the Jayhawkers nonetheless. The Bennett and Arcane families and their hired men constituted another group, in addition to which there were the Dale and Wade families and the "Georgia Boys" led by Jim Martin. They traveled sometimes together, but at other times went their several ways.

Through November and into December they moved in an irregular and snail-like course over a barren plain littered with oval buttes. Often the only water was "puddle water." As Sheldon Young put it: "There is no running water. . . . Grass, it is scarce, wood, there is none. It is a dubious looking country." In subsequent entries he amended the latter to read "dismal looking," "damned dubious looking," and "Damned hard looking." On what they called the five-day desert the Jayhawkers were saved by an opportune snowfall. The others had circled more conservatively to the southward, but, even so, had found it necessary to abandon some of their wagons.

By way of Furnace Creek Wash they all entered a "valley of salt," now known as Death Valley. The Jayhawkers moved north past several springs, made camp on Salt Creek, and there reluctantly decided to abandon their wagons. Here also they were overtaken by the Briers, who reattached themselves, and by the Georgians, who went on in the direction of Walker's Pass. After further tribulations the Georgians got to the diggings. The Jayhawkers left Death Valley by Towne's Pass and veered southwestward. Their suffering was grievous. Captain Asa Haynes on one occasion offered five dollars for a biscuit and was refused. At least three died on the trail. But in Antelope Valley the country began to improve. On February 1, at the head of the Santa Clara, Young was more cheerful, and four days later at San Francisquito Rancho he closed his dismal log with the words, "and we have got out of trouble at last."

Lagging behind the Jayhawkers in the entrance into Death Valley came the Bennett-Arcane party. From Furnace Creek Wash this little group turned south to a tiny oasis since known as Bennett Wells and went into camp. To take the wagons farther seemed impractical; but how to go ahead without them seemed equally impossible. As a solution of the dilemma they at length decided to send two young men, W. L. Manly and John Rogers, to explore the route and if possible to bring back assistance. These boys set off over the Panamints near Telescope Peak, overtook and passed the Jayhawkers, and, after a much longer journey than they had expected, arrived at Rancho San Francisquito.

With a mule and two horses, a small quantity of flour, and four oranges for the children, they immediately started back, an act of greater heroism when it is recalled that these were merely companions of the trail that they were going to rescue. In a steep and waterless canyon they had to abandon the horses, but with the mule they at last got back to Bennett Wells.

In the twenty-six days of their absence the camp had shrunk to just the Bennett and Arcane families. The Wade family had driven off southward to an unknown fate—though as a matter of fact this was the way they all should have gone. It went past bad water and barren desert but eventually tied in with Hunt's trail and took the Wades to the southern California settlements. Three or four men had gone off separately and at least one of them died before getting out of the valley.

With their oxen rigged for packing and one of them as a carrier for the four children, this last remnant of the 500-man train from Salt Lake bade farewell to Death Valley and took the Manly-Rogers trail. They had all the hardships imaginable—short rations, dry marches, alkali water, no forage for their animals, difficult trails, and scrambles over sharp rocks that cut their moccasins to shreds and made their cattle sore-footed. Every few days they butchered an ox to get rawhide for new moccasins for themselves and for the other oxen and to eat. They were astonished at how little meat there was on an ox—no more than a packload for their little mule, which carried the entire commissary. At long last, on March 7, four months and three days after they had made their fateful decision at Mount Misery, this last remnant of the five hundred who had embarked under Jefferson Hunt got in to the comparative comfort of Rancho San Francisquito.

Because of the special heroism of Lewis Manly and John Rogers, the fortitude of Mrs. Bennett and Mrs. Arcane, the patient suffering of their four children, and the awesome desolation of Death Valley, the saga of this little group has a particular fascination. In conjunction with the experiences of the Wades, the Jayhawkers, the Georgia Boys, the Pinney-Savage group, the Stover party, those who stuck with Smith, the Rich party, and those who repented at Mount Misery and turned back to Hunt's trail but could not overtake their guide—linked to all these, the Manly narrative becomes an irrefutable argument against the folly of disregarding the established trails. None of the tracks of these experimenters developed into a regular emigrant route, but Hunt's trail was used by the Pomeroy–Van Dyke company later in 1849, by several late-season companies in 1850, and became a standard route for freighters and drovers throughout the 'fifties and 'sixties.

One other alleged short cut remains to be noticed— the Lassen Cut-off, which turned from the Humboldt into Black Rock Desert, rounded the Sierra by way of Pit River, and descended the Sacramento Valley. Poring over maps and documents at the national capital, J. Goldsborough Bruff had selected this route for the Washington City company. Other parties, disappointed and antagonized by what they found along the Humboldt, made a last-minute decision to switch to the Lassen trail.

They found it hard going. Black Rock Desert was broad and dry. There were steep hills to climb. The mountain pass was less elevated than those west of the Humboldt Sink, but the country was rough, the Pit River fords were a nuisance, the Indians were pestiferous, and the route was roundabout. Apparently no company by this trail got in before September. Bruff's train got stuck in the mountains, where he with undue magnanimity volunteered to stay as guard and watchman. And Delano, who had turned off on the Lassen trail with some misgivings, pronounces the epitaph not only on this route but on cut-offs in general: "Instead of avoiding the desert, instead of the promised water, grass, and a better road, we were in fact upon a more dreary and wider waste, without either grass or water, and with a harder road before us. . . . We had been inveigled there by false reports and misrepresentations."

The main roads pretty clearly would have been better, yet with twelve or fifteen thousand forty-niners traveling the various byways they shape up as a substantial feature of the gold rush.

CHAPTER 8

The Miner at Work

THE MINING season of 1848, as described in an earlier chapter, got off to a slow and diffident start, gained momentum in the summer, and came to a climax in the fall with several thousand miners hard at work. Onset of the rainy season closed down most of the diggings, forcing the gold seekers to hole up in camp or to move down to the valley towns or to San Francisco. Yet, as soon as winter relaxed its grip they came out of hibernation, ready to launch a new and bigger season.

At the start, of course, the new year's mining was done by a carryover crew of forty-eighters. Panama steamers and round-the-Horn ships brought early reinforcements, followed shortly by contingents which had chosen southern trails. By August and September the main overland trail was discharging thousands of laborers into the diggings, and in later months appeared the rear guard of this migration. Stragglers were still en route, by sea and by land, particularly on the confused march south-west from Salt Lake. In a spirit of broadmindedness the Society of California Pioneers, for membership purposes, later defined the forty-niners as those who had got across the line into California before the stroke of midnight on December 31, 1849. This action is a reminder that most of the forty-niners used up more of the year in traveling than in mining, and that whereas the year-end labor force was perhaps 40,000 or 50,000, the number employed throughout most of the year was far less.

In techniques as well as in personnel 1849 began with an exact carryover from the first year of prospecting. As an implement for mealtime and general purposes, but also for working a crevice or a pocket, each miner carried a knife. Of equal universality was the gold pan. Available as wash basin, laundry tub, or skillet, it was called into play whenever a new claim was being tested; in the more primitive working of claims it was continuously in use; and it was relied on for the final cleaning of metal salvaged by cradle, tom, or sluice.

Oftentimes the miners had to use whatever pans they could get. Their preference, however, was for the stamped-iron variety, flat-bottomed and with sloping sides, not quite three inches deep, and eighteen inches in diameter.

In mechanical principle, the process of panning was exceedingly simple. It was merely to employ water as the agent to induce the heavier gold to settle to the bottom while the lighter sand, gravel, and clay rose to the surface and was eliminated. In practice, a rather high degree of skill, patience, and muscular control was needed to achieve this result.

To start with, one shoveled in a quantity of pay dirt, thoroughly wetted and stirred it, and tossed out any pebbles or rocks. The pan was then submerged and, by gentle rocking, a whirpool current was set up which was allowed to wash the dross over the lip of the pan. The rotating was continued, with increasing caution, until only the color was left, or sometimes the gold mixed with a black sand which had almost the same specific gravity.

To wash fifty pans was regarded as a good day's work, which would seem to mean ten or twelve minutes to the pan. Heavier labor has been devised in field, forest, and factory, yet in panning one had to stoop or squat, at the water's edge or in the water, with hands constantly in and out of the ice-cold stream, and with unflagging attention to the nature of the overflow. Quite understandably, panning, though a challenge to one's skill, was esteemed as a necessary evil rather than an ideally pleasant or comfortable occupation. Furthermore, it was much too slow a way of recovering gold. Whenever they could, the forty-niners made use of machines that would operate on a larger scale.

The earliest and, for a time, the most common example in this latter category was the rocker, or cradle, much favored by the forty-eighters. The rocker consisted of a wooden hopper set over a canvas apron emptying into an open trough about four feet in length, crossed by small cleats, or riffle bars, and all set on rockers so that it could be given a rough, cradle-like agitation. One or more operators shoveled dirt into the hopper, bailed in water, and rocked the cradle. The water, gravity, and the weight of the gold were depended upon, however, to do the essential job of separating the precious metal from its worthless contexture. More gold went out with the tailings than was allowed to escape the skillfully manipulated pan. On the other hand, a far larger quantity of dirt could be washed, and therefore the day's earnings averaged much higher.

Other advantages were inherent in the rocker. Neither patented nor complicated in design, it was something that a moderately skilled handyman could knock together in a few hours. It could be improvised and reproduced in the diggings out of materials conveniently available. It was also reasonably portable, could be moved from one claim to another, or packed from camp to camp. Furthermore, if the bailing was done with reasonable care, the machine could be operated dry-handed; and by trading off at shoveling, bailing, and rocking, some variety of task could be had. Cradling was no more genteel than panning, but at least it could be done without assuming such awkward positions and without absorbing so much moisture. Having gained the ascendancy in 1848, the cradle dominated the scene throughout 1849.

Although rocker, pan, and knife were the crucial implements for recovering gold, the mines were called, significantly, the diggings, and the commonest labor was that of digging. Here the miners used the time-honored pick and shovel. Note also that the popular heraldic device of the forty-niner is a gold pan with crossed pick and shovel. The preference in actual picks was for

Sutter's Saw Mill
Monday April 16 1849.
The first discovery of gold was in digging this mill race. [?]

Courtesy of the Henry E. Huntington Library

SUTTER'S MILL AT COLOMA, 1849

CROSSING THE PLAINS

a light one; the shovel must be round-pointed and long-handled.

The forty-niners dug deeper than those who had preceded them. Many of their claims were in locations where a thick coating of clay or sand overlay the pay dirt. The initial task therefore was to strip off this topping in order to get at the stratum that would be worth washing. Another method, known as coyoting, involved sinking a hole to bedrock and digging side tunnels into the pay dirt. If the shaft was not too deep, the gold-bearing gravel was pitched out. If it was too deep, a windlass was rigged and the gravel was hoisted out in buckets. Coyoting was laborious. Since the tunneling was usually done without timbering, it was also dangerous, and many a forty-niner was crushed or smothered in a cave-in.

Usually, the pay dirt unearthed by coyoting had to be transported a few yards, or perhaps several rods, to the place of washing. Whether moved by bucket, in a shouldered sack, or by wheelbarrow, this factor added considerably to the toil of mining. Some other claims that could be stripped were also inconveniently distant from water. A few of the more resourceful miners attempted to solve this problem by digging ditches that would bring water to the dry diggings. Later seasons would see this idea much elaborated.

The forty-niners also made a beginning in river mining. Since it was alluvial gold that they were exploiting, and since the alluvial process tended to deposit the gold at the lowest attainable levels, it seemed logical to expect that the river bottoms would be the receptacles for the richest caches. The most practicable way to get at the river bottom seemed to be to build a wing dam, divert the water to a fraction of its channel, and then work the exposed bottom. The efforts of this sort in 1849 were on a modest scale. They were coöperative ventures. They could be best undertaken in late season when the streams were low, and they would certainly be washed out in the run-off of the first winter rain. Accordingly, the partners in river mining made a double gamble: first, that their particular section of riverbed would be rich in gold; and second, that the rains would hold off long enough to give them a chance to work it. In 1849 this method was merely experimental.

Other methods sometimes attributed to 1849 include ground sluicing and the long tom. The ground sluice was an open ditch with some irregularities of bottom into which the gold would settle. In the tailrace at Coloma, Marshall had unconsciously made use of this device. Some of the forty-niner ditch diggers may have made purposeful use of the same method. There seems to be no question that gold was at times collected from ditch bottoms. It may also be true, as has been asserted, that boulders were sometimes set in ditches to make a gold trap. Ground sluicing, however, yielded only a negligible fraction of the income of this year.

The tom came in as an improvement on the rocker; it was, indeed, not much more than a rocker enlarged and immobilized. The hopper was lengthened into a trough and fitted with a heavy sheet-iron sieve emptying into another long trough fitted with the usual riffle bars. The major improvements were that a stream of water—

its amount later gaining legal definition as a tomhead—replaced the process of bailing, and that the flow of water was made to perform the work hitherto done by manual rocking. Since it was larger and required a stream of water, the tom took longer to install than the rocker. It was not much more efficient in terms of gold caught or lost, but, like the rocker before it, it enabled a man to work a much larger cubic quantity and thereby raised his daily earnings.

Why the tom was so slow in appearing and so long in gaining favor is a mystery. The Californians were not waiting for it to be invented. The southern Appalachian miners had it in use as early as 1809, and Agricola and Pliny describe it in Old World use long before the discovery of America. Yet for some reason the Californians were content to pan and cradle until the winter of 1849–1850, and some of them, of course, long after that.

About a year later a further improvement came into general use. This consisted in stretching the bottom half of the tom by lining up a whole series of riffle boxes so that the gold-bearing gravel would be subjected to a longer process of washing and sedimentation. Again there were ancient precedents, yet the idea seems to have popped up in California invention-wise. Before long the miners got their sawmill men to turn out a plank four inches wider at one end, so that one sluice box could be tongued in to the next, and so on *ad infinitum*—or rather, and so on for several hundred feet. Given the water, the drainage, and room enough to dump the tailings, sluice mining was the most agreeable form of gold washing yet devised.

One advantage was that whereas the pan had to be cleaned up after each use, and the rocker or tom at least once a day, the sluice could run for a week without much hazard that gold would be washed away. True, it became necessary to station guards for the discouragement of loitering near the riffle bars, yet on the whole the weekly rather than daily clean-up was an asset. It was simple, too. With the water cut down to a moderate flow, the upper cleats were removed, which allowed all the gold to collect at the lower end of the sluice, where it was carefully rescued.

No matter how gold was gathered, the final cleaning of it was a problem. An early technique, apparently Mexican in origin, was to dry the pile and winnow in a light breeze or by blowing. Fine gold was apt to get blown away too. A better method was to apply quicksilver, which has the property of amalgamating with gold. The quicksilver, as a matter of fact, could safely be poured into the rocker, tom, or sluice, where it was especially useful in catching fine gold. By putting the amalgam in a chamois and squeezing, much of the quicksilver could be expelled. The rest could be boiled away or heated in a retort so as to recover the mercury. To the untutored this seemed a magical method of purifying gold. Yet it was not alchemy, or even chemistry; the whole procedure of gold recovery at the placers was a physical process of sifting and sorting by weight.

In retrospect nothing is more striking about the first seasons of mining than the traditionalism that prevailed, the resistance to new ideas, the preference for old and inefficient methods even when better methods were at hand. One explanation, of course, is that human nature is like that; another, that most of the gold seekers arrived as novices and learned how to mine by observing and imitating the methods that were in use.

The emphatic individualism of the miners also, though paradoxically, inclined them toward conformity. The majority worked on their own or in small partnerships which had no other assets than the simple tools and the labor of the partners. This was the smallest of small business, with capitalism present only in the aspirations of the diggers, each of whom hoped to strike it rich enough to become a captain of industry, of finance, or at least of a farm.

Had large-scale capitalism entered the picture sooner, the transition from cradle to tom to sluice would doubtless have been accelerated. Such a development would also have avoided the uneconomical pockmarking of the hillside at Grass Valley with a profusion of coyote shafts, some a hundred feet deep, each to work a claim only thirty feet square. In river mining likewise it would have been more efficient to provide for a stream a completely new channel which would have exposed miles of river bottom. Instead, through disorganized enterprise, as Rodman Paul describes, a ten-mile section of the Feather was cluttered with no less than ten dams; multiple diversion of about twenty-five miles of the Yuba in 1853 cost $3,000,000; and two years later seventeen different companies had river mining projects afoot on the Feather.

Still another reason for technological backwardness in the diggings was the general conviction that mining was a strictly temporary activity, that the mines might be exhausted any day, and that the thing to do was to grab as much gold as possible, as quickly as possible, and then rush back home. At the same time, the miners were buoyed up by hopes of finding a big nugget, a pocket lined with pure gold, or a pay streak that would yield several ounces to the pan. If such luck was to be his, no miner wanted to have to share it with more than a partner or two. This combination of pessimism (that the gold deposits would soon play out) and of optimism (that at any time the miner might strike it fabulously rich) was a powerful influence against the application of big-business methods in the diggings.

On the positive side, this philosophy of the miner's life expressed itself in an unwillingness to put down roots and a mercurial tendency to shift about in search of more promising diggings. First and foremost, the forty-niner was a prospector. Take, for example, the semiserious instructions on how to dig gold which James Heren penned for his friends in Missouri. Tie your blankets on your back, he said. Surmount them with your cradle, pick, shovel, pan, coffee pot, flint bread, and scurvy-producing pork. Take rifle in hand and start off. You will travel, he warned, "over some of the worst mountains I ever saw." Coming to a ravine, you unload, dig a hole four to eight feet square and three to six in depth. A test pan shows no color. You dig more holes and perhaps find a little color. At dusk, having cleaned up five dollars, or more probably only three, you build a fire, sup on hardtack, pork, and coffee without sugar, smoke a pipe, curl up in your blankets, and sleep soundly. "I can assure you," he writes, "gold digging makes a man sleep well." In the morning, rise from your couch, "shake yourself and you are dressed."

The next day, Heren has his prospector join some vagabonds in the "forlorn hope" of river mining. They toil manfully for days, digging a race to accommodate the water, making a dam to divert the stream, and then, in the bed of the river, "pick, shovel, and wash and get nothing."

No doubt unduly cynical, this description nevertheless touches on an experience altogether too common. The forty-niners were incorrigible prospectors. The man hours invested in moving about in search of new diggings, the labor expended in test holes and exploratory panning, the earnings forfeited as paying claims were abandoned in the hope of finding something better—all these debits of prospecting would add up to a fearsome total. On the credit side, of course, were occasional new strikes and the intangible boost to the spirit that came with a change of scenery and taking a new chance.

Not least among the justifications of prospecting, as it flourished in 1849 and the early 1850's, was the increasingly crowded condition of the diggings. In 1849 the mining population rose from four or five thousand at the start of the season to ten times that many at the close. By 1852 the number is generally admitted to have climbed to a hundred thousand. Some put it even higher. The mere pressure of numbers meant that there would be competition for places on the proved bars, ravines, and gulches. Furthermore, as certain of these diggings were worked over, the area eligible for exploitation was by that much diminished and the crowdedness of the diggings was correspondingly increased. Prospecting, therefore, was a valuable safety valve and one which at times opened new districts where a substantial number of miners could work.

The grand total of gold salvaged in 1849 was appreciably larger than in the preceding season, but not by the same ratio in which the number of men at work had increased. For '49 there are relatively fewer anecdotes of tremendous success. Hardly anyone found gold by the muleload or in thousands of ounces. Pound diggings disappeared even from conversation, and the adage came to be that if a claim paid an ounce a day it was wise to stay with it.

The prevailing wage at which competent day labor could be hired in the mines also leveled off at about this figure. This may seem to signify that the average return to the independent miner was an ounce a day. Actually they did not average so much, but there was always the chance of making a rich strike, and if that chance was to be surrendered, the miner wanted and got a premium wage.

Caution is also in order when it comes to computing from this average daily income to find the year's production. The unimpeachable formula would be $t = m \times d \times a$; that is, number of miners times days worked times average daily earnings equals total production. Unfortunately, all four elements are unknowns, or at least mere approximations. The number of miners rose at an unspecified rate from four or five thousand to forty or fifty thousand. The average daily income was less than an ounce. The days worked also varied widely. Losing some weeks in the winter, not working on Sundays, taking time off on holidays, indulging in some other interruptions, turning aside at intervals to prospect or to move camp, and kept from work at other times by sickness, the average miner came nowhere near a 365-day year. Moreover many forty-niners did not arrive in the diggings until midseason or later. The equation then becomes: $t = $ (4,000 or 5,000 to 40,000 or 50,000) $\times$ (200 to as few as 1) $\times$ \$16 or less. For the answer it is as well to go to the contemporary estimates as refined by later scholars. The figures suggested are twenty to thirty millions, an answer that the equation might be made to yield. To repeat: this was a better total than 1848's, but not on a per capita basis.

The year also witnessed a decline in optimism about the mines. The earliest reports, many of them echoing the conclusions of 1848, opined that the mines were inexhaustible, that there was gold for generations to come, the prospects excellent, the gold area enlarging daily, and no need to discourage Americans, or foreigners, for that matter, from coming to the diggings. Later in the year, the tenor of statement was that there was plenty of gold but that getting it called for hard work plus a tincture of luck. Still later, these remarks were seasoned with charges that the mines were a humbug; that overzealous advertisers, probably merchants or speculators, had bragged outrageously about the gold that was to be found. These disillusioned forty-niners advised no one to come to California, especially no one who had a good job or a family.

Imperceptibly and inevitably this attitude slipped over into a general tendency among the forty-niners to feel sorry for themselves, to bemoan their fate as the cruellest imaginable. En route, many of the diarists had fallen into this vein. For every one who wrote about the pleasures and comforts of overland travel or of life on shipboard, there seemed to be ten who, possibly as a way of boasting about success in accomplishing the journey, complained about its hardships and dangers. That the difficulties were so great as they made out may properly be challenged.

Similarly, with regard to the diggings, although a few descant upon the pleasures of mining, more writers of journals and letters seem to have been struck by the unpleasant side. Whereas in one of his sketches Alonzo Delano, cook for the week, holds the mirror to his partner's life of Riley, "with nothing to do but mine and wash his shirts," the average account is more doleful. "There is gold here, but it is the hardest work for a man to get hold of it that you have ever saw." "It is six weeks since I reached the mines, and they have been rendered memorable by the hardest work I have ever undergone." "A miner's life, I think, is the hardest in the world."

What they protested against were such things as daytime temperatures of ninety or a hundred degrees, having to slog about in ice-cold water, the endless picking and shoveling, the uncertainty of reward, the high cost of their living, the monotony of their fare, the badness of their cooking, their susceptibility to disease, and the lonesomeness of being far removed from home. These were complaints as much against the conditions of life in the diggings as against the work itself, but the two of course did tend to fuse.

With mining such an ordeal, it is permissible to ask why the forty-niners kept on digging. One answer, of course, is that many of them did not. Some had come with a fixed intention of plying a trade or profession and made no gesture toward mining. Others were satisfied with a brief fling. Collis P. Huntington, for example, delighted to tell how half a day at the placers was enough to convince him that mining was not his career. Many others turned quickly to some other enterprise or employment in California. Still others, having "seen the elephant," and being thoroughly disillusioned with the country, sought early passage home.

Yet the majority would not let go so easily. In the first place, they had youth on their side. Most of them were near the prime of life; they had stamina and resilience. Even those who arrived soft-handed from the Cape Horn ships, after about a week of puffing and blowing and of aches and blisters, were able to do a good day's work.

They possessed also a goodly store of optimism. The roseate hopes with which they had joined the gold rush were not easily dashed; the high purpose of accumulating a tidy fortune was strong enough to survive a few reverses. This strength of original intention kept some at work, the more so since it was coupled with pride. Having left home to make their fortunes, they were reluctant to go back empty-handed. Having made a substantial investment of time and money to get to the mines, they refused to give up until they had made a real try.

Another potent factor in keeping them at work was that they had to eat. Even at its near worst, in 1849 and the 1850's gold hunting in the Sierra foothills yielded enough to sustain life. In the gold country there still is talk of "mining for beans." The Argonaut who arrived flat broke, and likewise the miner who ran out of dust in sickness or at the gambling table, often picked up the tools of his trade to engage in "subsistence mining."

Furthermore, though for good and sufficient reason the style was to be close-mouthed about how a claim was paying, all the miners saw daily evidence of gold accumulating in others' pokes. Rumor did its part, too, in publicizing bonanzas and strikes. The general atmosphere, therefore, was liberally charged with the spirit of success, to the encouragement of all, including those whose efforts had been slightly rewarded. For this reason also the miners persisted.

As for the working of the mines, the seasons immediately following were repetitions of 1849, but with almost everything on a larger scale. Production mounted to fifty, sixty, and, in 1852, to eighty millions. The average daily return, however, showed a decline, and so did the prevailing wage. The working force kept on growing, but the area remained virtually constant and the mines therefore came to be more and more crowded. Coyoting extended to lower levels and required timbering. Rockers and toms receded in favor of sluices, which stretched out to still greater lengths. The projects for river mining grew to larger scale and thereby became bigger gambles. Positive diversion of water was also elaborated, with V-flumes and square flumes extending the simple ditches of the earlier days.

The earliest flumes were improvisations, as is illustrated by one which W. L. Manly describes. He and his partners spotted a promising claim and ran a ditch from a spring in order to have water with which to work it. They found, however, that the water soaked into the porous ground and none traveled to the end of the ditch. For two dollars a day they rented a crosscut saw from a near-by camp, felled some sugar pines, cut twelve- and sixteen-foot sections, split out planks, put a V-flume into their ditch, and had boards left over to make a sluice.

In subsequent years the waterworks were much elaborated, some being made large enough to dry up a whole stream. By 1855 there were said to be 4,493 miles of canals, ditches, and flumes in the state, and the water companies represented the largest investment in the diggings and the first manifestation of capitalism.

From the very beginning the gold seekers had speculated about where the gold came from and had made assorted efforts to trace it to its source. The gold they were recovering was placer, or alluvial—free rather than embedded in hard rock. Occasionally they worked back to hard rock, usually quartz, in which gold was imprisoned, and by 1850 there were some attempts to work such veins. The majority, doubting that it would be feasible, continued to work the loose deposits. By 1851 some success was being attained, and in another few years quartz was to become the kingpin of the California gold industry. Yet, to mine in quartz required heavy machinery and an industrial approach. It was a kind of mining that was in spirit far removed from the early attack upon the placers.

It may be significant, too, that when in later years the gold diggers reminisced about their experiences on the Mother Lode, they had little to say about these elaborate methods, but much to recount about their achievements with pan, cradle, and tom. Except as something to brag about, the tedium and discomfort of mining tended to fade away, and what remained was the memory, also valid, of placer mining as a great adventure.

CHAPTER 9

Life in the Diggings

IF THE reminiscences of the forty-niners are any criterion, the experience of life in the diggings was as memorable as that of mining itself. Picture any Argonaut arriving at the mines, early in the season or late, delivered by whatever route, sound of body or at the brink of exhaustion, utterly destitute or loaded down with elaborate equipment. Whatever his condition, his first thought was to get the necessary tools, find a place to dig, and start washing gold. Yet at day's end he had to pause and take thought of getting something to eat and a place to sleep. Thus early he began to face the realities of the miner's life.

By the middle and later stages of the golden era almost every camp boasted some sort of public eating place and a miner might solve the food problem by eating out. In 1852, for example, Hubert Howe Bancroft had a partner who disdained camp fare and took his meals at a Rich Bar boarding house. But the original gold seekers, and most of those who followed, shifted for themselves. Sometimes the results were sadly disappointing; as when Paul Chalfant invested his first gold in a candlelight purchase of hardtack, mixed it with water and salt pork, promptly ate half of it, and next morning found he had cooked up a hardtack and bug chowder. On other occasions the results were well-nigh fatal, as when a certain Gillespie broached a keg of oysters for his friend Pérez Rosales and poisoned them both.

With skillet, coffee pot, and perhaps a Dutch oven, the miners cooked over an open fire, or, if their camp was more permanent, at a fireplace or on a crude stove. Bread was the staff of life. Sometimes they bought hardtack or ship's bread. A few of them nursed along a culture of yeast and baked light bread. More often it was some form of quick bread, leavened with saleratus or baking soda, and skillet-fried or baked on a flat rock or in the oven. Salt pork or jerked beef was the usual accompaniment. In time, drovers brought fresh beef to the more accessible camps and hunters supplemented the food list with game, especially venison and bear, yet without vanquishing the salt-pork and jerked-beef pattern.

Beans and rice were available and were, of course, much favored by the Mexican and Chinese miners. Others used them rather sparingly, probably because of the longer time needed for their preparation. Potatoes and onions likewise had a subordinate role, and dried apples and dried peaches, though relished, were only incidental.

Dietetically, such meals ran high enough in calories; but they were deficient in elements which might have been supplied by fresh vegetables and fruits, dairy products, eggs, and fish, had these been readily available. The miners, none too expert in scientific dietetics, were occasionally reminded by sickness that something was wrong with their feed. Their more frequent complaint was at the monotony of their meals and at the drudgery of cooking.

Working with limited and unreliable ingredients, they were obviously at a handicap. It may well be, too, that hard work and the open air stimulated appetites and created an unfortunate tolerance for mediocre cooking. Yet the main trouble seems to have been that these chefs were uninspired. Looking upon gold digging as much more important, they all relegated cooking to an early morning stint and an evening chore, to be dispatched as quickly as possible and strictly as an incidental. Under these circumstances it is only natural that the cuisine of the camps was more often tolerated than enjoyed, more often berated than praised.

To the repertoire of gourmets the mines did contribute one recipe that has a measure of fame. It was conjured up, so we are told, by a miner who wanted a special breakfast, and, looking over the stock at hand, instructed the cook to fry a few strips of bacon and a can of oysters and, at the opportune moment, fold them into an omelet. The resultant "Hangtown fry" is still dispensed with a flourish at the Raffles in Placerville.

And in the ordinary housekeeping of the camps an occasional meal was of superlative excellence. One miner recalls such an occasion. He and his partner had been on a forced diet of rice and rancid bacon. Then they got hold of some flour which had been wet through and had soured. Grinding it to powder, they added saleratus, shaped the mixture into loaves, and popped it into the oven, fully expecting that it would come out as yellow sinkers. Instead, the result was wonderfully light and white—a triumph. Prentice Mulford immortalized another mouth-watering feast, which centered around a thick steak broiled on the coals of a mountain campfire. The day-to-day fare, however, was nothing to brag about.

To the problem of housing, the miners gave similar airy inattention. Arrived at Long Bar, in the summer of 1852, Bancroft paid a dollar to sleep at a hotel, getting not a room, nor even a bed, but a place in the dining room where he could roll up in his own blanket. Here he made his first close acquaintance with the men of the mines, "the great hairy unwashed," who, he said, were "strewed about on bunks, benches, tables, and floor." From their "loud snorings and abominable smells" he at length took flight to sleep rolled in a blanket on a pine-needle couch on the hillside. Early in 1850, Jacob Stover found lodging at Deer Creek for six dollars a day, American plan, and on credit because the innkeeper happened also to be from Iowa.

A few months earlier, when Chalfant arrived at the diggings on the Yuba, he spent one miserable night in the rain under an overturned bull pine, and another somewhat more comfortably under an oak bough thatched with pine bark. On a subsequent night, six strangers, who were stretched out on the sodden ground under a tent only large enough for three, took compassion on him and invited him in. The tent, he says, had a wash house odor from the steaming "middle men," while, he, on the edge, was soaking wet and cold on one side. Yet even this limited hospitality made him exceedingly grateful.

Chalfant's experience was more harrowing than the average. Had the Pit River Indians not killed his oxen he would have had more equipment than just a blanket and rifle. Also, he had the misfortune to arrive at the onset of the rainy season. It was routine, however, especially in the early stages of the golden era, that the Argonauts would have to fend for themselves.

The few who got their wagons all the way to the mines had a guaranteed minimum of shelter. Others brought tents. The majority had only a blanket or two, planning, when they got located, to contrive some sort of protection against the elements. Sometimes it was nothing more than a ridgepole, faced on one side by poles and brush. Or it might be a crude frame with canvas sides and roof. Pork-barrel shelters are on record; also caves and dugouts. Toward season's end some of the miners built more elaborate cabins of logs or split timber, sometimes with a field-stone fireplace and chimney, though most often with a canvas roof.

This sort of camping was often idyllic, especially through the long season of clement weather. Sarah Royce, for example, certainly one of the gentler residents of the diggings, gives an ecstatic description of a camp pitched in a grove of young oaks, a curve of bushes walling one side, a few yards of cloth tacked up on another, and an awning stretched for partial cover. With cookstove set up and cupboard fastened to a tree, she thought it ideally pleasant.

The other side of the picture is a general neglect and slighting of the matter of housing. The miners were willing to put up with cramped, uncomfortable, and unhygienic quarters; and the real reason that they did not achieve something better was because they did not want to turn aside from mining, which was their overweening interest.

As to clothing, the miners were equally offhand and nondescript. The preferred uniform was a flannel shirt, red or gray, but certainly not white, and wool trousers tucked into rough and wrinkled boots. A slouch hat topped off the costume, with belt, knife, and pistol considered part of the normal dress. Yet the most bizarre variations were to be seen. A top hat and an overcoat; panama hats acquired at the Isthmus; hunting shirts and breeches of fringed buckskin; sombreros and bandanas from Mexico; broadcloth coats, brocaded vests, and pumps or dress shoes as the remaining attire of some who had gone through their rougher clothes—these were common sights.

The diggings also featured a variety of national costumes: Indians with their ancestral near-nudity somewhat modified by whatever bits of civilized attire they had been able to acquire, Frenchmen in berets and blouselike shirts, native Californians in sashes and slashed trousers, Sonorans in serapes, Chileans, Kanakas, Chinese, and various others in the work clothes of their respective homelands.

As often happens when style is allowed to find its natural level, the prevailing attire was well suited to the circumstances. In the alternating dust and mud, boots were superior to shoes. In the alternating heat and cold, wool shirts had a corresponding advantage over cotton. The preference for darker colors was also inevitable in a society where every man was his own laundryman. The miners have much to say about this recurrent task—for example, Franklin Buck's understatement, "I don't use much starch."

Curiously, their talk is almost solely of washing shirts, though presumably they gave attention to socks, undershirts, and drawers, then perhaps regarded as unmentionable even in the mines. In time a few professional laundresses appeared on the scene, and usually earned more than their gold-mining spouses. Throughout, however, most of the miners continued to wash their own shirts. They did it grumblingly and, as might be expected, cavalierly, as the following description suggests: "Have two shirts. Wear one until it is dirty. Hang on a limb, exposed to wind, rain, and sun. Put on second shirt. Wear until dirty. Then change to the clean one." Plausible though this regimen may sound, at all the camps Sunday was a day of vigorous soaping, pounding, and scrubbing.

These efforts, nevertheless, were not adequate to combat the accumulated mud, sweat, and grime. Added to such habits as sleeping on the ground, wearing the same clothes night and day, and allowing the hair to get long and tangled, and coupled with the casual arrangements for housing, the miners were natural hosts for fleas, lice, mites, and other small vermin. The flea was already a venerable figure in California folklore, most closely associated with the coastal settlements—for example, Rancho Las Pulgas.

In the mines the louse was king. It became a recurrent ritual to inspect the seams of shirts and trousers. Society frowned on the practice of merely picking off the offenders and dropping them to continue their nefarious careers. An oft-repeated anecdote concerns a sailor, stretched out on a gambling table, who roused to observe a large specimen approaching him. Lashing out at this intruder with his knife, he shouted, "Ye'll place no bets." A more elaborate story is of a match race for a substantial wager, won by an Irishman's pet, for which he claimed "the blood of Irish royalty." Whereupon, the man who had backed the loser paid off without a murmur and then solemnly asked a favor—the loan of the champion. "I would like," he said "to improve my breed."

Verminous, exposed, malnourished, and many of them run down by the hardships of getting to California, the miners were likely prospects for disease. Some escaped entirely, but an untoward number suffered rheumatism, fever, chills, ague, cholera morbus, dysentery, diarrhea, typhoid, tuberculosis, smallpox, scurvy, and other less clearly diagnosed ailments.

To combat these ills the forty-niners depended mainly on self-prescribed doses of calomel, blue pill, quinine, laudanum, and physic. Although comparative neglect was almost inevitable, friends and partners were often as solicitous as the circumstances permitted. They did such favors as sitting up all night with a sick man, or taking a day off from mining to try to find a chicken with which to make a tempting broth.

The rush had attracted a certain number of physicians and others with a smattering of training in medicine. These doctors did a thriving business, at an ounce a visit and more for distant calls. The frontier has seldom attracted the cream of the profession. Many of the gold-rush doctors were doubtless quacks, and mercenary ones at that. On the other hand, some had a strong sense of social responsibility, as was true of John Frederick Morse, physician, surgeon, and partner in the first hospital in Sacramento, an institution for the most part charitable.

Even with the ministrations of such men, sickness in the mines was apt to be more serious than sickness at home. The hazard to life was also compounded by accidents in mine, camp, and cabin, and accident and illness, food poisoning and lead poisoning, carried off a substantial number. The mortality rate apparently was not so high as that inflicted by cholera at the outset of the gold rush, but the letters and journals are liberally sprinkled with mention of deaths, and simple rites of burial, with a blanket for a shroud, or a pine box for a coffin, were all too common.

One incidental consequence of this presence of deepest tragedy in the diggings was to intensify the rather general affliction of homesickness. As the more sensitive fraction of the group, the diarists no doubt incline today's readers to see more homesickness than actually existed. Some of the gold seekers, it is clear, felt no pangs for the scenes and the people they had left. Other evidence, however, substantiates the fact; not least the avid interest in mail from the States. The San Francisco post office always had a queue on steamer day, and private carriers were able to collect twenty-five cents to a dollar for their "special delivery" to the mines. The writing and the reading and rereading of letters was a standard divertissement for the diggers.

To while away the evenings they also resorted to other reading. Papers from New York fetched as much as a dollar. The Bible and the classics came in for attention. One miner wrote home ecstatically about his discovery of Homer. Another undertook to compare Dickens' workmanship in *David Copperfield* with that in *The Pickwick Papers*. Still another bargained to silence his banjo if his partner would read *Nicholas Nickleby* aloud. With great enthusiasm, likewise, the Argonauts rallied to the support of California newspapers and literary journals.

Whittling, which today is one of the lost arts, came in for a certain amount of attention, and incidental music, if there happened to be a fiddler or a singer in the group, was now and then invoked to while away an evening.

Card playing was a much more frequent time killer. Among themselves and at home in their cabins the miners played for nominal stakes or for none at all. At the end of a day's strenuous labor there was not much temptation to linger over the cards, but in the course of the winter lay-off some of the miners gave them serious attention. According to George F. Kent this is how Euchre Diggings got its name.

All up and down the diggings there was a tendency practically universal to limit the work week to six days and to make Sunday something apart. Basically, of course, this attitude stemmed from the fourth commandment, second clause, and the vogue of its observation in the States. The miners could faithfully intone, "Six days shalt thou labor and do all thy work."

"But the seventh day—" In time, ministers of the gospel penetrated to the camps, improvised sanctuaries, and held services, which were attended, so many informants state, by rough-looking but remarkably alert, attentive, and openhanded congregations. Meanwhile, the miners' Sabbath had already fallen into a pattern as a day devoted to washing, to going to the store to lay in the week's provisions, to sampling whatever amusements the town had to offer—possibly a horse race, or a foot race, or a dog fight,—to testing the wares of the local saloon, to risking part or all the week's earnings against the luck and skill (and percentage) of the professional dealer of faro or monte.

Sunday in the mines was at least in contrast to the ordinary workday. The prudent miner came back to his claim refreshed and invigorated. The imprudent or unlucky, as depicted adeptly in one of Delano's sketches, came back with no other choice but to get to digging again.

At less regular intervals the Mother Lode towns had something extraordinary to offer as recreation. The act of naming the towns and camps, though a rather fleeting amusement, was often approached in that vein, as is evidenced by such names as Red Dog, Poker Flat, You Bet,

Fiddletown, Humbug, and Poverty Hill. Election of town officers and assemblages to draft a set of claim laws for the district were breaks in the monotony. Oftentimes this attitude carried over to occasions when the miners assembled as a popular tribunal to pass judgment on someone accused of high crime.

When the calendar brought round a major holiday, such as the Fourth of July, the miners could be counted on to take time out to celebrate. Such a day became an extra Sunday, usually with additional trimmings. The popping of pistols and the banging of larger guns substituted for firecrackers. Bigger charges were also set off. At Weaverville in 1854 lawyer Tevis read the Declaration of Independence and was orator of the day. At Rich Bar in 1852 Dame Shirley was distressed to observe that almost the whole camp, including many of the most respected citizens, went on a binge that lasted two nights and left a community hangover. At Downieville a year earlier a miner who had indulged too freely broke down a door and intruded on a certain Juanita. The next day he went to her place, assertedly to apologize, but gave further insult, and she stabbed him. The miners thereupon added business to pleasure, convened to try this young Mexican woman, resisted the pleas of Dr. Cyrus D. Aiken and a Mr. Thayer that they proceed more slowly, and carried out the hanging.

The men of Downieville, on second thought less sure about the justice they had meted out, and the sobering celebrants at Rich Bar stand on the debit side of the ledger. The Downieville episode was in some respects exceptional; that at Rich Bar, reasonably characteristic.

Throughout gold-rush California social restraints and inhibitions were weaker by far than in any of the eastern communities from which these men had come. Yet with or without a post session for repairing the damages, the Fourth of July celebrations were memorable. As late as 1857 Franklin Buck could sit down and recount to his sister how he had spent each Fourth since his arrival as a forty-niner.

In the intervals between the calendared celebrations, or in observance of an occasion such as St. Valentine's Day, the miners now and then staged a dance. They tried to do it with as much decorum as possible; their aim was to make the function reminiscent of those they had attended at home. At first, of course, they worked under great difficulties. Some of the earliest dances were handicapped by an absolute lack of women and girls, and it was necessary to choose up sides, perhaps on the basis of patched or unpatched trousers. Later the diggings boasted a limited number of women. Still it was not quite the same as at home; one participant remarks that it was odd to have a dance interrupted so that his dancing partner could go and nurse her infant. By the end of the decade, though the women in the diggings were still not more than an eighth or a tenth of the total, dances could be more high-toned, and the invitations were carefully screened.

Still another response to the miners' evident craving for amusement was by professional entertainers. These ranged from promoters of bull-and-bear fights or bear-and-jackass combats, through vaudeville acts, to much more ambitious concert and theatrical performances. The valley towns, and particularly San Francisco, had more varied and continuous theater. Inevitably, the commercialized theater could succeed in the mining camps only after a fair number of gold hunters had arrived on the scene and had accumulated some store of gold. As the mines began to play out, in the later 'fifties and 'sixties, the Sierran circuit went into a corresponding decline.

The excellent patronage of a stage which represented "the finer things of life" is perhaps surprising in the light of the cultural variegation which the miners represented and their ruling absorption in gold getting. Quantitatively considered, their efforts at self-amusement were comfortably in the lead. Chat, reading, desultory card playing, and such music as they could generate in camp served to while away most evenings and many a winter day. In town, the saloon and the gambling establishment had precedence over theater and concert hall and served to pass much more time than was devoted to straight drinking and gambling. The bar, in other words, was the miners' club; some say his home. Church, theater, and all else tended to be merely supplementary.

Now and then the gold harvesters quit their claims to go as far as Stockton or Sacramento or all the way to San Francisco in search of relaxation. The purpose might be to see if some letters were not stranded in the post office. It might be to remit part of the gold thus far accumulated or to look into a California investment. Often it was simply to taste again certain elements of civilization that were not available in the mines. All too often the miners found that these desiderata were not in supply in San Francisco either.

Masonry, the Odd Fellows, and other fraternal orders came early to the diggings. After all, the men of the mines were, most of them, Americans and ready joiners. Other more specialized fraternities also appeared, the most famous of them, though apparently not known to Bancroft, being the ancient and honorable order of E Clampsus Vitus, its name usually rendered without the troublesome middle "s."

Just when and where E Clampus Vitus first appeared in California is a moot point. The honor long was accorded to Sierra City for a lodge opened in 1857. Placerville, however, has unearthed evidence which suggests an earlier cell at Hangtown. According to Carl Wheat and G. Ezra Dane, the official historians of the organization, such questions are mere peccadillos, for the order dates back to 4004 B.C., the Garden of Eden, and the first clampatriarch Adam, while the roster of members includes such luminaries as St. Vitus, Solomon, the Caesars, the Louis, Henry VIII, Hee-Lai, Sir Francis Drake, and assorted Presidents and Senators. Once it did reach the Far West, the fraternity spread like an epidemic until throughout the diggings every town of any consequence possessed a chapter.

There are several good reasons for this popularity. The order could boast lofty and benevolent purposes. It was dedicated to the care of widows and orphans, especially widows. It was outfitted, too, with an elaborate and impressive ritual. Many details of the purposes, practices, and ceremonies are properly shrouded in secrecy. It is public knowledge, however, that when the Royal Grand Musician sounded the hewgag to assemble the Brethren at the Hall of Comparative Oblations, it was invariably for the purpose of an initiation, and that for every initiate the final indignity was the opportunity to stand treat. Some would say, as a matter of fact, that the convivial, raucous, fun-loving Clampers best embody the spirit of gold rush society.

With rare exceptions the recorded accounts of life in the diggings are from the perspective of the bearded, booted, red-shirted young fellows from the States, who loom up as the typical forty-niners. Such were in the majority. Yet the citizenry of the mines was highly cosmopolitan. The gold fever had been no respecter of national barriers, and men from all quarters of the earth had joined in the rush. The presence of assorted foreigners introduced enlivening contrasts and occasionally raised problems of some complexity.

Certain classes of foreigners amalgamated almost immediately with the American majority. The English and Australians, for example, though they might preserve peculiarities of speech to the end of their days, fitted into the prevailing society with hardly more adjustment than was necessary between New Englanders and Missourians. The Irish, though furiously resented by many an ardent nativist, immediately felt at home. And in spite of the language barrier, the Germans melted rapidly, as is suggested by the quite incidental trait often remarked as distinguishing them among the miners—their penchant for monstrous watches and heavy gold chains.

Others were more distinct to start with. Some resisted assimilation. Just as few of the American forty-niners had joined the rush with the intention of becoming permanent Californians, so many of these other gold seekers had no intention of becoming American citizens. They had come in quest of gold, and once they had made their pile they would go home again. Among the Mexicans and the Chinese this attitude was the rule. Oftentimes, also, the privilege of melting into the general population was denied.

Among the various colors, creeds, and cultures represented, the mere fact of cohabitation in the diggings led to a certain amount of interchange of ideas and influences. Thus the Indians began to appear in hats, coats, shirts, and trousers, though not always fully rigged. Thus the French began to turn from Parisian and peasant styles to rough boots and shirts. Thus the American forty-niners began to talk of arrastres, bateas, piojos, and frijoles, while basic American profanity enriched the speech of Indians and Chinese. These were lendings and borrowings made without volition and without charge or prejudice.

Nevertheless, the climate of opinion toward the foreigners in the diggings is perhaps best described as variable. From a thoroughly democratic willingness to accept individuals on the basis of ability as demonstrated in performance, the attitude ranged through amusement at outlandish practices, to indifference, condescension, discrimination, and cruelty.

The old-line Californians appear to have fared quite well. They benefited, no doubt, from several decades of living with and doing business with the Americans and others who had come as foreigners to the Mexican province. After the first season of mining, it is also true that many of these Spanish-speaking Californians went back to their farms and ranchos, leaving relatively few in the mines.

Thanks in part to the famous lotteries for passage to California, Frenchmen were a much more common sight in the diggings. They tended to be clannish and the common opinion of them was that they were a bit impractical and therefore not ideally suited to the mining life. The miners had a nickname for them, the "Keskydees," growing out of their oft-repeated question, "Qu'est que se dit?"

In the summer of 1851 the French in the southern diggings were thrown into a ferment over the newly enacted Foreign Miners Tax. Hearing of violence to one of their countrymen at Jackson, they rallied from the near-by camps, particularly Murphy's and marched on Jackson, apparently intent on wreaking vengeance. After much oratory and copious draughts of brandy, they sallied forth, made a night camp on the trail, and marched on in the morning to the outskirts of Jackson, where they learned that the supposed *casus belli* had no basis in fact. A few went into Jackson for refreshment; the majority slunk back to Murphy's. The affair has a certain immortality as "The French Revolution." It became part of the folklore of the gold country and, with suitable embellishments, was written up in Gerstäcker's *Californische Skizzen*.

Mexicans and Chileans commanded respect because of their expertness in mining. Yet the sentiment toward them lacked full cordiality, and this became evident whenever one of these nationals was haled before a

From J. M. Letts, California Illustrated (*1852*)

THE ROAD TO THE MINES

PASO TIEMPO

popular tribunal. His punishment was apt to be more severe. It is significant, too, that when Pérez Rosales was taken to be a Frenchman, he thought it wiser not to disclose that he was really a Chilean.

Still farther down the line, as the forty-niners measured it, stood the Chinese. The first Celestials to show up in the diggings were regarded tolerantly as curiosities. The first reaction to them was even favorable. Franklin Buck found them good customers and got one to paint him a sign in Chinese characters which he could hang out as an invitation for their trade. But as more and more came, until at length one miner in every five was Chinese, they began to be resented and subjected to petty discrimination and major harassment. They were the primary target of the Foreign Miners Tax, and it was only upon them that this impost was really enforced. Furthermore, the Caucasian miners saw to it that they got only the leftover claims or reworked the tailings that the whites had discarded.

Pigtails, shapeless dress, singsong language, and other peculiar practices gave most forty-niners the impression that the Chinese were irresistibly comic. Accordingly, in the summer of '54, when the Chinese at Weaverville fell into discord and announced that the point of honor would be settled by doing battle, the populace eagerly awaited the spectacle. The week-long preparations added to the interest, for the men of the Yangwa and Canton companies besieged the hardware stores and the blacksmith and tinsmith, to get properly accoutered for the fray. They particularly wanted round sheet-iron helmets, shields, short swords, long spears and tridents, two-handed swords set in generously long handles, enormous squirt guns, and noise-making equipment such as gongs and horns. On Tuesday the Yangwa company demonstrated in a boisterous parade. They were 110 strong, plus one American in military attire and mounted on a fire horse. On Friday both companies went into camp near the chosen battlefield.

On Saturday morning the sheriff made a final effort at preserving the peace, but fellow Americans talked him down. The Chinese, they said, had made elaborate preparations, they wanted to fight, and two thousand spectators had rallied to witness the spectacle. Let the show go on.

The battle began with seemingly meaningless maneuvers, with the Yangwas in one compact group and the more numerous Cantons in three separate divisions. Then, about three o'clock, the Yangwas made a furious charge on the Canton center. One of the flanking forces attempted to come to the rescue, but some of the American onlookers drew their pistols and held them off, in the interest, so they said, of a "fair fight." Thus aided, the Yangwas put their foes to flight.

There were wounded enough to keep the doctors busy for days. The dead included two of the victors and six of the vanquished and one bystander, a not so innocent young German who was hit by a stray bullet just after he had fired into the Canton troop.

After the battle the Weaverville Americans professed to have greater respect for these Orientals who, in an affair of honor, had been willing to fight to the death. There were other Chinese traits, it might be remarked, that were more deserving of praise. After the battle the more thoughtful men of Weaverville did reproach themselves for not having prevented the gladiatorial combat. Their excuse continued to be that they had not believed the Chinese would go so far. It stands, therefore, as an episode in racial misunderstanding. For the Chinese as a whole, the rising tide of objection to their participation in mining was far more significant.

In the society of the mines the group held in lowest esteem was unquestionably the Indians. In the first season, it is true, these original denizens of the gold country were allowed to work in the diggings either on their own or as gang labor for some white boss, but as soon as the mines began to fill up this sanction was withdrawn and they were ordered off.

The forty-niners took some note of these Indians. Their letters and journals have a good deal to say about the peculiar customs observed, such as grasshopper harvests, the cremation of the dead, the accompanying ceremonies of mourning, and the ingenious system of signal fires. Mostly the comments are about the extreme backwardness of the Indians, their simplicity in dress, the rudeness of their huts, their poor equipment for warfare, and the general poverty of their culture.

Except for Sutter's initial negotiation with the Coloma Indians for a leasehold on their valley, there was hardly a recognition of the Indians as owners of the mining area. The Argonauts had a more convenient theory that the land was American by conquest—the federal government backed them up in this attitude through its interpretation of the treaty of Guadalupe Hidalgo,—and that the Indians were as much interlopers as the Chinese or any other "foreigners." With occasional exceptions they treated the Indians thus, pushing them aside and wasting no charity or kindness upon them.

The mere presence of ten, twenty, fifty, and eventually more than a hundred thousand miners was enough to upset the pattern of Indian life. The miners killed off much of the game and scared away most of the rest. They muddied the streams and ruined the fishing. They chopped down many of the oaks and nut pines to get timber for their cabins, dams, flumes, and sluices, and later to fuel the stamps used in quartz mining and to timber shafts and drifts. Even had this mining been carried on by the best-intentioned friends of the Indians, it almost inevitably would have laid waste the sources of food on which these people had for many years based their life.

Yet, as any student of the American frontier could have predicted, the men of the mines were not kindly disposed toward the Indians. From the earliest days of the colonial frontier on the Atlantic Coast, all across the continent, the Indian had been thought of as an inferior being, an obstacle to the proper development of the land, and a nuisance to be cleared away to make room for the oncoming whites. Among the overland gold seekers en route, especially after 1849, this feeling of antagonism was intensified by their troubles with the tribesmen on the western plains, the Humboldt, and the Pit. Without logical warrant many were inclined to visit this traditional and aggravated hostility upon the hapless natives of the Sierra foothills.

On their part, the Indians looked upon these streams, mountain valleys, and hillsides as ancestrally theirs. The gold seekers, as they saw it, were trespassers, and although they had only primitive means of resistance, there was a limit to the forbearance that they could be expected to exercise.

The relationship of whites and reds in the diggings was that of a powder keg with fuses laid in both directions. In the over-all picture the whites are properly charged with the first violence. In certain localities, on the other hand, it was the Indians who struck the first blows. Whatever the start, retaliation was the normal sequel. Consequently, the California Indian frontier from Yuma to Klamath Lake was soon bathed in the bloodshed of a series of ruthless Indian wars, so-called.

These conflicts were all of a pattern. They began with some individual wrong, whereupon the friends and compatriots of the aggrieved set out to pay back the damage, with interest. By Indian practice the group was more significant than the individual; a retaliatory blow at the group was therefore as satisfying as one which landed upon the offender's own person. The whites, perhaps because to them all Indians looked alike, gravitated into this same way of reasoning. To a real or alleged Indian atrocity they responded by organizing a posse and going on the warpath against whatever Indians they could catch. Thus they were able to surround and kill or capture whole villages that with a little warning might have been able to put up a defense or to escape. By reason of superior arms, too, the whites could deal out much more punishment than they took. They had practically no burden of women and children to defend; within a year they outnumbered the Indians; and before long they were able to draw pay from the state for serving in these Indian-hunting excursions. Small wonder, then, that history balks at calling them "wars," finding more accuracy in such labels as "brutal butcherings."

A generation ago, Frederick Jackson Turner posited that the American frontier had been especially conducive to a number of traits fundamental in Americanism, notably democracy and tolerance. In certain respects the California gold camps offer evidence in support of this assertion. Yet the attitude that prevailed toward the French and the Latin Americans and more pointedly toward the Chinese and the Indians makes it apparent that the full blessings of these two principles were not available on an intercultural basis, but were mainly reserved for Americans and for such others as by slight modification could pass as Americans.

In the light of the enthusiastic advertising of the year-round excellence of the California climate, it is not easy to understand why the miners a century ago were driven from their claims by the rigors of winter. The explanation is twofold. They were at work in the Sierra foothills, not in the southern and coastal parts of the state where nine-tenths of the modern population lives. Also it was not so much the cold that interrupted digging as the excess of water cascading down the gulches and canyons and over the gold-impregnated bars and beds. The winter rainy season, at any rate, spelled a general shutdown of mining and thereby radically modified the pattern of life in the diggings.

From the northern (and wetter) part of the diggings so many miners departed that the gold towns had at least a hint of their ghostly future. From the southern mines there was a lesser but sizable exodus. Others prepared to stick it out in the diggings.

Those who had been camping in tent or lean-to tried to devise more satisfactory shelter. Those whose wardrobes had worn thin tried to get new outfits. All had more time to devote to cooking—in fact, on many days there was little else to do. Yet, except where hunters were especially active, the winter menus were not much more appetizing than those of the mining season. Flour and salt pork, jerked beef and hardtack continued to be the staples, and when mud and snow stopped the freighters even these bare necessities sometimes gave out.

As to recreations, the situation might with some exaggeration be described as every day a Sunday. The idle miners could do a great deal more reading, and those who wanted to could catch up on their writing. The card players put in longer hours. More elaborate bits of horseplay were devised. There was more hanging around grogshops and gambling tents, and probably more patronage of them. It might all have been thoroughly enjoyable, like the vacation of the New York clerk, or the slack season on an eastern farm, except that so many of these gold hunters could ill afford the lay-off from breadwinning toil. They were so anxious to resume digging that they could not relax and enjoy their time off.

CHAPTER 10

Catering to the Miner

THE SUDDEN pyramiding of population in the diggings
created a large market for goods and services where previously there had been an economic void. The gilding
of that pyramid with a thick crust of real gold backed
up this demand with a buying power that was even more
fabulous. Out of these twin circumstances issued, therefore, a stimulation of commerce that was the most intense
the American frontier had seen. It set in motion a chain
reaction that spread from the storekeepers in the mines;
through transport, as represented by packers and wagon
freighters, and lighters on bay and river; to wholesalers
on shore and on ship; to importers from depots as near
as Oregon and as distant as England; to producers in
California fields and forests and in industry wherever it
could flourish; and to all sorts of supporting activities,
including those of drover and slaughterer, banker and
usurer, investor and speculator, realtor and insurer,

restaurateur and launderer. Some of the consequences were worldwide; the most striking were visible on the California scene.

The lowly and industrious miner, whose quick-emptying poke oiled the whole elaborate machinery, often saw little more of it than the plank-and-barrel counter over which the mining-camp storekeeper ladled out flour and salt pork in exchange for an agreed-upon heft of gold. In the beginning, these stores were as impromptu as everything else in the diggings. Supplies were often sold right off the wagon or the mule's back on which they had arrived. If no merchant came of his own accord to a new camp, the miners sometimes importuned one of their number to drop his pick and pan, go get a supply of the necessities, and open up for business. In their extremity the miners were tolerant of limited stocks and inferior quality. They did not insist on commodious premises or elaborate display. The merest excuse for cover would do, and the only absolute necessity was some sort of balance on which to weigh the circulating medium.

Boys from the farm set up as businessmen alongside men who had been ministers or teachers or clerks in the States. As time went on, some of these amateurs were able to make their business pay in competition with the experienced tradesmen who also invaded the diggings, but increasingly the business passed into the hands of careful, canny, astute, not to say sharp, traders of the Yankee breed.

These provisioners were not the most popular men in the diggings. Of necessity, they had to run their shops in a rather heartless fashion. Since their customers were restless and footloose, here today and off to some other gulch on the morrow, they could not extend credit, but had to insist that purchasers "come down with the dust." The miner's liability to accident and disease and the unpredictability of his reward also militated against selling on time.

The miners accepted this feature as inevitable. On the other hand, instances of short weight, the palming off of spoiled merchandise, and such tricks as blowing fine gold from the balance onto the canvas counter made them skeptical of the business ethics in vogue. The extremely high prices were resented. And the sure profits of the storekeeper as contrasted to the gamble of the gold hunter, widened the rift. A frequent plaint was that the miners were doing all the hard work while the merchants were the only ones getting ahead. An occasional miner struck it rich, but it must be admitted that quite a number of California fortunes—for example, those of Stanford, Huntington, and Hopkins—had their initiation in gold-rush merchandising.

Although he had the advantage of cash-and-carry sales to free-spending customers, the mining-camp merchant was up against exasperating problems. At the start he had to stock whatever goods he could get. Even well into the 'fifties he still had to buy in a limited and uncertain market. Having bought from some dealer at San Francisco or Sacramento or Stockton, or direct from a ship on the bay or river, he still had the major problem of getting his goods transported to his store. Here he relied on wagon freighters or, if his camp was less accessible, on packers. The willingness of the miners to pay is doubtless the big reason for the fantastically high prices current in the diggings. The cost factor that went furthest toward justifying the prices was the charges of the carriers.

Charles Bennett and Jacob Wittmer will be recalled as teamsters hauling to Coloma before the news of gold leaked out. They represent a very meager equipment in wagons and draft animals previously assembled by Sutter and a few of his neighbors. Yet California as a whole had put little stress on wagons. Building with adobe, which could be made on the spot; settling near the coast, where water transport was available; and in its agriculture stressing cattle, which could be delivered on the hoof, it had neatly sidestepped dependence on wheeled vehicles and was not in good position to meet the sudden demand for cartage to the mines.

Fortunately, the gold rush itself brought in part of the equipment needed. Some of the overland emigrants arrived with serviceable wagons and teams which could be put to work. Others, especially from the southern routes and particularly from Sonora, came with strings of saddled pack animals. It was largely in this fashion that transport in the mines was outfitted and recruited.

In the horse-and-buggy days of the mid-nineteenth century the spectacle of wagon freighting was so much a matter of course that few forty-niners bothered to set down descriptions. The peculiarities of this work, apart from the phenomenally high charges, seem to have been that it was done at first with makeshift equipment, that the hauling was over unimproved trails, and that in the wet season the roads were bottomless. In time, the outfit came to be standardized in a large wagon, usually with a smaller wagon trailing behind, six or eight mules as the team, and the mule skinner either walking alongside or astride the near wheeler. Until comparatively recently, when trucks took over, freighting outfits of this general type were a common sight throughout the American West.

Mexican in its genre, the pack train was more picturesque. Several graphic descriptions exist, notably that by Carl Meyer in *Nach dem Sacramento*. En route from Monterey to the mines, he fell in with a 150-mule train to which he allots several pages. After tributes to the short-coupled Mexican horse, now better known as the western pony, and to the more humble but durable mule, he sketches the events of a day on the trail.

It begins with a breakfast consisting of a pot of beans, cooked tender the night before, and corn-meal tortillas, slapped thin by skilled hands and cooked for a minute on a slab of sheet iron. The night herders, meanwhile, have brought in the stock and the work of saddling and packing commences. The *arrieros* affix a balanced load, lashing everything securely in place. If they are expert, the procession is soon ready for the trail and troops off after the bell mare. If a pack slips, an arriero quickly lassos the mule, slips a hood over its eyes, refastens the cargo, and gets the animal back in line.

The noon stop for cold tortillas and perhaps cheesecakes is a short one, and the packs are not removed. On then for the afternoon march, until the night camp is reached. Packs, aparejos, and saddles are pulled off and neatly piled. If a saddle sore is detected on one of the mules, it is rubbed with the sovereign remedy, dried horse manure. The animals are then turned out to graze. The cooks, meanwhile, are busy with pot and frying pan, and *charqui*, or jerked meat, fried in well-peppered *mantequilla*, together with frijoles and hot tortillas are soon ready. After a round of cigarettes those not on watch curl up in their ponchos and sleep.

In the mines the meals of the packers were soon Anglicized and the vocabulary partly so, yet many of the features that Meyer most praised—the nimbleness of the mules, their ability to follow a shelving trail over mountain and chasm, and the sound engineering of the aparejo—continued to be the justifying factors for packing. On the level, or wherever wagons could go, the wheel conferred a decided mechanical advantage. Packing was best for the upper reaches of the mining country and its less accessible parts.

The drover was another important actor in the supply of the mines. At first it was merely a matter of driving up a few head of stock from Sutter's ranch or one of his neighbors'. Before long the magnetism of demand was felt in Oregon and southern California, and in time it produced sheep drives from Chihuahua and New Mexico and cattle drives from points as distant as Texas.

Isaac J. Wistar was one of the importers from Oregon. Collecting a herd in the Willamette Valley, he drove it south to Scott's Valley, where he left the animals on good grass and guarded by a couple of hired men. Then in lots of three or four he drove his cattle over a forty-mile scramble to the mines on the Salmon River, where he butchered and sold for a dollar a pound. This work, he says, was mostly done by the customers themselves, who lent a hand with the hanging, skinning, and cutting up, partly because they wanted first choice of the cuts, but mainly because they wanted to hear the news from the outside world.

The rancheros of southern California, accustomed to raising cattle for hides and tallow, enjoyed a fabulous boom when a market opened for beef. Few realized a dollar a pound, and not for long, but the price leveled off at several times the figure of the hide-and-tallow days. Volume was large, too; in the season of 1852 Los Angeles County was estimated to have sent 25,000 head north at an average price of thirty dollars.

Sometimes the rancheros staged their own drives. At other times they sold to cattle buyers who made up trail herds to be sent north by Santa Barbara and the Salinas Valley, or by Tejon Pass and the San Joaquin. A far greater measure of fame, of course, attaches to the long drives of a later epoch from Texas to the central and northern plains. These drives to the diggings and to San Francisco have laid no such hold on literary and popular fancy. Yet they flourished almost two decades earlier; they covered a respectable mileage and moved thousands of head of stock. Some day, perhaps, they will have an Andy Adams or an Emerson Hough to tell their story.

Their first effect was to help feed the gold miners and the urban forty-niners. A secondary effect was to spread the profits of gold mining to the cow counties of southern California. A third consequence was to bring about the rise of a new business. Henry Miller did not become a Swift, an Armour, or a Cudahy, but, with his abattoirs and outlets at San Francisco and his ranches spread from the Mexican border into Nevada and Oregon, he was, without exaggeration, the Cattle King.

By a more gradual process the food demands of the diggings stimulated other branches of agriculture. At the missions there had been a measure of attention to gardens and grain fields. With secularization this activity went into sudden decline. A few men like Sutter gave it attention, but at the time of the gold discovery California was not distinguishing itself except in the production of hides and tallow. The hungry miners, with their special fondness for flour, suggested a back-to-the-farm movement and particular attention to grain raising.

Before long, therefore, the grasslands of the lower Sacramento and San Joaquin valleys and those of the Coast Ranges, such as Sonoma, Napa, Livermore, and Santa Clara, were being put to the plow and sowed with wheat. The soil and climate proved thoroughly congenial to the small grains. In the San Joaquin Valley, in particular, there were no obstructions to the plow, the winter rains supplied adequate moisture, the dry summers turned the kernels flinty-hard and stretched out the harvest season so that a large acreage could be handled. From a mere 17,000 bushels in 1850, this crop mounted to 5,900,000 in 1860 and went on to make California first in wheat production by 1890. From an importer of flour and ship's bread, California turned to become a large exporter. California flour was especially popular in the tropics. During the Crimean War and the Civil War it got additional access to the European market. The beginning, however, was pointed toward the local market in the diggings.

On a more modest scale, farmers began to plant potatoes, turnips, onions, melons, grapes, berries, and fruit trees of practically all varieties. The annuals among these—the potatoes and onions, for example—found their way to the mines in a slight trickle in 1849 and in somewhat larger volume thereafter. The fruit of the more leisurely developing plants was not available until later and was more important in the fare of the San Franciscans. But again gold was clearly the catalyst that got California off to a good start on the road to becoming the state with the most diversified agriculture.

From agriculture to industry was only a short step. The grape growers who turned wine makers are a good example. They likewise did not get into production fast enough to become much of a factor in the gold fields, but by the 'sixties they had caught up with the local market and were shipping pipes and barrels round the Horn to the States. Flour milling grew by similar schedule. By 1869 California had some two hundred mills, several with capacity of a thousand barrels a day.

Such businesses as wagon making may be taken for granted, since it was a practically universal fact that wagons were made near their place of use. The tanning industry was one of more marked development. Cowhides were abundant. There were oaks throughout much of the state that could be drawn on for tanbark. The miners wanted boots; the packers had to have saddles; the freighters needed harness; and the machinery of mills, pumps, stamps, and industry in general depended on power applied through leather belting. At San Lorenzo in Santa Cruz County, at San Francisco, at Sacramento and Benicia, and at several other places good-sized plants were erected to meet this particular demand.

Textile mills turning out woolens and grain sacks, powder factories, sugar refineries processing island-grown cane, and cigar making were other successful ventures. Iron working had a greater significance. From routine blacksmithing it advanced to the processing of iron into pipe, wire, cables, pulleys, and machinery of various sorts ranging up to locomotives and iron river boats. The gold rush and, to quite a degree, the very process of mining itself made this development more rapid than it would have been on an ordinary frontier.

For cabins, stores, sluices, flumes, piling, and shoring, the gold rush set up a prodigious market for lumber. In part it was met by importation, especially from Oregon and Puget Sound, but an entirely obvious response was to make use of California's stands of timber. Small sawmills, rather on the order of Marshall's at Coloma, were set up in the gold country itself, but there were difficulties in competing with the mines for labor and for water, and the timber resources of this area were not the best. The more favored lumbering areas therefore came to be the Santa Cruz Mountains with their redwood, and Mendocino, Humboldt, and Del Norte counties. Exigencies of terrain and species led to certain distinctive features, such as the chutes for offshore loading along the northern coast. The ease with which some of these varieties could be split also suggested that method of turning out fence posts, rails, beams, planks, shakes, and shingles. A fair number of intended gold seekers dropped by the wayside to fell trees and saw and split lumber. Others, after a fling at mining, came back to this more stable employment.

Remarkable though these developments of agriculture and industry were, the immediate wants of the gold seekers at the start of the rush and for quite a while thereafter were met, if at all, by importations. This, to be sure, was nothing new. For most of the comforts and many of the necessities of life the province had always depended on deliveries from abroad—first in the Spanish ships from San Blas, then in the ships of the smuggling sea-otter hunters, then in the hide ships, and most recently in the traffic that was supplying the American military. Prior to receipt of word of the gold discovery, additional commercial ventures to California had been planned in New England.

As the gold-rush market became a reality, merchants and shipowners in the Pacific exerted themselves to meet the opportunity. Voyages were undertaken to Hawaii and to Oregon to load foodstuffs. Other ships sailed to more distant Pacific ports. At the height of the gold fever it was difficult to get enough men to form a crew, but sailings of this sort increased in number. Hawaii continued to be the most favored destination, but other ships went to the west coast of Mexico, to Peru and Chile, to the Galápagos Islands for turtles, to Tahiti and the islands of the South Pacific for pork and potatoes, and to China and the Pacific Northwest. In the annals of Seattle, which was founded in 1849, it is recorded that the first profitable enterprise for its residents was to work up a cargo of lumber for a ship from San Francisco.

Fewness of ships, reluctance of sailors, and the industrial benightedness of the Pacific area made these supplying efforts inadequate and forced dependence on goods from the States. The merest trickle came by the overland routes. Panama contributed a small amount of fast freight, but it was essentially a route for passengers and mail. Practically, therefore, it was by the Cape Horn route that the goods of Atlantic industry and commerce would reach San Francisco and its golden hinterland.

Argonauts choosing this route could bring along cargoes of goods. With the gold fever rampant, merchants who wanted to venture a shipload of goods had no trouble signing on a crew—at least for the voyage out. Also, except for the time that the investment would be tied up, the costs were moderate.

In the Californians' view, the principal defect of this dependence on round-the-Horn shipments was their unpredictability. Instead of filling orders, eastern merchants shipped whatever they thought might be in demand. The West Coast customers neither knew what was coming nor when it would arrive. To have these fundamentals so completely in the lap of the gods was an irresistible invitation to speculate. It also led to the adoption of certain business methods that were at least extraordinary.

Appearance of a ship entering the Golden Gate, for example, signaled a rush of merchants and commission men to board it, inspect the manifest, and bid on the cargo. Thus a warehouse and a sales organization might be less essential than an alert lookout and a good pair of oars. The merchant who first reached the incoming ship gained an advantage over his competitors. He was also able to take advantage of the newly arrived captain or supercargo before the shipman came to a full realization of California prices.

San Francisco's early business history is lit up with many examples of ingenious merchandising, such as Sam Brannan's inspiration to invest heavily in carpet tacks, which turned out to be much in demand in the era of canvas and muslin housing. It is also illuminated by successive attempts to corner the market in some particular commodity. Early in the gold rush, Collis P. Huntington is credited with going after shovels, which he bought for $2.50 a dozen on up to $125 a dozen. He encouraged his last supplier to boast about this transaction, and thus he was able to peddle his whole stock of shovels at a big advance over their average cost.

Another merchant prince set out to get a corner on rice. He bought up all that was on hand; but just as he was ready to cash in, two whole shiploads arrived, breaking the market, bankrupting the ambitious enterpriser, and upsetting the balance of his mind. He went on to greater fame as San Francisco's favorite eccentric, Norton I, self-styled "emperor of the United States," and humored in this foible by an indulgent society.

On the whole, gold-rush California is to be thought of as a scarcity market—one in which demand built up much more rapidly than the counterpoise of supply. Often, however, the opposite was true, particularly at the wholesale level in San Francisco. We are told that consignments of tobacco poured in until a stock sufficient for sixty-five years had accumulated. The series of big fires helped to restore a balance here. Glutted markets also led to use of cookstoves and tierces of tobacco for sidewalk paving. The stoves are especially praised—so long as the lids stayed put.

In the light of the uncertainties confronting trade, it perhaps becomes more tolerable that there was a big markup from wholesale to retail. It is an oft-repeated observation by men who had known something of business in the States, that whereas California wholesale quotations were not much advanced over those in the East, the retailers' margin was tremendously greater. Objection to extortionate charges by middlemen and distributors is, of course, a plaint which has been voiced again and again, by Grangers, Populists, muckrakers, the labor press, and by organized and unorganized consumers. The early California spread—justified in part by uncertainties and instability—did not draw determined criticism, but it was remarked, and some wondered if the law of supply and demand had been suspended.

In the panorama of business there was another phase in which a fundamental economic law seemed to have lost its effect. This was in moneylending. As gold production mounted and persisted, Californians came to have more money per capita in hand and in circulation than any other people anywhere. Such an abundance ought to have depressed interest rates. But the rate stood at three to five per cent *a month*, sometimes higher, and not much lower until well into the 'fifties.

True enough, most borrowers counted on quick profits. In the eyes of the lender, at the same time, the proposition was apt to look speculative and full of risk. If any collateral at all was offered, it was seldom of the sort to inspire confidence. Even land, which is usually regarded as the best underwriting, was doubtful security because most titles throughout the state had been thrown into jeopardy by the change in regime and soon were to be still further clouded by the Land Act of 1851. Many California loans of the gold-rush epoch were therefore unsecured except on the basis of the borrower's personal integrity.

At the time of gold discovery California had no banks. The proprietors of the hide ships, through extending credit, had acted as a primitive substitute. Certain merchants also began to accept deposits, to make loans, and to perform some of the other functions that normally go with banking. The banking service most in demand by the forty-niners was one peculiar to the time and place. The miners wanted their California money—gold dust and nuggets—changed into that of the nation and transmitted to the States.

Many an Argonaut circumvented this need by hiding his gold in camp, secreting it in a money belt, and standing guard over it as he made the long journey home. Soon, however, California firms sprang up and eastern companies moved in to engage in gold buying, issuance of drafts payable in the States, and shipment of gold via Panama to cover those drafts.

Henry Schliemann in later years the archaeologist who exhumed ancient Troy, operated such a bank in

Sacramento in 1851, in a stone house at the corner of Front and J Streets, with a tremendous safe bought from Barton, Lee and Company, and with three $250-a-month clerks, one from Ohio, one from Spain, and the third an eminent German geologist, who, however, was a bad calculator and made many mistakes. The bank bought an average of 180 pounds of gold a day. Banking hours in those days were from six in the morning until ten at night, and clerks and bankers went armed, day and night, with long bowie knives and Colt's revolving pistols, which, Schliemann asserts, "can kill 5 men in as many seconds."

Gold buying might logically have been the business of a government mint, had one existed in California at the time. There was vigorous agitation for such an establishment, and finally, in 1854, the hope was realized. In the meantime, private bankers invaded another of the roles usually monopolized by the government—the coining of money. A number of them struck off ten- and twenty-dollar pieces and, what was more characteristic, octagonal slugs rated at fifty dollars. These private coins were looked upon with some suspicion. Some were short weight, others got clipped, and some may have been debased. But in the absence of an official coinage they were a great convenience, for the most time-consuming part of doing business in California was commonly the weighing of the gold.

In other respects it is clear that the business of banking was more essentially what we now classify as express. Here was a line of endeavor that blossomed quickly, more than a hundred companies cropping up to serve the mines and the miners, though in time Adams and Company and Wells Fargo got most of the business. The express companies had as their prime function the shipment of gold. This they accomplished in the mines by pack mule, by courier, by the famous "box" that was sent by stage, and by escorted shipments on local and Panama steamers. By easy transition the express companies also became mail carriers. Their offices outnumbered and preceded the post offices, and their franks covered more of the early local correspondence than did Uncle Sam's postage.

Associated with the express companies there arose a machinery for public transportation within California. A certain Alexander Todd is mentioned as the real pioneer. Acquiring a whaleboat, he offered passage from San Francisco to Sacramento to those who would pay one ounce and pull an oar. In the autumn of '49, John Whistman, with an old French omnibus and a mixed team of mules and mustangs, offered an adventurous ride from San Francisco to San Jose; the time nine hours, the fare two ounces. At Sacramento, James Birch was the first stager. He began with a light emigrant wagon and a team of fractious mustangs and hauled passengers the thirty miles to Mormon Island for two ounces.

From these modest beginnings gold-rush California went on to develop a remarkable system of public transportation. The waters of San Francisco Bay and its tributaries were soon churned by paddlewheels and propellors, as a fleet of river boats was built up for the purpose. Some were fabricated on the spot. Others were brought out in pieces and were assembled locally. Still others, such as the *New World*, a palatial craft designed for Hudson River excursionists, were sailed out by way of the Strait of Magellan. Another was sailed out in a floating drydock, built round the steamer in New England and shucked off once California was reached. With the *Senator*, the *McKim*, the *New World*, and a host of others, it was not long until bay and river boats were providing the essential linkage between San Francisco, Sacramento, Stockton, Marysville, San Jose, and the towns of the northern and eastern shores of San Francisco Bay.

Other vessels, slightly more seaworthy, plied the coast north and south of San Francisco. Working northward, the fleet consisted chiefly of small lumber schooners hauling northern California redwood and Oregon pine and fir to San Francisco and the mines. Southward, such ships as the *Goliah* and the *Seabird* gave Los Angeles, San Diego, and Santa Barbara their chief contact with the civilized world. In all these towns the most important time marker was steamer day.

The sea lanes likewise were the state's chief link with the rest of the world. For passengers, express, and mail, the Panama steamers, checked and stimulated by intermittent opposition on the Nicaragua route, were the primary carriers. For freight the Cape Horn ships were predominant. Here the gold rush touched off a glorious epoch in American shipbuilding, as New England and New York craftsmen vied in turning out sleek, sturdy, and ever larger clippers, soundly engineered and vigorously sailed—in both senses of the word. The *Sea*

Witch, the *Sovereign of the Seas,* the *Flying Cloud* set record after record for day's run, for outward passage, and for homeward voyage. Not uncommonly such a ship paid out its cost in a single voyage. Except that her gold and distance stimulated this type of ship construction, California's role in the clipper ship era was merely to reap some of its most spectacular advantages.

Beyond the limits of inland navigation the stage was the thing. In the course of a few years Birch's springless wagon to Mormon Island and Whistman's French omnibus from San Francisco to San Jose had burgeoned into 3,000 miles of regular schedules, equipped with the finest Concord stages and matched and blooded horses, and handled by skilled whips and managers. Notwithstanding the roads, which were rough and tortuous and unimproved, these stages took the miners to their destinations at speeds comparable to those of the Royal Mail. The business was highly profitable, too; the California Stage Company in 1854 incorporated at a million dollars.

Later in the decade these California stagemen entered a bid for the federal contract for an overland mail. They did not get it. Some allege special influence in favor of John Butterfield. Yet California staging had developed rapidly enough to be competent to handle a line all the way to Missouri. It actually stocked the line as far east as El Paso.

To the tradesmen, farmers, industrialists, and transporters should perhaps be added the professional men. The gold rush brought lawyers in abundance—they had been relatively scarce and inactive before. It brought doctors in less adequate number and some who were bitterly criticized by their patients, though there is no question that there was present far more medical and surgical skill than had previously been available. Teachers and men of religion also put in an appearance. One forty-niner twitted his New England relatives for sending missionaries to heathen lands and not to California, where, he said, they were sorely needed. In actuality missionaries were sent, and in addition there were ministers who came simply as ministers. These people, together with professional entertainers, helped satisfy the wants and sometimes the needs of the miners.

Then there were still others in what might be called the service trades who patently were catering to the miners and to those who supplied the miners. In San Francisco a number of disillusioned gold seekers had turned porter. They particularly greeted passengers from newly arrived ships in order to pack their luggage to the place of lodging. There was nothing menial about these fellows, as is illustrated by the incident of a pompous individual who addressed one of them with "Here's a quarter; carry my bags." The stalwart fired back, "Here's a dollar; carry them yourself."

For cook fires and warmth wood was the standard fuel. Accordingly there were men who made their living by chopping wood and delivering it at the towns. Similarly, others worked as hunters, supplying the hotels and restaurants, and private customers as well, with venison and bear, ducks, geese, brant, quail, rabbits, or whatever game was available. A hunter's life is traditionally idyllic and independent, and perhaps especially so in a land where game was so plentiful as in most of California. Yet, significantly, hunting was seldom the first choice of those who were doing it for a living. Like the porters and the bootblacks they were mostly men who had tried their luck at prospecting and found it bad.

A more substantial though not necessarily more honorable calling was that of operating a hotel or restaurant. Both ordinarily began with skeleton equipment, had frequently to improvise, and relied heavily on the indulgence of their patrons. Sarah Royce, for example, describes the Montgomery House when it was one of San Francisco's finest. Its light frame was covered with boards and canvas, patched here and there with zinc. Aside from the kitchen stove there was no heat except in the bar. All interior partitions were of cloth; and the bedrooms, each with double-decker bunk, had just enough space for a person to stand and dress or undress. Valiant efforts were made to build more adequately, but for a long time hotel life in the towns as well as in the mines was but a step removed from camping out.

The restaurateurs likewise had initial handicaps to overcome, but seem to have risen above them with greater éclat. Perhaps it was that the forty-niners relished good eating rather more than luxurious shelter. Perhaps it was because French, Italian, Southern, Spanish, and Chinese styles of cooking were brought into close juxtaposition, with a consequent stimulation and interplay. Perhaps it was that California gardens provided a year-round supply of toothsome viands and that a wide variety of fish and game was usually on tap. The ecstatic echoes of marvelous food are mostly from the middle 'fifties or later and principally of San Francisco. In the beginning and in the mines the fare was more Spartan, though with an occasional display of genius.

In the towns as in the diggings the real show places were the emporia of drink and chance. They usually occupied the largest tents or buildings in the community. They employed every known device to attract: bright lights, free lunch, a band or orchestra and frequently a singer or dancer, lavish works of art with strong leanings to size and to nudes, and, whenever it could be arranged, young women to deal vingt-et-un or to act as croupier. Throughout gold-rush California these were the places of common resort, the most likely spot to find one's friends, the place to hear the latest news, the place where many a business deal was arranged or where it was made official with a drink. If we can believe the letter writers, a good many dropped in who neither drank nor gambled.

A larger truth, of course, is that the myriad forms of supplying and trafficking with the miners set up many forms of enterprise and employment. They gave birth to a number of towns specifically designed to provision and accommodate the miners, while other older towns were made over completely and vitalized far beyond their founders' wildest dreams. It was, of course, San Francisco that most thoroughly adjusted to the new order and moved forward with it, until soon the city by the Golden Gate was not just a point on the supply line of the gold hunters, but the metropolis to which the entire interior, the mines included, was tributary.

CHAPTER II

Architects of Law and Government

CALIFORNIA of the gold-rush epoch is a famous example
of men finding themselves beyond the pale of the law
and being so uncomfortable in that nakedness that they
concerted to erect a system of law and a machinery of
government. The *Mayflower* passengers, in a similar
predicament in 1620, had responded with their famous
compact, thereby endearing themselves to political the-
orists. The gold seekers attacked the problem of improving on the state of nature, not once but repeatedly. How
well they wrought may be another matter.

En route to California some of the forty-niners had
a taste of government making. The constitutions and
rules drafted by the Cape Horn companies are sometimes cited, but they are less than genuine examples.
They were essentially business agreements, and where
they ventured into definition of governing authority it
was not so much to fill a void as to circumscribe the

power which the tradition of the sea and the law of nations assigned to the captain of the ship.

On the overland trail the travelers would be equally out of touch with established government. From the veterans of the plains they copied the device of organizing as a company and electing a captain to whom a measure of power was assigned. This officer wielded a hesitant scepter. His sailors could desert anywhere along the line, not just in port. If his leadership grew unpopular, it was also a simple matter to demand a meeting and call for a new election. The covered-wagon commanders, therefore, were perhaps unduly responsive to public opinion.

Their realm of government also tended to be limited to such matters as setting the watches, choosing the camp sites, and determining the line of march. Whenever a more serious crisis arose, such as the commission of a high crime, group action imitative of what would have been done in the States seemed called for. Thus in 1849, when a murder was committed on the Gila, the travelers organized a court with judge and jury, conducted a trial, and on the following day carried out the sentence with a firing squad of twelve, of whom half had blank loads. Again, at Bear River in 1852, when an old man was killed in an altercation, his young assailant was tried, found guilty, and sentenced to death or banishment. Although offered an outfit sufficient to see him through to the gold fields, he replied that he was a Kentuckian and would rather die an honorable death than run. Accordingly, a firing squad of seven did the honors. Thus justice was invoked where no regular court could reach.

Meanwhile, in the diggings the forty-eighters had set a pattern in claim law. At the time of their entrance upon the scene, California was in transit from Mexican to American sovereignty, such government as it had was provisional and fragmentary, and the general land system that was to prevail had not been decided. It was not in the cards that the military governor should promulgate a code for the mines, and had he laid one down he could not have enforced it.

The diggings, furthermore, were in the interior where hardly a rood of land was claimed and occupied by a white man. The Indians perhaps should have been regarded as the rightful owners, but there was little disposition to accept this premise. Instead, the forty-eighters, and the courts after them, preferred to look upon the whole region as government land, part of the public domain. They moved in on it freely and without asking anyone's permission.

So long as they were few and the bars and gulches unlimited, they operated simply as individuals. But as soon as prospectors began to crowd the area and competition developed for mining sites, these pioneers saw the need for a system of regulation. Obviously they would have to work it out themselves.

The device they hit upon has been praised as the simplest possible. It was so logical that it came into use all through the gold country, not just in one or two camps but everywhere. The records do not prove whether the several camps got it by independent invention or by contagion—probably the latter way chiefly, though there were variations from camp to camp. Yet the degree of uniformity permits us to speak in the singular of claim law effective throughout the more than five hundred camps scattered over the diggings. In essence the law was that a man might claim a reasonable square footage of workable ground, and that to continue his claim he must mark it and work it.

The permissible size varied from camp to camp, somewhat in terms of the nature of the diggings. It might be as little as a hundred square feet, or it might be several times that much. The intention, however, always was to allot what a man could actually work, rather than a surplus that he would be tempted to sublet or hold for a speculative profit.

The title, furthermore, was usufructuary rather than absolute. Sometimes a shovel or a pick left on the spot was sufficient for maintaining ownership. But in most camps, if a claim was not worked at least one day a week, it was forfeit and might be taken over by anyone.

The earliest codes, some of which were not even put in writing, stuck closely to these fundamentals. Later sets of claim regulations became much elaborated; first, with provisions designed to implement or reinforce the basic principles; second, with incidentals that were outgrowths of the claims system; and third, with matters that were quite extraneous.

The most common implementing device, and one that came to be well-nigh universal, was the election of a claims officer, variously called alcalde, recorder, arbitrator, or chairman. In many camps he was the only officer. If a registry of claims had been ordered, he was the one who kept it and collected a fee for each entry. His major function was to settle disputes. Again, a fee was involved, to which some camps added a dollar a mile as the alcalde went to and from the disputed digging.

Conciliation or arbitration of disputes was the technique everywhere relied on to make the system work. Some camps used a panel, allowing each contestant to name two men. If the four could not come to a decision they chose a fifth arbiter. In other camps disputes were merely put up to a mutually acceptable referee or submitted to the alcalde. Since the question was usually over conflicting boundaries or claim jumping, inspection and one short hearing were ordinarily enough. The decision, furthermore, was final.

Benefiting from experience, the miners in the late 'fifties and 'sixties were able to write in additional provisions that took care of almost all contingencies. Sickness and jury duty were recognized as valid excuses for not working a claim, though the former was to be attested by a physician. A claim might not be laid out to encroach closer than twelve feet to any building, nor was digging to be done in such a way as to cut off access to a building. If a miner dug up a road, he must construct another—in today's terminology, a detour. The discoverer of a new placer should be rewarded with a double claim. No one else could file on more than one claim, and although buying and selling of claims was permitted, no person could possess more than two—one filed upon and the other by purchase.

By the limitation on number of holdings and by the insistence on continuous working, these codes effectively ruled out absentee ownership. By the simplicity and finality of the arbitrations lawyers were rendered non-essential. In some of the codes the alcaldes were specifically warned that they had tenure of office only during good behavior. Whether specified or not, every camp had the means easily at hand to recall any official who had lost the people's confidence. All that was necessary was to call a camp meeting and put the question to a vote.

A less commendable but equally modern feature, the restrictive covenant, appeared in several of the codes. Columbia's, for example, contained this regulation, "Neither Asiatics nor South-Sea Islanders shall be allowed to mine in this district"; to which were added these teeth, "Any person who shall sell a claim to an Asiatic or South-Sea Islander shall not be allowed to hold another claim in this district for the space of six months."

At the time of their initial drafting, the claim laws of any camp occasioned a camp meeting which some have compared to a New England town meeting, others to the old Teutonic folk moot. The miners' camp meeting was perhaps even more democratic. It asked no questions about church membership or previous condition. It did not even inquire what a man's age was; anyone who worked as a miner could hold a claim and could vote.

With slight modification, the claims system designed for placers was adapted to tunnel mining; to dry diggings, where a common practice was to throw up a mound of pay dirt in preparation for the season when there would be water—ownership of such piles was recognized and protected; to water rights; and to quartz mining. With even less modification, it could fit group enterprises such as wing damming. An early concession was that several men could work as a crew on one claim without forfeiting their individual claims.

Practically without modification the California claim law was transplanted to Nevada's Comstock Lode, to Oregon and Idaho, to Arizona and New Mexico, to Montana—in fact, throughout the Rocky Mountain West wherever mining flourished. Writing in 1884, Charles H. Shinn predicted that the system would continue to flourish wherever Americans mined gold or silver. Another significant endorsement came from the state of California, which permitted the claims associations of the camps to govern mining long after the machinery of state government had been set up, and which adopted a mining code that was a composite restatement of the claim laws of the various camps.

The fashion is to extol the miners for outstanding achievement in creating a code of self-enforcing laws where none had existed before. Several elements suggest an indebtedness to Spanish-Mexican practice: the mining titles based on use, the bracketing of water rights, and the stress on conciliation. At least as notable were the thoroughgoing democracy and the safeguards thrown up to protect the individual workingman against monopolists.

At a moderately early stage some of the camps slightly enlarged the functions of their claims officers by allowing these worthies to act as alcaldes or justices of the peace to handle minor and noncriminal actions. Some of these men dispensed orthodox and evenhanded justice. The ones most remembered, however, were those without legal experience, many of them unlettered and eccentric. They are credited with injecting much unconscious levity into the courtroom.

The first case in one such court was an American's complaint against a Mexican for stealing a pair of old leggings. The alcalde remonstrated, but the miner insisted on justice. The verdict: a fine of three ounces for the theft, and against the miner a fine of one ounce for bothering the court with such a trifle. The second case was like unto it. A miner sued for a stolen pick. He was awarded one ounce as the value of the implement, but was assessed the costs—three ounces.

A few magistrates gained a reputation for arbitrary decisions, gross discrimination against Mexicans and other foreigners, uncouth manners in conducting court, and overweening interest in lining their own pockets. So far as these attributes are unprofessional they characterize frontier justice in general, not just that of the mines. Indeed, the most notorious of the early California judges were men like Reynolds of Stockton, an expert marksman with tobacco juice and a rapid calculator in fining Mexicans, and Blackburn of Santa Cruz, hero of many quaint decisions.

Except for the simple machinery for adjudication of disputed claims, most of the camps at first boasted no other mechanism of government. Through much of the first season they remained crime-free, and, since the assumption was that each man could look out for himself, an established court seemed unnecessary.

There came a day, however, when a crime of the first magnitude was committed. Such an event jarred the miners out of their exaggerated individualism. Particularly if the culprit or a suspect had been caught, they flocked together, in a camp meeting such as had drafted the claims regulations, and prepared to do business as a court of justice. Here likewise, although there was a studious effort to approximate the forms of a regular court, the mode was to cut through the intricacies of the law and the pettifogging of lawyers and to get immediately at the vital question of guilt or innocence.

Thus, at Dry Diggings, near Coloma, five men were caught in the act of robbing a Mexican gambler. The time was January, 1849, which was long before any official agencies of justice had penetrated the region. The options seemed to be to let the culprits go or for the miners to act as a court. Choosing the latter alternative, the miners impaneled a jury of twelve and promptly executed its sentence of thirty-nine lashes. New charges were then made against three of the men for crimes committed months earlier on the Stanislaus. Hanging was the popular verdict, against which E. Gould Buffum lodged an energetic protest, but the assembled miners had their way. The corpses dangled from a convenient oak and Dry Diggings was ready for its new name, Hangtown.

Up and down the gold country other crimes led to similar performances. The procedure was not standardized. Some camps preferred juries of six, others of twelve or twenty, and others merely put the question to a vote by all present. These courts would listen to testimony but had little patience for argument. And lacking jails and reformatories and personnel to stand guard indefinitely, they specialized in quick punishment: whipping, hanging, ear-cropping, branding, or banishment. At times a traveler on State Highway 49, overpowered by all the hang trees there commemorated, suspects that folklore has embellished the record. Yet history also asserts that the oaks were "tasselled with the carcasses of the wicked," and documentary evidence supports the assertion.

Milus Gay describes a typical case: "I was called up last night 11 or 12 o'clock to assist in taking and trying a man for stealing money—George Gillin late of Ioway—Took him up to Dry Town—went into the 'Southern House'—I was appointed Judge—selected 12 men for Jury—tryed him—found him guilty—sentenced him to 39 lashes on the bare back—blind folded. Tryal occupyed the night—Jury rendered their verdict about sun up—took him out—tied him up and applyed the lash—required him to leave by 3 p.m."

"I was present," forty-niner Richard J. Oglesby recalls, "one afternoon . . . , and saw with painful satisfaction, as I now remember, Charley Williams whack three of our fellow citizens over the bare back, twenty-one to forty strokes, for stealing a neighbor's money. The multitude of disinterested spectators had conducted the court. . . . I think I never saw justice administered with so little loss of time or at less expense."

Other typical performances may be summarized as follows: On the Cosumnes, on March 7, 1851, two New Englanders were found with stolen horses in their possession. Without so much as a jury trial, they were "condemned by acclamation" and hanged at once. At Shasta

City a fortnight later a man who had been drinking too heavily quarreled with his partner and killed him. Immediately put to trial, he was in a few minutes sentenced to die. Contrite, he submitted with resignation, with the rope around his neck addressed the crowd on the evils of drink, and stepped off into space. At Drytown in Amador County in June, 1851, a Mexican killed a Chinese. His guilt was so obvious that a trial was not deemed necessary. No proper rope was to be had, however, and he was bunglingly hanged with a rope noose spliced to a log chain.

At Sonora that same month a band of Chileños plotted to rob and kill one George Snow. Enticing him to their tent, where they had dug a grave for his body, they fell upon him with knives. Mortally wounded, he managed to call for help, which came running, and the assailants fled. Two were overtaken, tried simultaneously by separate juries, and pronounced guilty. They were conducted by fully a thousand men to the scene of the crime, were duly hanged, and buried in the grave they had thoughtfully prepared.

A number of times the punishment-minded miners were confronted by suspects against whom no tangible evidence could be summoned. The citizens of Oregon Bar, for example, looked upon a man named Walden as the probable thief of a hundred dollars and a piece of meat. They fitted a rope around his neck and swung him off the ground in hopes that he would confess. The camp doctor then administered an emetic, which, however, did not yield positive evidence. The man was then released on the chance that he would uncover the gold.

This failing, the miners once more applied the rope, whereupon Walden demanded that if they were going to hang him they do it speedily and respectably, "without humbug, harangue, or torture." The crestfallen miners let him go.

Accused of stealing a thousand dollars from his partner, a man named Seymour was taken to the Weaverville hang tree and given two trips on the rope. He still denied guilt and was released, after which the partner found that his gold had merely been misplaced. A man named Henry Lorenze was given two hours of such treatment by the citizens of Mokelumne Hill, but would not oblige with a confession. A posse of Columbians applied similar pressure to an elderly suspect with such good effect that he confessed his crime and produced the stolen gold.

On several most unfortunate occasions the miners' tribunals got hold of the wrong man. At times the proof of innocence came too late. G. Ezra Dane tells of a sheepish delegate going hat in hand to a newly bereaved widow and saying, "We just hanged George for murder. But ma'am, the joke's on us; he didn't do it." On other occasions the fates intervened just in time. In Vaca Valley, in 1857, pursuit of a horsethief led to a young Mexican, who was strung up and strangled almost to death before it was realized that he was not the right hombre.

Besides having been impetuous and informal, the direct action of the miners often had an element of sadism in it. The Downieville mob that hanged Juanita is a famous instance in point. So was the affair of gambler

John Barclay at Columbia. Entering his wife's none too respectable saloon one day, he discovered a miner pummelling his wife. Out came his pistol, and the miner dropped dead. Too late Barclay learned that the scuffle was over nothing more serious than a broken pitcher. But the drunken and now dead miner suddenly had a host of friends who roused the town and demanded a hanging.

This was in 1855; regular government had come to the diggings, and Barclay was soon in the sheriff's custody. But the aroused townspeople were in no mood to wait. They broke into the jail and carried the prisoner away. A trial, or at least the formality of a trial, ensued, with judge and jury and counsel for the prosecution and the defense. The defense wanted Martha Barclay brought to testify, but the crowd hooted him down. The judge asked if there were character witnesses from Chinese Camp, where Barclay had lived. The crowd protested derisively, and some wag shouted, "Send him to hell for witnesses." Counsel were then allowed one minute apiece to address the jury. The prosecuting attorney was listened to and applauded. The counsel for the defense was constantly interrupted and shouted down. The jury's verdict was a foregone conclusion.

Sheriff James M. Stewart created a diversion by trying to rescue the prisoner, but for his pains was cracked over the head with a pistol. A rope lowered from the high flume was now hastily adjusted and Barclay was yanked into the air, while the thousand men below yelled their satisfaction. His arms had not been pinioned and he tried to save himself by grasping the rope. The men above responded by jerking the line and letting it drop suddenly. One of them yelled to the poor unfortunate, "Let go, you damned fool! let go!" Strangled at length, Barclay did let go. His body quivered and hung motionless.

This particular mob scene illustrates a principal defect in the impromptu justice of the mining camps, the tendency to continue it and prefer it after legal courts were available. True, the regular courts did not always inspire confidence. Some of the early governors also were too free—though free is not quite the word—with pardons. But most of the later resorts to extralegal action rested on such flimsy grounds as wanting to have the performance in the camp rather than transferred to a rival camp which happened to be the county seat. Or they expressed the vengeful, bestial quality that characterizes lynchings, which is what they really were.

The general reputation of the miners' handling of crime and punishment also takes a drubbing in the literary treatment usually accorded it. Clarence King has a story in which a jury reports not guilty. Willing hands lock it up again with the enjoinder, "You'll have to do better than that." Half an hour later the verdict is guilty. "Correct," say the boys, "we hung him an hour ago." Bret Harte presents almost the same theme, but with the variation that he has the jury deliberate too long, whereupon one of the boys calls in, "Take your time, gentlemen, but remember, we want this room to lay out the corpse in."

Inevitably, the political impulses of the foothills tended to trickle down to the valley towns and the people around the bay. When gold was discovered, California languished under military government with local authority delegated to Mexican-type alcaldes, most of whom were Anglo-Americans. In August the province learned that it had indeed been transferred to American ownership. Thereafter it became a favorite indoor sport for editors and outdoor sport for orators to declaim against the ignominy of military rule, to insist that the Constitution followed the flag, and that California was immediately entitled to civil government. The golden harvest in the mountains and the avalanche of Argonauts gave these protestants mighty arguments which they used with much zeal. They were, however, up against an implacable rule of procedure in the American system, namely that provision of civil government, whether territorial or state, would have to be by federal action; and the authorities at Washington, rendered timorous by the bugaboo of slavery extension and the balance of slave and nonslave votes in the Senate, were reluctant to touch the nettle.

The gold rush did not create this problem. Without it, Californians would still have raised the question of ending military government and erecting one on the civilian pattern. But gold accelerated the issue and at the same time complicated it by reason of the cosmopolitan crew that it brought in and the allegedly unstable citizenry that it gave California.

How the issue was fought out in Washington may be left to the national historians. Agitations in California built up sentiment in favor of a convention to draft a state constitution, and in July, 1849, the military governor coöperated by calling an election of delegates. The mining camps, it must be admitted, showed less acute interest in the proposal than the people of such places as San Francisco and San Jose, but they voted, and what is perhaps more surprising, they found delegates who would quit the diggings and make the journey to Monterey for a six-weeks session of constitution making.

By the time the delegates assembled, in September, the gold-mining forty-niners far outnumbered all other Californians. It was natural, however, that "old-timers" should dominate the convention. There were a few native Californians such as Vallejo and de la Guerra and a number of Americans of long residence such as Stearns and Larkin. Others, like Semple, had moved in before the War with Mexico, or, like Halleck, had come in uniform while the war was being fought. Of the forty-eight delegates not more than a dozen were forty-niners. Gold did not particularly influence the content of the constitution, but it did play a large part in determining the early date, and it supplied the numbers, wealth, and confidence that led these Founding Fathers to vault over the customary tutelage of territorial government and design instead the foundation of a state.

The constitution thus fashioned has been prized by many learned men. Four years later it served as the principal inspiration and model for Juan Bautista Alberdi's constitution for Argentina, and of it Alberdi remarked, "Without universities, without academies or law college, the newly-organized people of California have drawn up a constitution full of foresight, of common sense, and of opportunity."

By popular vote the Californians had promptly ratified their constitution. Nevertheless, Washington's politicos looked upon it askance. They regarded the Californians as distant and irresponsible. Since President Taylor's military governor had connived with the constitution makers, they suspected it as an executive conspiracy. There was the larger problem of providing government for the entire Mexican cession, and beyond this the most vital issues of slavery extension and sectional rivalry. Congress, therefore, delayed almost a year before it acted on the California proposal, and its final approval was linked to several other measures which made up the Compromise of 1850.

Meanwhile, General Riley had stepped aside in favor of a civil government under the constitution. In the closing days of 1849 the first legislature assembled at San Jose, installed Peter H. Burnett as the first elected governor, and began to function. The wheels of government creaked. No one knew whether the state would be legitimatized by Congress or disallowed. No one knew, therefore, whether to pay taxes or to take the risk of lending money to the infant state. These uncertainties perhaps help to explain why Senator Thomas Jefferson Green repeatedly moved adjournment for liquid refreshment, and why this legislature is immortalized as the "Legislature of a Thousand Drinks."

From this start, both glorious and boisterous, California went on in the 'fifties to a checkered political career. The successive legislatures wrangled over whether the capital should be at San Jose, Monterey, Vallejo, Benicia, New York on the Pacific, or, as finally decided, at Sacramento. Repeatedly, the election of United States Senators was the all-engrossing question, to the sad neglect of the problems of the state. On the whole, these legislatures came in for sharp criticism, as, for example, that of 1851, which a San Francisco journalist categorized as an "infamous, ignorant, drunken, rowdy, perjured and traitorous body of men." The governors, such as John Bigler, the Chinaman's friend; "I, John" McDougal, a redoubtable pardoner; and Know-Nothing J. Neely Johnson, were not much better.

The Democratic party almost always prevailed, but it was torn by bitter strife between the "Chiv" or Chivalry faction, headed by William M. Gwin and other Southerners, and that led by David C. Broderick, a product of New York's Tammany Hall. This fight came to a climax in 1859 in the duel between Judge David S. Terry and Broderick, in which the Tammany leader was shot down.

No one glosses over the imperfections of state politics in this initial decade. Excuse is offered, none the less, that a host of men had come to California with the simple intention of gathering gold and then departing. Such persons could hardly be expected to take the most conscientious interest in the obligations of citizenship. Furthermore, the intended permanent residents were exceedingly busy with their money-making ventures and were sorely tempted to forget their responsibilities to the state.

Anecdotes abound on vagaries in electoral method. The newspapers of the day preserve the editorial advice offered the voters, record the issues that were current, and reproduce some of the political oratory. Other sources testify how campaigning for office contributed to the entertainment of the populace. A Weaverville correspondent, for example, estimated a successful candidate's champagne bill at about five hundred dollars. Of a particular contest he reports that if there had been one more candidate hardly anyone in town would have been able to step up and cast a ballot.

Occasionally the miners let themselves go with a full-scale burlesque on politics as it was practiced. At Rough and Ready in 1850 a man named Brundage conceived a violent distaste for the state government as organized. He called a meeting, sounded a diatribe against the government, and reminded his hearers that their camp had had no delegate at Monterey and no voice in drafting the state constitution. Apparently in dead earnest, he went on to propose that the camp secede from the iniquitous state of California and organize as the "State of Rough and Ready." A hundred of his amazed and delighted listeners gave the proposal vociferous support, some perhaps with serious intent. In short span, however, the State of Rough and Ready was the butt of guffaws all up and down the diggings, none more hearty than those of Rough and Ready itself.

Grass Valley's "Hunger Meeting" in the winter of 1852–1853 was a worthy sequel. Thoroughly rained in and reduced to short rations, the miners called a meeting to see if something could not be done. Since the conclusion was soon reached that the only remedy was to wait for the roads to dry, the meeting dissolved into a burlesque. Inflammatory speeches called for action, breathing dire threats against the hoarders at Sacramento and San Francisco. A committee on ways and means went into a huddle, emerged with a declaration of war on San Francisco, and a resolution to get the supplies "peaceably if we can, forcibly if we must."

In their dealings with the federal government the Californians exhibited comparable bravado. The volume of gold production probably gave them an exaggerated idea of their importance. At any rate, they bombarded the federal authorities with demands for better mail service, larger Indian patrols, a mint, a railroad, and a free hand in local affairs. Whenever Washington was lax or remiss, or whenever it verged on an unwanted interference, the Californians were apt to threaten a westward secession and the setting up of a Pacific Republic. How many were serious in this threat, and how often, it is difficult to say; but certainly without the reservoir of gold these Californians would not have been so petulant. It took the larger issues of the Civil War and the completion of the transcontinental railroad to scotch this idea permanently.

The most famous political manifestations of gold-rush California were the popular tribunals of San Francisco. As early as 1849 a hoodlum element, styling itself the Hounds or Regulators, terrorized various minority elements. A raid on Little Chile incensed the community, which rose en masse, donated for the relief of the victims, insisted on the arrest of several of the Hounds, and frightened the rest into decamping. This business accomplished, the citizens went back to their own affairs.

From these pursuits they found themselves diverted again early in 1851. In the course of eighteen months San Francisco had been devastated by six fires, the worst of them thought to be incendiary. Crime was on the increase too, and the regular courts seemed powerless or unwilling to convict footpads, robbers, and murderers. A group of leading businessmen decided, therefore, to organize a popular tribunal, on the order of those that flourished in the mines. They abstracted from jail two men charged with assaulting a tradesman in his store. Unfortunately for the vigilance committee, there was doubt that they had the proper culprits on trial, and their own jury could not agree. They returned the two men to the custody of the authorities and were well pleased to have done so because just in the nick of time the real Jim Stuart was caught and the man who had stoutly maintained that he was Thomas Berdue thereby got reprieve, release, and reward.

Next on the committee's list was a certain John Jenkins, unmistakably caught while robbing a safe. Its confidence shaken by the Stuart-Berdue affair, the committee wavered, but Sam Brannan spoke up for vigorous action, Jenkins was judged guilty, and forthwith, in the middle of the night, the committee marched to the Plaza and hanged its man. This committee of 1851 sat on ninety other cases, hanging three, whipping one, deporting twenty-eight, delivering fifteen to the regular authorities, and releasing forty-one. Perhaps most notable was its abandonment of secrecy. After the coroner's jury had listed nine men involved in the midnight hanging of Jenkins, the committee published its full roster of 180 members. Even with this publicity it was still an extra-legal court, operating in defiance of the regular channels of justice.

Five years later San Francisco found itself again at the mercy of active criminals and venal courts. Two acts of spectacular violence—gambler Charles E. Cora's killing of a federal marshal, and Supervisor (and ex-convict) James P. Casey's shooting of editor James King of William—led to the summoning of the second vigilance committee.

In the half decade since 1851 both the local and state governments had become much more thoroughly established. Neither could be expected to sit idly by while a vigilance committee protractedly flouted the regular courts. It was possible also that federal interference might be invoked. The sponsors of the tribunal of 1856, therefore, proceeded with much caution. First they advertised that names would be enrolled. Establishing a headquarters, Fort Gunnybags, they gathered arms and ammunition, effected a military organization, and then marched to the jail to requisition Casey and Cora.

After careful, deliberate trials in which the defense, through witnesses and capable counsel, was given full opportunity to be heard, both men were declared guilty. At the very hour of King's funeral they were hanged. The committee, like its predecessor, now began to work through a long list of suspects, hanged two, banished a larger number, turned some persons over to the regular courts, and frightened still others from the city.

From the Law and Order group, which included many prominent citizens, especially members of the bar, the second vigilance committee came in for harshest criticism. If officials were not doing their duty, the proper remedy, said these men, was to vote them out and put honest men in. If, in the meantime, certain criminals escaped punishment, that was far less of a menace to society than the committee's own action in going beyond the law.

Among descendants and historians this debate still goes on. The vigilante group felt thoroughly justified. It justly averred that the provocation was great, that it acted with dignity and without passion, and that after a few months it surrendered to the authorities a thoroughly cleansed San Francisco. The committee does stand as a model of vigilance, though some will insist that this is still no compliment.

Encouraged by the patterns set in the mines and inspired by the example of the San Francisco committees, provincial California also made vigilante action the order of the day. From San Diego to the Oregon border, horse thieves, cattle thieves, murderers, lesser criminals, and occasional victims of mistaken identity were unceremoniously hanged. Trial sometimes preceded the execution, but increasingly it was thought sufficient that a posse had caught a suspect or that the man was in jail.

Even when a notable such as the mayor of Los Angeles took the lead, this rustic vigilance lacked much of the urbanity that characterized the work of the San Francisco committees. The avenging groups almost always gathered on the spur of the moment. Their action was hasty. There was no such thing as a responsible membership. Passion and sadism often affected their work, which was, in other words, more akin to that of the later tribunals in the mines.

To be sure, the courts in the rural areas were weak, and crime was made the worse by the proximity of the mines and the expulsion of desperadoes from San Francisco. Yet the so-called vigilante actions in the provinces were crude performances—in actual fact, lynchings rather than anything more respectable.

Popular tribunals degenerated into lynching mobs represent the seamy side of political endeavor in gold-rush California. For the innocent who were made to suffer and for the wicked ushered prematurely into eternity nothing can atone.

There is, however, a better side to the picture, which proved in many respects the more enduring one. For the men of this epoch wrought exceedingly well in their system of claim law. They did passably well in their first responses to crime. And they established local governments and a state government on a foundation that has endured to the present. They proved themselves notable architects of law and government.

CHAPTER 12

Mining as an Industry

INFLUENCED by the circumstances of the discovery, California gold mining at first was closely tied to the watercourses. Practically all the metal recovered in 1848 and 1849 came from the bars, banks, benches, and beds of the permanent streams or from ravines and gulches which flowed only intermittently but were nevertheless a part of the drainage system of the Sierra foothills.

Since these deposits were relatively shallow and were of free, or loose, gold, they were well adapted to individual working. That is the way the early miners went at it, either completely on their own or joining forces with a partner or two.

The only major departure from this norm in the early years was in the practice of river mining. To dig a diversion channel and build a dam, or even to construct a wing dam, was too big a job for an individual or a small partnership. It was accomplished by a group called a company. What was invested, however, was usually not money or capital, but the labor of a substantial number of sharers. It was, in other words, a larger partnership in which a dozen or a score of men pooled their labor in an enterprise that would keep them busy for months and, in the end, might pay them off.

Similarly there was occasional banding together to dig a ditch or build a flume to carry water to a particular digging. At the outset these were also partnership efforts.

Both river mining and water development had potentialities for the industrial rather than the partnership method. In time a number of such properties were constructed or acquired by investment capital and were operated by hired labor. Yet in the placers this intrusion of the capitalist system was fairly belated and hardly more than incidental.

Although the miners often voiced the fatalistic saying, "Gold is where you find it," many of them evinced a healthy curiosity about where it came from. Pretty obviously, the alluvial gold they were working had got where it was by being washed down. Accordingly these prospectors kept working upward, hoping to find the ultimate source. They speculated about volcanic action that might have scattered the precious metal over the favored area, and about other mysterious geological processes which perhaps had done the deed. Meanwhile, they inched along uphill and came upon, not just one source, but two.

On hillsides far above existing stream levels they found sedimented gravels rich in gold. Geologists at length explained that these gravels had been deposited in the Tertiary by the watercourses that then drained the area. Because of different slopes of the drainage courses, the alluvial action of this earlier age had produced some stupendous deposits—as much as two or three hundred feet in depth—and often overlaid with other sedimentary or volcanic material. The superimposed weight, together with an intermixture of sulphides, had compacted some of this gold-bearing gravel into what the miners called cement. Though not hard rock, it approached that consistency. Most of these Tertiary gravels were laid out along courses which do not always coincide with those of the modern streams.

In their placer workings the miners also came upon occasional chunks of quartz with gold firmly embedded in them. These finds led them to examine various outcroppings of this same kind of rock, some of which proved to be gold-bearing. This rockbound gold, deposited during an earlier chapter of Sierran history and by weather and erosion persuaded to release its captive metal, was presumably the source of the gold in the Tertiary deposits and likewise of those in the more recent placers. Presumably also the exposed leads or veins continued underground, perhaps for a considerable distance.

At Mariposa, within the area claimed by Frémont, a rich outcrop was discovered in 1849. Samples were chipped off, naturally from the richest part of the vein. Laboriously pulverized and washed, they yielded two ounces to every twenty-five pounds, or, by another computation, seventy-five dollars a bushel. Comparably rich ores were found at Grass Valley, and soon other finds were reported practically the entire length of the gold area. The assays approached and sometimes surpassed those of Mariposa. They were ten to a hundred times higher than those of paying ores elsewhere—in Georgia, for example. To the placer miner, accustomed to having to winnow his gold from a much larger bulk of dross, these concentrations sounded fabulously high. Volunteer oracles prophesied that the future of California gold mining was clearly in quartz, and a wave of excitement about locating veins and ledges swept the diggings. Projects were also set afoot to acquire the necessary equipment for hard-rock mining. The men of the placers made the first moves, but the contagion spread rapidly to the California towns—a Los Angeles company offered stock at auction in August, 1850—and kept on going to engulf the eastern states and particularly England.

Grass Valley had the honor of seeing the first quartz mill in operation. Brought out from the States for G. W. Wright, it went into operation in 1850. Before that season was over, other mills arrived by way of the Horn and a few by the Isthmus. A dozen or so were in operation by the end of the year, and more were on order.

Notwithstanding the optimism in which they started —some of these companies put as much as $100,000 into locations and equipment,—these first quartz operators had great difficulty showing a profit. They were beset, to be sure, by inordinately high transportation costs on all the materials that they needed. They had to pay exceedingly high wages to compete with the surrounding placers. They had trouble finding labor that was adequately skilled, and greater difficulty in lining up superintendents who really knew the business.

A common mistake was to erect a mill over a rich out-crop without any exploration to try to learn the extent of the ore body. Too often it proved to be only a pocket, or at most a vein that soon pinched out. Others built where even the surface indications were negative and frittered away their money in useless shafts and drifts. To a degree, of course, satisfactory location was a matter of luck. But even the mills that were fortunately placed disappointed their owners in the first few years. The real trouble was that quartz mining was an intricate business, and Californians needed to learn more about ores, machinery, and processes before they could make it pay.

The quartz miner had three principal tasks confronting him: first, the mining of the ore; second, reducing it to powder; and third, extracting the gold from the powdered rock.

For actually getting out the ore, they depended upon picks, hand drills, and sledges, mildly assisted by black powder. This was hard, slow work. The prime necessity was to follow the vein. For efficient operation, however, the shaft, whether vertical or inclined, had to be ap-proximately straight, and the reconciliation of these two requirements sometimes involved a good deal of extra digging. In the shallower workings a hand windlass was the standard device for getting the ore to the surface. As the work progressed, it was necessary to install don-key engines and winches. Up to 1852, however, none of these mines had reached a depth of more than 300 feet.

For the pulverizing of their ore the quartz miners had recourse to some form of stamp, or, less ambitiously, to the Mexican arrastre or a variant known as the Chile mill.

The arrastre consisted of a fitted stone bowl or tank, rigged with a center pivot and a boom which could be swept around the circle by a plodding mule. To the boom were hitched one or more heavy abrasive stones. The Chile mill differed merely in that a big stone wheel or roller was fitted onto the boom. Both were effective machines, relatively inexpensive to build and operate, but too slow to suit the Californians. Their continuing importance was chiefly for very small operations or as supplements to a battery of stamps.

The stamp, as its name implies, was a machine that delivered vertical, hammer-like blows. It, too, operated within a mortar-like container or box. Its heavy pounder was lifted eight to twelve inches and then released to come crashing down on the ore. By proper rigging, a whole battery of such stamps could be powered by a single steam engine and synchronized so as to impose a uniform load. As a device of considerable antiquity the stamp had been thoroughly tested before its arrival on the California scene, but unlike the arrastre it came in for substantial improvement at the hands of the Californians.

These included the substitution of cast iron for soft iron stamp heads and dies, making heads and stems round instead of square, allowing the stamp to drop free and to revolve instead of being held rigid, reinforcing the mortar with a cast iron bedplate, and better engineering of the lifting device. Some of these improvements came as early as 1851. They were enough of a change to justify calling the new machine the California stamp. And they were enough of an improvement to enable this type of mill to replace all the more complicated and expensive ore crushers of earlier importation.

Having mined and crushed his ore, the quartz operator had reached the stage where the placer miner began. His remaining problem was to separate the gold from the powdered rock with which it was mixed. Superficially the methods employed were the same as in the placers. Water and gravity and quicksilver, with its remarkable amalgamating quality, were called into action in sluices, riffle boards, shaking tables, and other such devices.

Unfortunately, the process was not so simple as it sounds. It is estimated, in fact, that the early millers lost two-thirds to four-fifths of the gold. Sometimes this was because the stamps did not grind fine enough. A remedy was to put the product of the stamps through an arrastre for more thorough pulverizing. Sometimes the difficulty was that the gold itself was reduced to so fine a powder that it got washed away. A partial answer was to line the sluice with blankets, which would catch particles too fine for the riffles.

Because the gold came from unweathered rock, some of it, too, was chemically imprisoned in sulphides. In the presence of these sulphides, furthermore, the gold that was free would not amalgamate with the quicksilver. For a decade or more this circumstance completely baffled the quartz miners. A process that would have solved the difficulty had been invented in Germany and also in England in 1848. The ore, after being heated in a furnace, was suffused with chlorine gas, which changed the sulphides to soluble chlorides, which were then precipitated. A group of Germans began experimenting with this process in California in 1858, went off to Washoe without perfecting it, but returned in 1860 and made the process work. Mill operators at Grass Valley and Nevada City put it to use, and eventually it was adopted in Amador County, but the spread was not as great as might have been expected. Later the cyanide process took over.

Through the 'fifties the graph of quartz mining is peculiar and instructive. The initial discoveries attracted widespread interest and heavy investment, with a profusion of mills being established and a large amount of complicated machinery brought in. A count in 1852 reported 108 mills, representing an investment of $5,876,000. Yet nine-tenths of these early plants were failures; most of them were shut down and their elaborate machinery sold for junk or allowed to rust away. The early reverses inevitably discouraged investors and led to a persistent skepticism about mining in quartz. By 1854 the number of mills was down to 32.

Then, thanks to the improving efficiency of some of the operators and to technological advances such as the California stamp, recovery set in. In 1856 the number of stamp mills advanced to at least 59, in 1857 to more than twice that number, to 279 in 1858, and to more than 300 by 1861. Many of these outfits were relatively small; some had been outfitted for as little as $6,000 to $10,000. Others were considerably more elaborate, as is indicated by the figure of $3,270,000 as the cost of the mills operating in 1858.

This development was all very encouraging and a harbinger of the future which would find quartz mining the most durable phase of the industry. To the end of the decade, however, quartz accounted for only a minute fraction of the state's gold production; one authority puts it at no more than one per cent. To the men of the 'fifties, therefore, the development of techniques of washing the Tertiary gravels was of more immediate interest.

This type of mining rested directly on the placer methods used in working the deposits along the contemporary watercourses. It at times made use of methods of tunneling, shoring, and timbering devised by the coyoters or the quartz workers or imported from the mines of Cornwall, Spain, and elsewhere. More especially, it was made possible by the diversion and harnessing of a fair fraction of the water in the Sierran streams. Ditching, damming, and fluming began as a means of supplying ordinary placer claims. Their more spectacular results were in the attack upon the Tertiary gravels.

One method of getting at these gravels was by tunneling into a hillside. Since in any such deposit the richest gravels were always at the bottom, the aim was to work in as close to the bedrock as possible, yet with a preference for going in straight and at a slight upward incline to facilitate drainage and emptying. Sometimes the exposed hillside gave pretty clear indication of where to start tunneling, but frequently the miners had to do a good deal of studying about how to proceed. They measured the surface indications as well as they could, asked advice from trained geologists when that could be had, and occasionally resorted to magic in such contrivances as the gold magnet, a small box worn over the heart and supposed to give a shock when brought close to gold, or the hazel-fork divining rod, which would point to the precious metal when manipulated "by an appropriately constituted person."

No complete tally can be made of the tunnels dug. Table Mountain was honeycombed by them; Iowa Hill in 1856 had ninety about equally divided between the abandoned, the still working, and the paying. Many other districts had a similar welter of tunnels. Digging into the gravels was less laborious than working in quartz, but because of the looseness of the formation the danger of cave-ins was much greater, and these tunnel drivers had to take the precaution of heavier timbering. This branch of mining consequently ran into a sizeable investment. To the more fortunate and sometimes to the more skillful it yielded good profits. It was also a ready avenue for plowing back into the mountains some of the profits gathered elsewhere in the diggings.

At places like Table Mountain, where a heavy basaltic crust overlay the gold-bearing gravel, burrowing seemed the only way of getting at the pay dirt. At other locations the overburden was not so formidable and a surface attack appeared feasible. Yet even then there might be a good deal of nonpaying topsoil to peel off, plus the upper part of the gravel, which was too poor in gold to be worth the miners' attention. Shovel, wheelbarrow, and dump cart were puny tools with which to undertake the task.

Some ingenious soul—his name lost to history—had the inspiration to open a ditch or flume upon such a formation, allow the water to course down its face, cutting a gully into the dirt and gravel. Actually this was no invention. Water had been used earlier to strip off certain placer claims. The hillside miner helped the water in its work by shoving dirt into the stream and by poking and digging here and there to speed the erosion. He also took some pains to channel the water in its lower course, lining the bed with stones as a ground sluice, and cleaning up occasionally a mixture of heavy sand and gold.

A number of such claims flourished in 1851 and 1852. In Nevada County in the latter year a Frenchman named Chabot devised an improvement by using a hose to bring water from the flume. Thereby he was able to direct the flow to the spot where it would do the most good. His idea was freely copied.

Early in the following year a neighboring miner, Edward E. Matteson from Connecticut, went a step further and put a nozzle on his hose. In retrospect this act seems absurdly simple and inevitable. Its consequences, however, were astounding. Now the gravel washer would be able to drill out the hillside with a pressure-propelled stream of water. His water would not only do the accustomed work of carrying off the loosened earth and sorting out the gold; it would also tear down the hillside.

Following Matteson's invention, the device of the nozzled hose gained quick popularity. Improvements also came rapidly, chiefly in piping water down from a greater height, which would increase the pressure, by shortening the hose to a mere neck to give slight flexibility, and by reinforcing the neck with a set of iron collars. Armed with this artillery, which shot a bigger and harder stream than today's fire hoses, these operators were ready for an all-out bombardment of the Tertiary gravels. They would get down to bedrock in a hurry.

Observers spoke with awe of the majestic power of the hydraulic, which literally ate into the hillside, undermining the higher part of the bank to bring it down in an immense slide, toppling stately trees, and loosening tons of earth, which were washed forthwith into the prepared sluice. Simply as an earth-moving performance, hydraulicking was almost incredible. The wonder of it all was made still greater when one stopped to consider how small a unit of man power sufficed for normal operations. Once the sluice had been set up and the pipe line and its monitor heads had been rigged, a man to each monitor, or nozzle, and a few to tend the sluice were all that were needed.

Hydraulicking thus cut the cost of working gravel to a fraction of a cent per cubic yard. Now it would pay to wash the low-grade gravels of the upper strata, while the profits from the high-grade lower strata would be stupendous.

Prompted by these inducements, this new type of gold washing spread rapidly. It could go no faster than the network of ditches and flumes that would deliver water to the various claims. Its feasibility was limited also to claims where the water could be brought in at sufficient elevation to deliver the necessary pressure. Another requisite was adequate space downhill for dumping the voluminous tailings. Actually, many places in the Sierra foothills offered all these facilities. The hydraulickers moved in, demolished grass- and tree-covered hillsides, left yawning rock craters in their stead, cleaned up fabulous quantities of gold, and spewed sand and gravel and slickens into the canyons and river beds, sometimes to the dire annoyance of the placer miners below.

It was possible to go wrong in this type of mining. Occasionally a hydraulic outfit was set up where there was not enough water or not enough outfall, or where the gold deposit disappointed. The general record was favorable enough, however, to make hydraulic companies a preferred investment in the later 'fifties and still more popular in the following decades.

Perhaps the knottiest problem in the 'fifties was how to break up the compacted gravel of the bottom-stratum gravel, the so-called cements. Even water under tremendous pressure did not do the trick. An arrastre could be set up, but this was awkward and out of step with the streamlined assembly line of the hydraulic system. A better technique was to drill in and set a blasting charge in advance of the watering. Still another method sometimes followed was merely to set the chunks of cement aside for a year, to give them a chance to weather into a less refractory mood.

More dramatic was the combination of hydraulicking and tunneling. By this system, a tunnel at the right pitch for a sluice was driven into the mountain so that its interior end would be perhaps two hundred feet below bedrock. A vertical shaft then ascended to this layer of rock and through it into the richest part of the gold-bearing gravel. Hydraulic monitors then attacked the bowels of the mountain, washing gravel and chunks of cement to the verge of the 200-foot sump. The force of the fall was usually enough to shatter the chunks of cement.

The whole torrent then went racing down an enormous sluice laid out in the tunnel. Some had cross dimensions as large as five feet by nine. They were cushioned against the wear and tear of the torrent and of occasional boulders by a lining of heavy wood blocks with the grain side exposed. The cracks between these same blocks served as riffles and, with the aid of mercury, caught most of the gold.

At the mouth of the tunnel there was usually a grizzly,—a grating of iron bars to deflect larger stones and boulders. Oftentimes an undercurrent was also installed at this point, a sluice of lesser gradient fed through a fine-meshed sieve set in the bottom of the main sluice. With other falls and sluices, the winnowing continued, until finally the residue was dumped into the canyon.

Setups as elaborate as this characterized the hydraulic operations of the 'seventies and 'eighties. It was then that the method came into full flower. In the late 'fifties, however, just when the ordinary placers were showing such exhaustion that they were beginning to be relinquished to the Chinese, this more gargantuan form of gold washing came in as a substitute. For a time it did considerably more than quartz to bolster the annual output of gold.

In the 'sixties and 'seventies the hard-rock branch of the industry recorded substantial gains, especially in Nevada and Amador counties. These included more vigorous ore searching, in which some of the richer veins were opened to depths far beyond the earlier 200- or 300-foot mark. Two Grass Valley mines, the North Star and the Empire, penetrated 1,000 feet on the incline, while Alvinza Hayward's Amador mine reached 1,350 by 1870. Better hoisting machines, cables in place of ropes, dynamite instead of the milder black powder, and more skillful operating were among the factors involved.

Milling and recovery likewise improved, especially the latter. Here, there was a measure of indebtedness to the mill operators on Washoe's Comstock Lode. Scientific metallurgy also made a contribution. Recognition of the importance of the scientific approach is contained in the insistence on mining as one of the things to be taught in the state university chartered in 1868. Yet most of the improvements effected in the 'sixties and 'seventies came by trial and error, out of experience; they represented practical knowledge and often rested on theories only dimly grasped. A tendency in the period was for big mines to get bigger and for many of the smaller mines to close down.

For the decade of the 'eighties the highlight unquestionably was the culmination of the campaign against hydraulic mining. From the beginning these operators had been targets of criticism because of the avalanche of waste that they spilled into the Sierra streams. First complainants were the placer miners who were their immediate downhill neighbors. Occasionally these men were able to force a slight modification of the dumping methods, but they were not in the best position to object. Their individual resources were much smaller and their organization loose-knit. Furthermore, though on a smaller scale, they were engaged in exactly the same sort of stream pollution, soil destruction, and erosion acceleration. Nevertheless the placer miners several times attempted, by intimidation or by court action, to put restraints upon the hydraulickers.

Before long the fight was taken up by the agriculturists and townspeople of the valley. These men pointed out that the damage was not merely to the placer diggings, such as the valley of Bear River from Dutch Flat to its mouth, filled in with as much as 140 feet of sand, gravel, and boulders, or Steep Hollow and the Greenhorn buried under 250 and 200 feet. Farm lands farther downhill were also in the line of march. Eighteen thousand acres along the Yuba, described as the choicest farm land in the state, were overwhelmed by as much as a hundred feet of this artificial detritus. And every winter flood that spread into the lower valley left a deposit of sterile sand and gravel, oftentimes enough to ruin farm lands.

Silt from the mines muddied the waters of the Sacramento all the way to its mouth, discolored Suisun Bay, and was discernible in San Francisco Bay and at the Golden Gate. Enough sediment was deposited to impair navigation above Carquinez Strait, make it more difficult on the lower Sacramento, and close many of the upper channels to steamboat traffic. There was a faction which condoned this disruption of navigation on the score that it would stimulate development of railroads, which they thought would be a better transportation system.

Perhaps more alarming was the aggravation of the flood danger. Before mining was much advanced, Sacramento had had some rousing floods that drove her citizens to refuge in the upper stories and permitted steamboats to navigate her streets. A system of levees gave precarious protection, but with the river silting in until its channel was raised six and a half feet, Sacramentans were disturbed and infuriated at the prospect of having to raise their levees higher and higher.

The state legislature was importuned to act. Complaints were laid before the United States Land Commission. Injunctions were sought from the courts, and suits for damages were brought against specific hydraulic operators. Finally the whole issue was brought to a crux in the case of the State against the North Bloomfield Mining Company. After exhaustive investigation and prolonged argument, this suit, which had been recognized as a test case, was decided in 1884 by a permanent injunction restraining the hydraulic miner from working in such a way as to discharge waste matter into a navigable stream or onto the property of another.

Hydraulic mining was not brought to a halt, but it could no longer operate untrammeled. Some companies were able to acquire satisfactory dumping grounds. Others developed methods of shoring up their dumps in such a fashion that the whole countryside was not overflowed. Since 1892, when Congress set up a commission to regulate hydraulic mining and the state established a like commission, hydraulic mining has been carried on only under license.

In the first years of the gold rush a gold dredge was shipped around the Horn and put to work on the bed of the Feather River. It did not prove effective. Subsequently the idea was revived, better machines were designed, and in recent years the floating, clanking dredge is a common sight in the lower reaches of the gold country. Given enough water to float it, the dredge is at home in the alluvial plain. Its course is marked by land turned upside down, the topsoil buried under a thick layer of gravel and boulders, so to remain until nature has a geological eon or two in which to repair the damage. By way of extentuation it is said that the land dredged, like that subjected to hydraulicking, is usually not highly productive in its pristine state.

These have been the principal forms of California's gold mining. At the start, placer mining was the only way. Quartz and hydraulic works came in on a tentative basis in the early 'fifties, but up to 1857 or 1858, quartz had produced only an infinitesimal fraction and hydraulicking only a modest part of the half billion dollars' worth of gold that was on record.

Over the next six or eight years placer mining showed a decline. Quartz advanced gradually and hydraulic mining more rapidly, but, even so, the annual output dropped from $80,000,000 in 1852, to $70,000,000 in 1854, to about $45,000,000 at the end of the decade, and to $24,000,000 in 1864. The output of the placers was dropping much more rapidly, for quartz was increasing gradually and hydraulic production rapidly.

For a score of years after 1864, gold production was relatively stable at fifteen to twenty million dollars per year, mostly from hydraulic claims. Interruption of this type of work brought the average down to between twelve and fifteen millions for the next two decades, after which it rose again temporarily. In modern times the industry has fluctuated with wars, depression, debasement of the currency, and the like. In summary, however, it is not far wrong to say that the first half billion produced was almost entirely placer gold, the second half billion mostly hydraulic, and the second billion chiefly quartz.

With river mining and tunneling and the water companies, and more especially with quartz and hydraulics, the mines entered a new economic and social pattern. Instead of a throng of individual adventurers, each gambling his time and energy for whatever gold he could produce, mining came to signify men working for specified wages; entrepreneurs and plant managers; and, oftentimes, absentee ownership. The change was not made at a single instant all through the diggings, and it was not absolute. A fair number of hydraulic mines were worked by a crew consisting of the owning partners, and the same is true of many of the smaller quartz mines and mills. Yet on the whole the waning of the placers meant that the industrial type of capital-labor relationship would prevail.

An inevitable corollary was that the population of the mining counties should decline. As the placer deposits played out, prospectors drifted away to the valley and the coast, went off to the mines of Australia or British

Columbia or the mountain states, or headed back home. Hydraulic mining, which by its very essence was a labor saver, was not to be counted on to hold up the population. Quartz was advancing more slowly, but it also was more a matter of skill and machines than of a large labor force.

With the departure of the miners there was less demand for freighting, packing, storekeeping, innkeeping, etc. Some of the counties had a nucleus of lumbering. El Dorado profited from the traffic with Washoe, and in the 'sixties Placer County acquired a few railroad towns. Farming was attempted, but too many of the mountain valleys, which would have been the most productive plots, had been ripped up by the placer miners or buried under gravel and boulders by the hydraulickers.

Throughout the diggings, therefore, the booming 'fifties were succeeded by a gloomier pair of decades. Many camps lapsed into ghost towns, while others persisted but with no more than a fraction of the life and business they had previously enjoyed. In recent years the automobile, tourists, Sierra-bound sportsmen and vacationers, and history-conscious visitors have stimulated business in these mining counties, yet hardly a one can boast as large a population today as it had in the glorious 'fifties.

CHAPTER 13

Cultural By-products

BY GENERAL observation, if not by definition, frontier communities are characterized by cultural poverty. That such a condition should exist is natural and almost inevitable. At the edge of settlement population is sparse. The few who are present have their hands full with such elemental tasks as clearing the land, breaking the sod, erecting shelter, and gathering food. Problems of defense and those of shaping a government usually demand attention, leaving little energy for such luxuries as art and letters. Usually, too, the material resources necessary to cultural development are lacking.

Through its first three centuries of recorded history, from Cabrillo to American annexation, California was a normal and therefore a culturally benighted frontier. The missions, besides giving some attention to art and music, did introduce a massive architecture well suited to the land. Occasional officers wrote reports that merit a

[269]

place in California letters. In the dance, in guitar strumming and improvisation of song, and above all in the artistry of horsemanship, the pastoral Californians injected grace into a life that otherwise might have been simple to the point of drabness. Non-Spanish recruits—hide droghers, beaver trappers, traders, settlers, sailors, and soldiers—contributed much to California's store of business skill, political aptitude, and military confidence, but they were not ideally selected to exalt the cultural level. Indeed, it was not until the time of the War with Mexico that they produced any noteworthy innovations.

During the war years, artists such as William R. Hutton and John Mix Stanley journeyed the length of the province, sketchbook in hand. At Monterey some of the men of Stevenson's regiment, bored by garrison duty, rigged a theater for performance of old English farces and Shakespeare. This first theater was followed by another amateur playhouse at Sonoma, likewise a soldier enterprise. Early in 1848 San Francisco saw a few plays, and in the fall there was serious talk of building a theater.

Except for the Anglican service read by Drake's chaplain in 1579, Protestant church work also made its entry in the course of the war. The Rev. Walter Colton, going ashore from the U.S.S. *Congress* at Monterey on July 30, 1846, became the first ordained minister resident in the state. His work, however, was as alcalde. A day later, Elder Sam Brannan of the Church of Latter-day Saints landed at Yerba Buena. He is credited with the first Protestant sermon, preached the following Sunday. In April, 1847, two Methodist missionaries en route to

Oregon stopped off at San Francisco, launched a Sunday School, but had no minister to leave in charge. Before the year ended, other clergymen had arrived: T. M. Leavenworth, chaplain, and alcalde at San Francisco; Chester S. Lyman, working as a surveyor; Adna A. Hecox, preaching at Santa Cruz; and "a reverend gentleman," probably Elihu Anthony, who preached two or three sermons in San Francisco's new schoolhouse on December 26.

Meanwhile, in December, 1846, a dirt-floored stable at Santa Clara was requisitioned by Mrs. Olive Mann Isbell to house an American-type school. Another followed soon afterward at Monterey, taught by this same pioneer settler, and in April, 1848, at San Francisco by the first public school. Here one Thomas Douglas, a graduate of Yale and former head of the Young Chief's School in Honolulu, gave instruction in reading, writing, spelling and defining, geography, arithmetic, grammar and composition, mental and moral science, ancient and modern history, chemistry and natural philosophy, geometry, trigonometry, algebra, astronomy, surveying, navigation, Latin, and Greek. A gratifying enrollment of thirty-seven greeted this versatile teacher. By the end of the second month, however, gold fever had carried off four of the five school commissioners and all but eight of the pupils. Douglas reluctantly closed the doors of his little redwood schoolhouse and adjourned to the mines.

The beginnings of journalism were in accordance with this same formula. At Monterey on August 15, 1846, Walter Colton and Robert Semple brought out the first issue of the *Californian,* a small, four-page weekly. Moved to San Francisco, this sheet competed with Sam Brannan's *California Star* until both succumbed in May, 1848, drained of subscribers, advertisers, and pressmen by the gold in the foothills of the Sierra.

Yet, whereas gold dealt roughly with the rudimentary beginnings in journalism, education, religion, and the arts, it soon redressed the damage. The golden alchemy that caused stage and steamer lines, banks and business houses, farms and factories, courts and legislatures to blossom where had been a desert, performed like miracles in the realm of things cultural. Letters, the creative and ornamental arts, the schools, and even the churches put forth vigorous new growth and fruited precociously.

Long before the gold rush the Spaniards had made California a Christian land. By mid-nineteenth century some of the missions had fallen into decay, but others, along with such structures as Los Angeles' plaza church, were serving parish congregations. These centers of Roman Catholicism were the largest and most impressive buildings in the landscape; they represented a functioning religion.

Nevertheless, the majority of the gold seekers came from an environment in which Protestantism was the prevailing faith. It is not surprising that their impingement upon California included steps toward organizing Methodist, Baptist, and other such churches, the more so since their number included a goodly sprinkling of clergymen. One observer, doubtless exaggerating, estimated the preachers at one in ten.

As early as November 1, 1848, the people of San Francisco gave tangible evidence of their interest in religion. Assembling at the schoolhouse, they invited Timothy Dwight Hunt, a Presbyterian divine just arrived from Hawaii, to be city chaplain on a nondenominational basis at $2,500 a year. Hunt accepted the call. In December his work was supplemented by that of a Methodist minister, the Rev. C. O. Hosford, sent down by the superintendent of the Oregon missions.

Thereafter the work expanded rapidly. Ministers moved themselves to California, preached on the streets or in tents, assembled a flock, and, if things prospered, built a church. The state also profited from the missionary zeal then current. Missionaries arrived by transfer from Hawaii and Oregon. Others were sent out from New England and New York under the sponsorship of the various missionary boards. The *California*, which landed the Rev. S. H. Willey at Monterey on February 23, 1849, had three other missionaries aboard. The roster of missionaries and pastors soon included such names as John W. Douglas, Osgood C. Wheeler, Albert Williams, Ezra Fisher, William Roberts, Isaac Owen, William Taylor, and Samuel Damon, and for the close of 1849 Clifford Drury is able to tabulate twelve bona fide ministers established in their work.

The process continued, until by the middle 'fifties San Francisco could boast thirty-two churches, ranging from the African Methodist to Welsh Presbyterian, other principal towns were correspondingly equipped, and most of the mining camps possessed at least one structure dedicated to divine worship.

The earlier stages were admittedly more colorful, as when a street preacher like William Taylor appealed to the passing throng in San Francisco, or when a circuit rider in the diggings got some saloonkeeper to clear a space before the bar for a Sunday morning discourse. Except in the accommodation to such surroundings and in the suddenness with which organized churches sprang up, California's experience was in step with that of the West in general. Her pioneers included many who took no interest in such matters. There were others, however, who out of conviction or homesickness wanted the solace of the church. They sought to achieve as close a reproduction of their accustomed church as they could.

How well they succeeded is variously attested. Sarah Royce, certainly no unbiased observer on this point, remarks on the "fixed attention," the "intense earnestness," the "reverence, devotion, and glow of intelligence" that characterized the congregation she first observed in San Francisco. Visiting that city in 1859, twenty-four years after his famous sailing before the mast, Richard Henry Dana encountered a Harvard man, a regular churchman in New England, who could not even direct him to Bishop Kip's church. But when he did locate it, Dana found that the congregation was "precisely like one you would meet in New York, Philadelphia, or Boston." In mundane terms, this was the exact objective of those who transported Protestant Christianity to the Pacific Coast.

The California school record is in most respects parallel. To this new scene the American forty-niners brought the studied conviction that education is a bulwark of the nation and that society must make provision for proper schooling of youth. Upon those Argonauts who were merely temporary Californians this obligation rested lightly, and since so many had no children, nor even any wives, the emergency did not seem immediate. Yet there were children in the towns and in some of the camps, and, with as much dispatch as was possible in the dearth of suitable buildings, supplies, and qualified teachers, schools were opened.

A listing of them would seem almost endless. The beginning was usually with a private school, often under the auspices of a religious body and perhaps taught by a clergyman, but in due course quite a number of these schools were transformed into public schools. Thus a certain John C. Pelton, having rounded the Horn with the express purpose of conducting a free school at San Francisco, enlisted the aid of various citizens, arranged for the use of the chapel of the Baptist church, and on December 26, 1849, began instruction. The following April the city took this free school under its wing, voting Mr. and Mrs. Pelton a joint salary of $500 a month, paid, unfortunately, in scrip.

The tribulations of teaching in these early schools have been much written about. They were those of the country schools of nineteenth-century America: classrooms crowded, many grades in one room, inadequate equipment, long hours, and some of the bigger boys harboring ambitions to thrash the teacher. Shinn tells of one teacher in the diggings who quelled insurrectionists by reminding them that in the schoolroom he was the alcalde. In a tin-roofed church room at Jimtown, Prentice

Mulford presided over the destinies of sixty youngsters of all ages. Ere long he decided that his labors with pick and shovel had been much easier.

Besides the trials of the classroom these teachers had to undergo various other ordeals. One was the gantlet of arbitrary examination by the school board, with questions that ranged from farcically easy to monstrously difficult. Another was payment in scrip. In a hard-money country such as California, and with prices ranging high, this system was painful. John Swett, who comes near to being the patron saint of the state's early educational system, once was reduced to doggerelize a protest:

> As well suppose that a game of Euchre
> Will fill your pockets with filthy lucre,
> As think that teaching the city's scholars
> Will line your pockets with silver dollars.

By local effort and state encouragement a system of private, public, and parochial elementary schools was brought into being. In due course high schools were added, not without debate over whether public responsibility extended so far, just as there had been debate about public provision of elementary schools for pupils whose parents could afford to pay the costs.

The next step was to embark upon higher education. The Methodists took the lead, chartering California Wesleyan College, which, by September, 1851, when it opened at San Jose, had been renamed University of the Pacific. It migrated in 1852 to Santa Clara, went through various changes, including the absorption of Napa College in 1895, and in 1924, as College of the Pacific, moved to a new campus at Stockton.

Under the mandate of Bishop Alemany, a Catholic school was opened at Santa Clara. The preliminary work began in 1851, but not until a few years later was it properly called a college. The curriculum was similar to that of the neighboring College of the Pacific. The faculty was Jesuit, and for years enrollment was limited to students who would agree to abstain from tobacco. They were restricted further to a twenty-five cent weekly allowance, any other pocket money was to be deposited with the college treasurer.

A school for girls operated by the Sisters of Notre Dame; a boys' school first called St. Ignatius College and now the University of San Francisco; a college annex to Dr. W. A. Scott's Calvery Presbyterian Church, known first as Dr. Burrowe's School, then Dr. Burrowe's High School, then in 1861 incorporated as City College; Pacific Methodist College at Vacaville; the Petaluma College School; Hesperian Collegiate Institution; Pacific Female College; St. Vincent's College, now Loyola—these are some of the early institutions.

Probably there would have been an even larger number except that several of the more active advocates of higher education showed strong preference for a nondenominational school. In 1853 these men opened Contra Costa Academy in Oakland. Two years later it expanded into the College of California. In 1860 its trustees dedicated but did not occupy a new site with an inspiring vista out the Golden Gate. In 1864 the College of California had its first class of graduates, and four years later its trustees wisely and unselfishly arranged for the transfer of their property to the state and the incorporation of their college in the state university to be built on the Berkeley site.

In this general development gold-rush influence may be seen in the rapid strides and perhaps in the popularity of the nondenominational approach. Otherwise, the procedure was typical of the American West at the time.

The theater, as must readily appear, was a culture form that could respond much more bouyantly to the stimulation of gold. A rolypoly little Englishman, Stephen C. Massett, who liked to bill himself as Jeems Pipes of Pipesville, apparently was the first professional to take a turn. On a June night in 1849 he put on a one-man show at San Francisco. In a rich baritone he sang several of his own compositions. Shifting to a clear falsetto, mimicked an operatic diva, then did a series of monologues, imitating Yankee characters, and ended up with a seven-part reproduction of a New England town meeting. Here in miniature was a foretaste of Gold Coast theater: a variety show, with a touch of sentiment, a vein of broader humor, some burlesque, and a demonstration of versatility.

After Massett, San Francisco was visited by a minstrel company, but its run was broken off when one of the "bones" was killed at the Bella Union. The other minstrels took the first ship for Hawaii. On Kearney Street near Clay, Joesph Rowe erected a large tent and billed a circus which consisted of nine acrobats and equestrians and a posing horse. For the rest of 1849 that was all the theater that San Francisco enjoyed.

Sacramento was a long step in advance. In a large tent labeled Eagle Theater a company opened a dramatic season with "The Bandit Chief; or, The Forest Spectre." Such plays as "The Wife," "Dead Shot," "Othello," "Bachelor Buttons," "William Tell," "Rent Day," and "Charles II" also adorned their repertoire. Night performances were the invariable rule, with a nightly change of bill and an afterpiece almost always added to the more ambitious drama with which the show began.

In mid-January, 1850, the Eagle Theater company gave San Francisco a sample of legitimate theater. Although there were mishaps, such as the manager's losing the first week's receipts at monte, the popularity of this type of entertainment prompted Rowe to throw a platform across one end of his circus tent and substitute thespians for gymnasts and animal acts. Other impresarios came forward. As a second-story annex to the Parker House saloon and gambling hall, Tom Maguire opened a theater which he called the Jenny Lind— though the Swedish Nightingale never came to California. When this theater burned, he built a second. When that burned, in 1853, he built a third, even more magnificent, which the city fathers promptly bought for two hundred thousand dollars and converted into a city hall. Another redoubtable figure in the city's early theatrical history was Dr. David Robinson, to whom a citizens' committee entrusted fifty thousand dollars in 1851 to build the Adelphi. He also built the first American Theater and was a partner in backing the Bryant Minstrels, later enlarged to San Francisco Hall and, after a change of ownership, renamed Maguire's Opera House.

Besides these various stages, of which not a tithe has been mentioned, the troupers played a circuit of the min-

The proprietors of these places of amusement, especially the larger ones in the towns, soon installed additional attractions: a free snack bar, musicians, Spanish dancers, variety performers, and minstrel acts. To compete successfully the theater had to outdo itself.

Nevertheless, the tidings of flush days on the coast intrigued artists and their managers, and ere long top-flight stars were staging a gold rush of their own. Included were Ed Christy and minstrel headliners such as Eph Horn the end man, Dan Bryant the soft-shoe expert, and Thomas F. Briggs the banjo virtuoso. Songsters such as Elisa Biscaccianti and Kate Hayes joined the trek. So did a host of noble actors, including the Booths, father and sons, the Chapmans, Edwin Forrest and Catherine Sinclair, and, a bit later Lola Montez, Adah Isaacs Menken, and Matilda Heron.

Of these the most noteworthy was perhaps Edwin Booth, because he arrived an unknown, introduced almost contemptuously by his father as a good banjo player. When he left the state a few years later, Edwin had come into his own as a Shakespearean actor. The wildly enthusiastic reception accorded Biscaccianti is most significant in its demonstration that the rough-hewn men of the mines would sit enthralled by a strictly classical program—at least from one possessed of winsome face and graceful figure.

Lola Montez' fame ensured a first-night sell-out. Her beauty did not disappoint, nor did her skill at repartee, but, quickly exposed as neither actress nor dancer, Lola wisely retired to a cottage salon at Grass Valley. Her most notable effect upon the California theater, aside from becoming a legend in it, was the inspiration of burlesques written by guitarist Robinson, M.D., and romped through by the irrepressible Caroline Chapman.

After all else is said, it may be that Lotta Crabtree is the best exemplar of the gold-rush theater. Her debut was at a tiny log theater at Rabbit Creek. Dressed in long-tailed green coat, knee breeches, and tall hat, she tossed aside a shillelagh and danced a vigorous Irish jig and reel, laughing infectiously the while. After many encores she came back on stage looking angelic in white dress with round neck and puffed sleeves and sang a plaintive ballad. The hardened miners went wild, showering the stage with coins, nuggets, and a fifty-dollar slug. Black-eyed, red-haired Lotta, all of eight but looking no more than six, was their darling.

Under the tutelage of her ambitious mother, versatile Mart Taylor, and other willing helpers, Lotta embarked on a rapid tour of the mining camps. She learned new songs and steps. At Placerville a Negro minstrel taught her how to do a soft-shoe breakdown. Lola Montez introduced her to Spanish dancing. From others she picked up hornpipes, buck and wing, new bits of pantomime, and a comic way of picking up the largess of coins and nuggets, while from Jake Wallace she learned how to make a banjo ring.

Thus equipped, she could have emulated Massett's early example of putting on a whole show. By the middle 'fifties, however, talent had become abundant and the real problem was to get a chance to perform. But with barrel-top numbers at auctions, with variety-show billings in the mines and at San Francisco, with bits in the regular plays, and with specialties between their acts, Lotta had as busy a childhood as one could ask. In one little bundle vibrant with energy, she represents the contradictory elements that the miners most prized: humor and pathos, high skill and less high buffoonery, mastery of the traditional forms and indulgence in individual pyrotechnics.

Lusty, opulent, wonderfully diversified, star-studded, attracting the best from the boards in the States, and remolding actors and vehicles to fit the less trammeled milieu of the Gold Coast, this chapter of theatrical history is one of the most distinctive features of the Argonaut generation. Without the gold of California only the merest fragment of its pageantry could have existed. To what extent it influenced the future is less patent, but the heritage of passionate interest in the theater is readily discernible.

Less spectacularly, the gold rush encouraged the pictorial arts. Here the record is partly preserved in illustrated books, in canvases hung on widely scattered walls, and in such out-of-the-way places as Bruff's sketchbooks and the lithographed letterheads sold by gold-rush stationers. Charles Nahl's landscapes and group scenes, W. S. Jewett's portraits, J. W. Audubon's travel sketches, and Edward Vischer's lithograph prints are examples of this workmanship. Realism and romanticism are in obvious conflict, with realism gaining moderate advantage.

More widely heralded than any of these art developments is the rush of writing that the gold discovery touched off. One beginning was with travel reporting, as hundreds and perhaps thousands of forty-niners, in journals, diaries, or letters, set down for friends, relatives, and posterity a narrative of their great adventure. Necessarily uneven in literary quality, this mass of writing is graced by occasional masterpieces: Bayard Taylor's *El Dorado*, Alonzo Delano's *Life on the Plains and among the Diggings*, and Lewis Manly's reminiscent narrative of mistake and tragedy and heroism on the Death Valley route. Continued in the diggings, this same type of writing produced Louise Amelia Knapp Smith Clappe's fluent description of life in camp at Rich Bar, the often-quoted Shirley letters.

Another outgrowth was the revival of journalism. On January 4, 1849, newspaper publishing was reborn at San Francisco with the issuance of the *Alta California*. The pattern spread to the mines and to all the intermediate towns, and soon California was teeming with newspapers—more per capita than any other land could boast. As journalistic ventures these papers were characterized by much personalized comment, by glaring inadequacies in news coverage, and, on the contrary, by faithful mirroring of the local scene. Their files are historical sources of the first magnitude.

As an incidental function these papers opened their columns to creative writing in the form of verse, story, essay, and anecdote. Before long they were supplemented by weeklies such as the *Golden Era* and monthlies such as the *Pioneer*, the *Californian*, and eventually the *Overland*, which were professedly literary. In these publications California writers and editors sought to turn out the kind of reading matter that gold-rush California wanted. The attunement to the region was more express and purposeful than in any subsequent western journal; in the *Pioneer* and, more emphatically, in the *Overland* a remarkable success was attained.

The *Golden Era,* so unpretentious that it is often charged with catering to the low tastes of rustics and miners, launched the experiment. Its editors preferred California themes and treatments and followed this line through five decades, concerning themselves almost always with matters that were within the comprehension or even the experience of a majority of their readers.

The durability of the *Era* is a vindication of this choice. Another is the way in which this paper served as a starter and a stepping stone for practically every California writer of the time. Old Block, Caxton, and Yellow Bird (Delano, William A. Rhodes, and John R. Ridge) were frequent contributors, as were Ina Coolbrith, Charles W. Stoddard, and Charles Henry "Inigo" Webb. Mark Twain submitted enough sketches to make a small volume, and Bret Harte, entering "by the back door" as compositor, used this journal for his "M'liss," archetype of the California short story.

In January, 1854, Ferdinand C. Ewer launched a competitor, the *Pioneer,* which he promised would be devoted to literature, politics, science, belles-lettres, poetry, and "the more flowery paths of Literature." Though it survived only two years, the *Pioneer* lived up to this promise. Its pages were adorned by some of Edward Pollock's best poems, by a series of sparkling pieces by Jeems Pipes of Pipesville, by the Shirley letters already cited, and by ten contributions with the signature John Phoenix. This alias cloaked a portly young army officer, George H. Derby, already famous as a jester and punster and the state's foremost humorist. His ten pieces were miscellaneous. One proposed and illustrated a number system for more exact measurement of adjectives and adverbs. Another was a broad burlesque on the program notes that purport to describe musical compositions. Still another parodied the reports of military reconnaissances then the rage. Derby plotted a course through the canyons and deserts of the heart of San Francisco, describing a band of baffling natives (street urchins) encountered along the way.

Much of his humor was too dated, too historical, to endure. Through the *Pioneer* and through eastern reprintings it impinged on the nation, even upon General Grant, and some regard Derby as having been, for a brief moment, the nation's favorite humorist.

The *Pioneer* gave way to *Hutchings' California Magazine,* full of nature writing and occasional bits of mild humor such as the famous parody, "The Miner's Ten Commandments." Then, in uneven succession, came the *Hesperian,* the *Pacific Monthly,* the *San Francisco Pictorial Magazine,* the *Sunday Mercury,* the *Golden Gate,* the *California Mountaineer,* and the *Californian.* These fleeting literary journals, the old reliable *Golden Era,* the daily and weekly press, and a sprinkling of locally written and manufactured books were California's contribution to its readers in the first twenty years after the gold discovery. Quantities of books, magazines, and even newspapers were imported, but on the whole it was the local output that was preferred.

The books included such compendia as *The Annals of San Francisco,* by Soulé, Gihon, and Nisbet (printed in New York), *The Resources of California,* by John S. Hittell, and *The Natural Wealth of California,* by Titus Fey Cronise, and two anthologies of western poetry. Two thrillers were far more widely read: John R. Ridge's *The Life and Adventures of Joaquin Murieta* and Royal B. Stratton's *Captivity of the Oatmen Girls.*

Stratton interviewed Olive Oatman shortly after her rescue from the Mojaves. He did full justice to the harrowing story of the Apache attack on the emigrant train, the barbarity of the Apaches toward Olive and her sister, the kindlier treatment by the Mojaves, and the eventual ransom. Ridge's dramatized biography glows with an intensity of feeling that traces back to a tragedy of his childhood, when his father was assassinated in a vendetta rising out of the Cherokee removal. Apparently as a means of sublimating his own feelings, Ridge idealized Murieta, elevating him from a petty bandit to a folk hero, a California Robin Hood, and this is the interpretation that Bancroft, Hittell, Joaquin Miller, and most subsequent writers have echoed.

In the 'fifties the writers whom the miners considered their best spokesmen were probably Alonzo Delano and Prentice Mulford. Delano was esteemed because of his nose, which he proclaimed was California's largest, and because of his integrity, dramatically in evidence when his employer failed in 1855. His writings, like Mulford's, struck a vein of good-natured irony at the expense of the noble miners. The miners applauded as if they had just discovered how droll they really were.

Much of the California writing of the 'fifties was self-centered, but it was not until the 'sixties, when placer mining was practically a thing of the past, that the gold rush theme was really exploited. Mark Twain took the lead with "The Notorious Jumping Frog of Calaveras County." It was a tale that had been knocking around the mining camps for some time. Twain told it better, put it into print in the East, and awoke to find himself famous. *Roughing It* was a specific follow-up of this western theme, and other reminders of his apprenticeship in Washoe and California cropped up in his lectures and in his later writings.

Bret Harte had a longer contact with California, though his experience in the diggings was as superficial. His contributions to the literary celebration of gold-rush California were two. First, in 1868 he was Anton Roman's choice to edit the *Overland*, a monthly conceived in western emulation of the *Atlantic Monthly* and generously backed by Roman so that it might live up to its promise that it was "devoted to the development of the country." Through stressing western subject matter and commissioning western writers Harte made this policy a reality, at least so far as the realm of letters was concerned.

His second contribution was to work the bonanza of the gold-rush theme. This he did incidentally in some of the verse that he sold to the *Overland*, but much more effectively in his short stories. In "The Luck of Roaring Camp," "The Outcasts of Poker Flat," "Tennessee's Partner," and other tales in the same genre, he brought facile artistry to bear upon the remarkable society that flourished in the early days of the gold rush. In point of fact, he was picturing good old times that had never been, and the life he describes is idealized and romanticized. Nevertheless, what he wrote was tremendously effective, and it had this accuracy: it jibed perfectly with what the miners preferred to remember about that glorious epoch.

As to literature, there is a special temptation to mark the end of California's golden era in 1869 with the completion of the transcontinental railroad. The rails carried away Harte, Twain, Mulford, and others. They brought in all manner of eastern wares, the literary included, and sharply reduced California's peculiarities. Although culture changes are too complex for such precise dating, on a broader basis there is good reason to discern the end of an epoch at approximately this time. Other factors contributed. More orthodox employment replaced prospecting. Frontier roughness wore off. Time corrected the youthful and masculine imbalance of the population. As of 1870 or 1875 it was possible to look back upon an age that had run its course.

In terms of cultural institutions, arts, and letters, gold-rush California had enjoyed a most remarkable flowering, the like of which was not achieved by a single generation on any other American frontier. Some achievements, to be sure, were due to individual genius; others stemmed from the unrestrained boyishness of the forty-niners, their isolation, excitement, and nostalgia. In largest degree, however, the rapidity and the character of this growth trace back to the gold itself.

CHAPTER 14

Assay

USEFUL only for beauty and dentistry, gold has a social inferiority in comparison to iron, which can be the backbone of an industrial development, to coal or petroleum, which can power industry and commerce, to copper with its great tensile strength and its superiority as a conductor, or even to sand, asphaltum, clay, and cement, which can be converted into buildings, dams, and highways.

That gold mining is not the ideal foundation for an enduring economy is suggested by the records for Minas Geraes, Siberia, the Rand, the Klondike, and even California's Mother Lode district proper. Of all the localities in the world that have been favored with great gold rushes, California is unique in having used hers as a springboard to a rapid and a gratifyingly consistent development. How this happened is worth inquiring.

The irreverent, it must be admitted, sometimes ask whether the gold of California did not do more harm than good. Anyone who follows the boulder-strewn trail of the dredger, visits the gaping holes and barren debris piles of the hydraulickers, and contemplates the unsightly dumps of the hard-rock mines will be conscious of some of the damage done. Add then the muddying of the streams that made the salmon stop running, the silting of the lower rivers that slowed and then stopped the river boats, the devastation of farm lands by flood-waters and tailings.

The Indians of the Sierra foothills were early victims, first in having their sources of food supply laid waste and then in the "wars" of extermination. Marshall got no profit from the discovery and Sutter lost his all. On the sea routes, shipwreck, cholera, and Panama fever claimed victims; on the overland routes, cholera, mountain fever, traffic accidents, and Indian attacks. In the mines, mishaps and illness afflicted the gold seekers, and another untold number went to their graves. The gold rush, it must be admitted, was responsible for more bereavements, more broken homes, than the War with Mexico.

For many forty-niners, perhaps for the majority, the proceeds of gold hunting turned out to be a paltry return on the investment of time and capital that went into getting to California and working the mines. Farm wagons burned in Death Valley, the carcasses of oxen strewn along the Humbolt, ships rotting in San Francisco Bay—these were tangible reminders of the vast outlay required to deliver the labor force of the diggings.

In the next hundred years, to be sure, two billion dollars' worth of gold was to come out of the California gold fields, the first part in a torrent, the rest more gradually and regularly. Even allowing for the cost of production hinted in the saying, "It takes a gold mine to work a gold mine," the two billion dollars total is impressive—impressive until one recalls that the ultimate fate of this metal was to be sterilized and buried at Fort Knox.

Still others deplore the gold rush on moral grounds. The miners, they say, were rowdy; their epoch a field day for liquor dealers, gamblers, and harlots. Standards of conduct got out of hand at the very outset, making it an uphill fight to bring them to the level of the East. Speculative instincts were overstimulated, and the California spirit came to be too strongly implanted in the get-rich-quick pattern.

Admittedly the gold rush led Californians to hasty decisions where longer tussling with the problems might have produced a better solution. Admittedly also, California's present material success is to a large extent the result of fertile soil, climate, position, and ingenuity not directly derived from its golden beginning. Nevertheless, there are tangible proofs that gold was the touchstone that set California in motion on the course that made her what she is today, and that her gold did things for the West at large and the Pacific basin that otherwise would not have been done for a generation or perhaps at all.

Gold mining itself provides clear examples. In July, 1849, roused by a shipment of 1,200 ounces of California gold that reached Port Jackson, a party of Australians sailed by way of New Zealand and Pitcairn for San Francisco. After a trying experience with an unreliable teamster, they got to the southern diggings, where by trial and error and by observation they learned how to pan and cradle and where to look for dirt that would be worth washing. One of these men, E. H. Hargraves, more observant than the rest, was struck by the geological resemblance to a locality in New South Wales. His companions scoffed at the idea of going back there to do their mining, but Hargraves on reflection became more and more convinced that he was correct. He wrote to friends in Sydney on the subject, and then, as Bidwell had gone from Coloma to the Feather in 1848, he went home to Australia.

February, 1851, found him across the Blue Mountains in New South Wales, with pick, pan, and trowel, riding off with a black boy to discover Australia's gold. Arrived at a California-looking spot, he scratched the gravel off a schistose dyke, which ran across a dry creek, dug a panful of earth, and announced to his companion that he would now wash out the gold. Sure enough it was there. He continued his prospecting, proving to his own satisfaction that the gold deposits were extensive and rich.

Then, instead of rushing into secret production, as might have been the California way, he went to Sydney, sought out the colonial secretary, broke the news to him, and asked for official recognition as the discoverer, and a suitable reward. Although the secretary was reluctant to believe, he did admit that if Australia proved to be a gold country it would stop England from sending any more convicts and would stop the drain of men to California. Hargraves now publicized his discovery assiduously, accepted appointment as commissioner of crown lands, and returned to the diggings to show others how to use pan and cradle, but without stooping to steady mining. A grateful government rewarded him with a donation of £10,000, with which he went to England and wrote a book about his experiences. For the mining methods employed, as well as for the discovery, Australia was clearly indebted to California.

In February, 1858, a Hudson's Bay Company ship arrived at San Francisco with $800,000 in gold from the Fraser River. From the city and from the mining camps a horde of gold seekers promptly sailed for the new El Dorado. According to one count, 23,428 Californians set out in less than six months. The Hudson's Bay Company factor and governor, James Douglas, succeeded in imposing a system of government and a mining code, but the Californians far outnumbered all other exploiters of these diggings. Naturally they brought with them the full pattern of mining method.

Colorado's 1858 rush, with its slogan of "Pike's Peak or Bust," drew a lesser complement of Californians, but the state was represented in the Cherokees, who had panned the first gold when they were California-bound in 1850, and some of whom now returned to prospect the Cherry Creek district more thoroughly. These sands disappointed, but a rich vein of quartz near Central City and placers with scale gold the size of watermelon seeds revived the excitement in 1859. Here also, mining techniques benefited from the California experience, and the life of the camps tended to reproduce that of the farther West of a decade earlier.

To the mining frontier of Baja California, Sonora, and Sinaloa, California shipped thousands of prospectors and tens of thousands of dollars' worth of mining equipment in the 'fifties and 'sixties. On Bill Williams Fork in Arizona in 1861, it was deserters from the California Column who started the mining rush. In eastern Washington, Californians participated in prospecting along the Columbia and the Snake, and they made the advance to the Clearwater and the Salmon, Alder Gulch, Grasshopper Creek, and Last Chance Gulch largely an eastward-moving frontier. On the Stikine, in the Klondike, and on the beach at Nome a few veterans of forty-nine were still active, while the use of California practices was a stronger carryover.

From the early 'fifties, California gold hunters had carried their prospecting across the Sierra to the drearier wastes of the Great Basin. Returns at first were modest, but as the miners worked up Gold Canyon toward Mount Davidson the color increased. There in the spring of 1859 partners Peter O'Riley and Patrick McLaughlin made a real strike, on which a shiftless, loud-mouthed Virginian, Henry Thomas Paige Comstock, horned in and subsequently gave his name to the mine and lode. The Riley-McLaughlin gold mine was cluttered with a heavy dark substance that settled with the gold. They thrust this bothersome "blue stuff" indignantly aside, but after a while a Californian took a sample across the Sierra to the assayer at Nevada City. When he reported that it contained to the ton $1,595 in gold and $4,791 in silver, eager Californians began to swarm across the mountains.

Most of them arrived too late to do much mining in 1859, but they forthwith staked out claims, incorporated mining companies, and began to peddle stock. Silver mining, they soon found, was not the same as washing gold. Elaborate machinery, capital, and technical knowledge were requisite. The tested arrastre was put to work, to which veterans of silver mining in Mexico added patios and adobe furnaces. Germans, also from California, introduced the "barrel" process, and the California stamp was an early import.

In 1860, no fewer than 10,000 Californians stampeded to the Comstock. For supplies and equipment they depended on California. San Francisco banks and merchants, in turn, became heavy investors in the Washoe mines and, with Comstock silver as the coveted prize, they embarked on an era of speculative investment that made William Ralston a multimillionaire and then broke his bank, elevated William Sharon to be King of the Comstock, built fabulous fortunes for James G. Fair, John W. Mackay, and their partners Flood and O'Brien—Californians all. Adolph Sutro with his tunnel, George Hearst and John P. Jones—these were other Californians who rose to stardom on the Comstock.

The lode drew from all mining countries. It was a German named Deidesheimer who introduced a method of square cribbing that made it possible to work the vast ore body of the big bonanza. Cornish miners deserve credit for demonstrating how to work the lower levels. Yet the history of the Comstock has many reminders of the influence of California and the indebtedness to the arsenal of men and methods built up there.

In matters other than mining the boost that the golden era gave to California is equally unmistakable. The sudden influx of enough persons to justify statehood and the prompt erection of such a government were a start. San Francisco, placid hamlet of 812 souls at the time of the discovery, soon became the largest city west of the Missouri, a hive of commerce and industry, and the metropolis of the entire West and much of the Pacific.

Transportation facilities, demanded by the gold miners and financed out of their earnings, spread up and down and across the state. Because of the gold, San Francisco became the terminus of the mail steamers instead of just a way point on the line to Oregon. Gold gave force to the earlier arguments that the federal government should speed the mails across continent by stage and should improve upon that facility with a railroad. California's mineral wealth and its population mounting toward the half-million mark were most powerful considerations in its favor, and the line eventually built led to Sacramento and San Francisco. But it was called the Pacific Railroad, it bound the entire West to the nation, and it opened a window upon the Orient.

From a geographical curiosity that even informed persons might locate rather hazily on the map, gold lifted California to immediate and worldwide fame. Thereafter no one would be in doubt. From this moment, too, great and spectacular things would be expected of California. In the long run, the black gold of petroleum, the orange gold of the fruit growers, the silver screen of the movies, and the brass of the real estate boomers might overshadow the genuine article, yet no one can say what these industries and the tourist trade would have amounted to had there not been the initial impetus of the golden beginning.

Even in the realm of the intellectual and the artistic it was an inestimable boon that California started rich. The standard frontier experience was that there should be a starving time, a period in which every ounce of energy had to go into scraping together the bare essentials, with no possibility remaining for more ambitious strivings. In California the Spaniards had done most of the starving. Then the gold rush rolled up an early surplus, some of which went to the encouragement of letters and the arts, schools, and churches. Within a very few years San Francisco had a bookstore that was better stocked than any other west of the Alleghenies. It was also a center of writing and publishing to a degree that would have been absolutely impossible except for the gold. In educational facilities, in libraries, in graphic arts, and in the sophisticated pleasure of the theater the acceleration that gold imparted is equally to be seen. The momentum of leadership thus provided is one of the state's choicest heritages.

Today's Californians, like relay racers handed a tremendous lead by their first teamsman, have a confidence that sometimes alarms strangers. They are in the habit of having great expectations, of entertaining roseate hopes and seeing them come true. In all this, gold is a fit symbol, the more striking since California appears to be the only place where a rush for gold was made to serve as the base for an ever-widening superstructure of attainment.

Bibliography

No ONE has published a comprehensive bibliography on gold-rush California. There are general bibliographies which are helpful, such as Robert Ernest Cowan, *A Bibliography of the History of California, 1510–1930* (3 vols., San Francisco, 1933), and specialized works which are useful, such as Henry Raup Wagner, *The Plains and the Rockies* (2d ed., enlarged by Charles L. Camp, San Francisco, 1937), and E. I. Edwards, *The Valley Whose Name Is Death* (Pasadena, 1940). In *The Maps of the California Gold Region, 1848–1857* (San Francisco, 1942), Carl I. Wheat describes three hundred maps and reproduces thirty. Some of the books listed below, notably Bancroft, Read and Gaines, and Potter, are rich in bibliographical entries.

THE DISCOVERY

On the discovery, most of the available testimony is discussed in the sixth volume of Hubert Howe Bancroft's *History of California* (7 vols., San Francisco, 1884–1890) and again in his *California Inter Pocula* (San Francisco, 1888). This latter volume, priceless in its title, is a book-length essay on many phases of the gold-rush epoch. Other general works which include narratives of the discovery are Owen C. Coy, *Gold Days* (Los Angeles, 1929), and, more sketchily, Stewart Edward White, *The Forty-niners* (New Haven, 1918). It is represented, too, in Valeska Bari's *The Course of Empire* (New York, 1931), a well-balanced body of excerpts from firsthand accounts of most aspects of the rush. A booklet issued by the California Historical Society in 1947, *California Gold Discovery: Centennial Papers of the Time, the Site, and Artifacts,* is now the most useful on its particular topics. It reports the results of archaeological as well as historical research and serves as a guide to the principal sources, such as the several versions of the Bigler and

Smith diaries, John A. Sutter, *New Helvetia Diary* (San Francisco, 1939), J. S. Brown, *California Gold: An Authentic History of the First Find* (Salt Lake City, 1894), and J. W. Marshall, "Account of the Discovery of Gold," *Hutchings' California Magazine*, Vol. II (November, 1857). See also Lawson R. Patterson, *Twelve Years in the Mines of California* (Cambridge, 1862), and G. F. Parsons, *The Life and Adventures of James W. Marshall* (Sacramento, 1870).

THE FORTY-EIGHTERS

Several forty-eighters chronicled their experiences, notably E. Gould Buffum, *Six Months in the Gold Mines* (Philadelphia, 1850), James H. Carson, *Early Recollections of the Mines* (Stockton, 1852), and William R. Ryan, *Personal Adventures in Upper and Lower California in 1848–49* (2 vols., London, 1851). These men were members of the regiment of New York volunteers. Peter H. Burnett's *Recollections of an Old Pioneer* (New York, 1880) describes his brief experience in the northern diggings late in 1848. Official reporting on the season is offered by Walter Colton, *Three Years in California* (New York, 1854), Richard B. Mason, *Report of the Gold Fields of California*, House Executive Document 17, 31st Cong., 1st sess. (Washington, 1849), and William T. Sherman, *Memoirs* (2 vols., New York, 1887). J. Tyrwhitt Brooks [pseudonym for Henry Vizetelly and David Bogue], *Four Months among the Gold-finders in California* (London, 1849), is often cited and sometimes followed, though made up largely out of whole cloth.

GOLD FEVER

Practically every gold-rush journal begins with a report of the incidence of the particular writer's case of gold fever. A number of such testimonies may be found in Walker D. Wyman, ed., "California Emigrant Letters," California Historical Society *Quarterly*, XXIV (1945), 17-46, 117-138, 235-260, 343-364. Bancroft's narrative of the spread of the mania is corrected and extended in Ralph P. Bieber, *Southern Trails to California in 1849* (Glendale, 1937).

PANAMA

John H. Kemble, *The Panama Route, 1848–1869* (Berkeley, 1943), is the principal reference on this most expeditious path of the gold seekers. There are several graphic accounts by forty-niners: Bayard Taylor, *Eldorado, or Adventures in the Path of Empire* (2 vols., London, 1850), Carl Meyer, *Nach dem Sacramento* (Aarau, 1856; translated by Ruth Frey Axe, Claremont, 1938), D. Knower, *The Adventures of a '49er* (Albany, 1894), A. Gaylord Beaman, ed., "Pioneer Letters," Historical Society of Southern California *Publications*, XXI (1939), 17-30, and Almarin B. Paul, "My First Two Years in California," Society of California Pioneers *Quarterly*, IV (1927), 25-54. Travel in following years is described in J. D. Borthwick, *Three Years in California* (London, 1857), Bancroft, *California Inter Pocula*, 121-224, Isaac Read, "The Chagres River Route to California," California Historical Society *Quarterly*, VIII (1929), 3-16, Sarah Meriam Brooks, *Across the Isthmus to California in '52* (San Francisco, 1894), Mrs. Cornelius Cole, "To California via Panama in 1852," Historical Society of Southern California *Publications*, IX (1914), 153-172, and J. E. Clark, "From St. Louis to San Francisco in 1850," *ibid.*, I (1890), 27-32. Joseph W. Gregory, *Gregory's Guide for California Travellers* (New York, 1850) stresses the isthmian route. Victor M. Berthold, *The Pioneer Steamer California, 1848–1849* (Boston, 1932), and Fessenden Nott Otis, *Illustrated History of the Panama Railroad* (New York, 1862), are monographs on two elements in the service. John C. Parish, "By Sea to California," in J. F. Willard and C. B. Goodykoontz, *The Trans-Mississippi West* (Boulder, 1930), assesses the contribution made by the Panama and Cape Horn routes.

CAPE HORN

Although not concerned exclusively with sailings on the Cape

Horn route, Octavius Thorndike Howe's *Argonauts of '49*
(Cambridge, 1923), a history of the emigrant companies from
Massachusetts, is the nearest approach to a monograph on this
aspect of the gold rush. See also Raymond A. Rydell, "The
Cape Horn Route to California, 1849," *Pacific Historical
Review*, XVII (1948), 149–163. Firsthand accounts range
from simple logs to semifictionized reminiscence. Examples are:
Albert Lyman, *Journal of a Voyage to California and Life in
the Gold Diggings* (Hartford, 1852), George Payson, *Golden
Dreams and Leaden Realities* (New York, 1853), Hinton
Helper, *The Land of Gold: Reality versus Fiction* (Baltimore,
1855), L. M. Schaeffer, *Sketches of Travels in South America,
Mexico, and California* (New York, 1860), Theodore Mes-
serve, "The Log of a '49er," *Overland*, LXIV (1914), 15-23,
187-192, 287-292, 397-403, 510-516, 606-610, *The Adven-
tures of a Captain's Wife* (New York, 1877), J. D. B. Still-
man, *Seeking the Golden Fleece* (New York, 1877), Samuel
C. Upham, *Notes of a Voyage to California via Cape Horn*
(Philadelphia, 1878), Joseph Lamson, *Round Cape Horn*
(Bangor, Maine, 1878), Prentice Mulford, *Prentice Mulford's
Story* (New York, 1889), C. W. Haskins, *The Argonauts of
California* (New York, 1890), Ezekiel I. Barra, *A Tale of
Two Oceans* (San Francisco, 1893), Frank Lecouvreur, *From
East Prussia to the Golden Gate* (New York, 1906), Richard
L. Hale, *The Log of a Forty-niner* (ed. by Carolyn Hale Russ,
Boston, 1923), W. Westergaard, ed., "Diary of Marcellus
Bixby," Historical Society of Southern California *Publications*,
XIII (1927), 317-333, Charles L. Camp, ed., "An Irishman
in the Gold Rush, the Journal of Thomas Kerr," California
Historical Society *Quarterly*, VIII (1928), 203-227, 395-404,
IX (1929), 17-25, 167-182, 262-277, Franklin A. Buck, *A
Yankee Trader in the Gold Rush* (Boston, 1930), Enos
Christman, *One Man's Gold* (New York, 1930), and Carroll
D. Hall, ed., *Journal of a Voyage from Boston to San Francisco
in 1849* (Redwood City, 1933). Edward E. Chever,
"Through the Straits of Magellan in 1849," Society of Cali-

fornia Pioneers *Quarterly*, IV (1927), 137-163, describes a less-favored route, and Mrs. D. B. Bates, *Incidents on Land and Water, or Four Years on the Pacific Coast* (Boston, 1857), describes an ill-starred voyage by collier.

THE OVERLAND TRAIL

The saga of the overland march of the main body of gold seekers is best read in some of their journals, notably Alonzo Delano, *Life on the Plains and among the Diggings* (Auburn, New York, 1854), Georgia Willis Read and Ruth Gaines, eds., *Gold Rush: The Journals, Drawings, and Other Papers of J. Goldsborough Bruff* (2 vols., New York, 1944), David M. Potter, ed., *Trail to California: The Overland Journal of Vincent Geiger and Wakeman Bryarly* (New Haven, 1945), Ralph P. Bieber, ed., "Diary of a Journey [by Bennett C. Clark] from Missouri to California in 1849," *Missouri Historical Review*, XXIII (1928), 3-43, William Kelly, *An Excursion to California* (2 vols., London, 1851), and Niles Searls, *The Diary of a Pioneer* (San Francisco, 1940). Certain reminiscent works, such as *Autobiography of Isaac J. Wistar* (2 vols., Philadelphia, 1914, and in one volume, New York, 1937) and Sarah Royce, *A Frontier Lady* (New Haven, 1932), are as vivid.

The migration of 1850 is well represented by John Steele, *Across the Plains in 1850* (Chicago, 1930), Eleazer S. Ingalls, *Journal of a Trip to California* (Waukegan, Illinois, 1852), Irene D. Paden, ed., *The Journal of Madison Berryman Moorman* (San Francisco, 1948), Georgia Willis Read, ed., *A Pioneer of 1850, George Willis Read* (Boston, 1927), Lorenzo Sawyer, *Way Sketches* (New York, 1926), Charles Smith, *Journal of a Trip to California* (New York, 1920), and Leander V. Loomis, *A Journal of the Birmingham Emigrating Company* (ed. by Edgar M. Ledyard, Salt Lake City, 1928).

Excellent recent treatments are Irene D. Paden, *The Wake of the Prairie Schooner* (New York, 1943), Owen C. Coy, *The Great Trek* (Los Angeles, 1931), W. J. Ghent, *The*

Road to Oregon (New York, 1929), and, with exaggerated drama, Archer B. Hulbert, *Forty-niners* (Boston, 1931).

BYWAYS

Friedrich Gerstäcker, *Narrative of a Journey round the World* (New York, 1853), and *Gerstäcker's Travels* (London, 1854) are translations of his account of the Pampas-Andes byway and of his experiences in California.

The route across Mexico to Mazatlán or San Blas is represented by Lewis C. and Elizabeth L. Gunn, *Records of a California Family* (San Diego, 1928), "A Pioneer's First Letter Home," *Overland*, LXXXIV (1926), 260-269, H. O. Harper, "To California in '49," *ibid.*, XXII (1893), 318-329, Rudolph Jordan, "Autobiography," Society of California Pioneers *Quarterly*, IV (1927), 174-201, and W. Augustus Knapp, "An Old Californian's Pioneer Story," *Overland*, X (1887), 389-408. The Lower California pilgrims are represented by Louis H. Bonestell, "Autobiography," Society of California Pioneers *Quarterly*, IV (1927), 117-135, and George H. Baker, "Records of a California Journey," *ibid.*, VII (1928), 217-243.

On the route through Mexico to the Gila see George W. B. Evans, *Mexican Gold Trail* (ed. by Glenn S. Dumke, San Marino, 1945), A. B. Clarke, *Travels in Mexico and California* (Boston, 1852), O. T. Howe, *Argonauts of '49*, pp. 27-37, John W. Audubon, *Audubon's Western Journal* (Cleveland, 1906), A. C. Ferris, "To California in 1849 through Mexico," *Century*, XLII (1891), 666-679, and the Durivage account in Bieber, *Southern Trails to California in 1849*.

On travel through Texas see Mabelle Eppart Martin, "California Emigrant Roads through Texas," *Southwestern Historical Quarterly*, XXVIII (1925), 287-301, C. C. Cox, "From Texas to California in 1849," *ibid.*, XXIX (1925), 36-50, 128-146, 201-223, William Miles, *Journal of the Sufferings of Capt. Parker R. French's Overland Expedition to California* (Chambersburg, Pa., 1916), and Charles Cardinell,

"Adventures of the Plains," California Historical Society *Quarterly*, I (1922), 57-71.

The most informing work on the Arkansas route is Grant Foreman, *Marcy and the Gold Seekers* (Norman, 1939). On the Santa Fe trail in 1849 Bieber's *Southern Trails* may be supplemented by H. M. T. Powell, *The Santa Fe Trail to California, 1849–1852* (San Francisco, 1931), Charles E. Pancoast, *A Quaker Forty-niner* (Philadelphia, 1930), and Benjamin Hayes, *Pioneer Notes* (Los Angeles, 1929). On the last division of the route see Cave J. Couts, *From San Diego to the Colorado in 1849* (Los Angeles, 1932).

The major reference on the attempted short cut southwest of Salt Lake is W. L. Manly, *Death Valley in '49* (San Jose, 1894). See also John Walton Caughey, "Southwest from Salt Lake in 1849," *Pacific Historical Review*, VI (1937), 143-164, "The Jacob Y. Stover Narrative," *ibid.*, 165-181, L. Dow Stephens, *Life Sketches of a Jayhawker* (San Jose, 1916), John G. Ellenbecker, *The Jayhawkers of Death Valley* (Marysville, Kansas, 1938), Carl I. Wheat, "Trailing the Forty-niners through Death Valley," Sierra Club *Bulletin*, XXIII (1939), 74-108, Carl I. Wheat, "The Forty-niners in Death Valley," Historical Society of Southern California *Publications*, XXI (1939), 102-117, Walter Van Dyke, "Overland to Los Angeles by the Salt Lake Route in 1849," *ibid.*, III (1894), 76-83, David W. Cheesman, "By Ox Team from Salt Lake to Los Angeles in 1850," *ibid.*, XIV (1930), 271-337, and W. Westergaard, ed., "Diary of Dr. Thomas Flint," *ibid.*, XII (1923), 53-117.

Delano, Bruff, and Bryarly describe Lassen's Cut-off, as does Harmon B. Scharmann, *Scharmann's Overland Journey to California* (n.p., 1918).

The Miner at Work

On the miner at work clear description is offered in Rodman W. Paul, *California Gold: The Beginning of Mining in the Far West* (Cambridge, 1947). *The Diary of a Forty-niner*

(New York, 1906), purportedly edited by Chauncey L. Canfield, has a fictionized plot laid over graphic description of the evolution of mining method. "How We Get Gold in California," *Harper's Magazine*, XX (1860), 598-616, is more explicit discussion by a veteran of '49.

Various diggers and visitors to the mines also describe the processes employed; for example: E. Gould Buffum, *Six Months in the Gold Fields*, J. D. Borthwich, *Three Years in California*, Daniel B. Woods, *Sixteen Months at the Gold Diggings* (New York, 1851), Alonzo Delano, *Life on the Plains and among the Diggings*, Vicente Pérez Rosales, *Recuerdos del pasado* (Santiago de Chile, 1890, and translated by Edwin S. Morby under the title *California Adventure*, San Francisco, 1947), Frank Marryat, *Mountains and Molehills* (New York, 1855), Lawson B. Patterson, *Twelve Years in the Mines of California*, Robert Allsop, ed., *California and Its Gold Mines* (London, 1853), Friedrich Gerstäcker, *Narrative of a Journey round the World*, and Edwin F. Bean, comp., *Bean's History and Directory of Nevada County* (Nevada City, 1867).

For technical or summary analysis see Philip T. Tyson, *Geology and Industrial Resources of California* (Baltimore, 1851), John S. Hittell, *Mining in the Pacific States* (San Francisco, 1861), Titus F. Cronise, *The Natural Wealth of California* (San Francisco, 1868), J. Ross Browne and James W. Taylor, *Reports upon the Mineral Resources of the United States* (Washington, 1867), and Charles S. Haley, *Gold Placers of California* (San Francisco, 1923).

LIFE IN THE DIGGINGS

The classic depiction of life in the diggings is from the sensitive pen of Dame Shirley, Louise Amelia Knapp Smith Clappe. Her letters, which first appeared in the *Pioneer* in 1854, are available in book form, edited by Thomas C. Russell (2 vols., San Francisco, 1922) and by Carl I. Wheat (2 vols., San Francisco, 1933).

Other illuminating descriptions are to be found in Sarah

Royce, *A Frontier Lady*, Alonzo Delano, *Life on the Plains and among the Diggings*, his *Chips from the Old Block* (San Francisco, 1853) and *Old Block's Sketch Book* (San Francisco, 1854), Prentice Mulford, *Prentice Mulford's Story* (New York, 1889), Vicente Pérez Rosales, *Recuerdos del pasado*, Friedrich Gerstäcker, *Californische Skizzen* (first published in 1856, and translated into English by George Cosgrave as *Scenes of Life in California*, San Francisco, 1942), Frank Marryat, *Mountains and Molehills*, William Kelly, *A Stroll through the Diggings of California* (London, 1852), and Ernest de Massey, *A Frenchman in the Gold Rush* (translated by Marguerite Eyer Wilbur, San Francisco, 1927). See also Henry De Groot, *Recollections of California Mining Life* (San Francisco, 1884), John Walton Caughey, ed., "Life in California in 1849, as Described in the Journal of George F. Kent," California Historical Society *Quarterly*, XX (1941), 26-46, George W. B. Evans, *Mexican Gold Trail*, John Steele, *In Camp and Cabin* (Chicago, 1928), Joseph Schafer, ed., *California Letters of Lucius Fairchild* (Madison, 1931), Franklin Buck, *A Yankee Trader in the Gold Rush*, and C. L. Canfield, *The Diary of a Forty-niner*.

Charles H. Shinn, *Mining Camps* (New York, 1885), Josiah Royce, *California* (Boston, 1886), and Hubert Howe Bancroft, *California Inter Pocula* are research reports tinctured with some personal recollection and observation. G. Ezra Dane, *Ghost Town* (New York, 1941), is an effort, on the whole successful, to recapture the atmosphere of the society of the diggings.

SUPPLY SERVICES

Most of the references grouped in the preceding paragraphs have information on the supplying of the mines and the miners. Franklin Buck, *A Yankee Trader in the Gold Rush*, and Alonzo Delano in his several books represent the perspective of the storekeeper. See also Shirley H. Weber, ed., *Schliemann's First Visit to America, 1850-1851* (Cambridge, 1942).

The weaving of a system of transportation is described in Jerry MacMullen, *Paddle-wheel Days in California* (Stanford University, 1944), John H. Kemble, *The Panama Route, 1848-1869,* William and George Hugh Banning, *Six Horses* (New York, 1930), Oscar O. Winther, *Express and Stagecoach Days in California* (Stanford University, 1936), Ernest A. Wiltsee, *The Pioneer Miner and the Pack Mule Express* (San Francisco, 1931), and Felix Riesenberg, Jr., *Golden Gate: The Story of San Francisco Harbor* (New York, 1940).

The agricultural changes in response to the stimulation of gold are best described in a long chapter by Frank Adams in Claude B. Hutchison, ed., *California Agriculture* (Berkeley, 1946). The general economic development of the state is described in Bancroft's *History of California,* Volumes VI and VII, in early surveys such as John S. Hittell, *The Resources of California* (San Francisco, 1863), Titus F. Cronise, *The Natural Wealth of California,* and J. Ross Browne, *Resources of the Pacific Slope* (San Francisco, 1869). More recent analyses include Robert G. Cleland and Osgood Hardy, *March of Industry* (Los Angeles, 1929), and Ira B. Cross, *Financing an Empire* (4 vols., Chicago, 1927).

For San Francisco see Frank Soulé, John H. Gihon, and James Nisbet, *The Annals of San Francisco* (New York, 1855), and John S. Hittell, *A History of the City of San Francisco* (San Francisco, 1878).

LAW AND GOVERNMENT

Charles H. Shinn, *Mining Camps: A Study in American Frontier Government* (New York, 1885), is a thorough exposition of the miners' elaboration of law and government; at times it becomes unduly laudatory. Josiah Royce, *California, from the Conquest in 1846 to the Second Vigilance Committee in San Francisco: A Study in American Character* (Boston, 1886), is a philosophical interpretation of the same epoch. The most recent discussion of the law of the camps is in Rodman W. Paul, *California Gold.*

Mining law is the theme of Gregory Yale, *Legal Titles to Mining Claims and Water Rights in California* (San Francisco, 1867), Charles H. Shinn, *Land Laws of Mining Districts* (Baltimore, 1884), Curtis H. Lindley, *A Treatise on the American Law Relating to Mines and Mineral Lands* (2 vols., San Francisco, 1897), and Samuel C. Wiel, *Water Rights in the Western States* (3d ed., 2 vols., San Francisco, 1911).

On the rise of extralegal justice the most voluminous work is Hubert Howe Bancroft, *Popular Tribunals* (2 vols., San Francisco, 1887). Mary F. Williams, *History of the San Francisco Committee of Vigilance of 1851* (Berkeley, 1921), James A. B. Scherer, *The Lion of the Vigilantes: William T. Coleman* (Indianapolis, 1939), and Stanton A. Coblentz, *Villains and Vigilantes* (New York, 1936), applaud the vigilantes. A few works, such as James O'Meara, *The Vigilance Committee of 1856* (San Francisco, 1887), take the opposite point of view.

On the fashioning of civil government see Cardinal L. Goodwin, *The Establishment of State Government in California, 1846–1850* (New York, 1914) and Joseph Ellison, *California and the Nation, 1850–1869* (Berkeley, 1927).

Quartz and Hydraulic

The geology of the California gold deposits is authoritatively discussed in Adolph Knopf, *The Mother Lode System of California* (U. S. Geological Survey, Professional Paper 157, Washington, 1929), Clarence A. Logan, *Mother Lode Gold Belt of California* (San Francisco, 1934), William D. Johnston, Jr., *The Gold Quartz Veins of Grass Valley, California* (U. S. Geological Survey, Professional Paper 194, Washington, 1940), Waldemar Lindgren, *The Gold-Quartz Veins of Nevada City and Grass Valley Districts, California* (U. S. Geological Survey, Seventeenth Annual Report, Washington, 1896), and Waldemar Lindgren, *The Tertiary Gravels of the Sierra Nevada of California* (U. S. Geological Survey, Professional Paper 73, Washington, 1911).

Information on mineral deposits and on mining is available

in the general works of Hittell, Browne, and Cronise, in Rodman W. Paul, *California Gold*, and in Thomas A. Rickard, *A History of American Mining* (New York, 1932). Numerous articles appeared in *Hutchings' Illustrated California Magazine*, 1856–1861, the *Overland*, 1868–, the *California Mining Journal*, 1856–1858, and the *Mining and Scientific Press*, 1860–. On mining operations see J. Arthur Phillips, *The Mining and Metallurgy of Gold and Silver* (London, 1867), and William P. Blake, *Notices of Mining Machinery and Various Mechanical Appliances* (New Haven, 1871).

On hydraulic mining the standard references are B. Silliman, *Deep Placers of the Yuba River* (New Haven, 1865), Aug. J. Bowie, *Hydraulic Mining in California* (Easton, Pa., 1878), his *A Practical Treatise on Hydraulic Mining in California* (New York, 1885), and Eugene B. Wilson, *Hydraulic and Placer Mining* (New York, 1901). On dredging see D'Arcy Weatherbe, *Dredging for Gold in California* (San Francisco, 1907). Grove K. Gilbert, *Hydraulic Mining Debris in the Sierra Nevada* (U. S. Geological Survey, Professional Paper 120, Washington, 1917), is a brilliant analysis of the consequences of hydraulic operations.

CULTURAL BY-PRODUCTS

A number of California's early churchmen recorded their experiences, for example, William Taylor, *Seven Years' Street Preaching in San Francisco* (New York, 1857), and *California Life Illustrated* (New York, 1858), Samuel H. Willey, *Thirty Years in California* (San Francisco, 1879), and *The History of the First Pastorate of the Howard Presbyterian Church* (San Francisco, 1900), Albert Williams, *A Pioneer Pastorate and Times* (San Francisco, 1879), and James Woods, *Recollections of Pioneer Work in California* (San Francisco, 1878).

The educational record is assembled by William Warren Ferrier, *Ninety Years of Education in California, 1846–1936* (Berkeley, 1937). See also John Swett, *History of the Public School System of California* (San Francisco, 1876), and William G. Carr, *John Swett: The Biography of an Educational Pioneer* (Santa Ana, 1933).

Works on the early theater include: G. R. MacMinn, *The Theater of the Golden Era in California* (Caldwell, Idaho, 1941), Constance Rourke, *Troupers of the Gold Coast* (New York, 1928), and Pauline Jacobson, *City of the Golden 'Fifties* (Berkeley, 1941). To the California Historical Society *Quarterly* in recent years Lois Foster Rodecape has contributed several articles on gold-rush drama, for example, "Celestial Drama in the Golden Hills: The Chinese Theater in California, 1849–1869," XXIII (1944), 97-116.

Pioneer journalism is recorded in Edward C. Kemble, *A History of California Newspapers* (reprinted from the Sacramento *Daily Union* of December 25, 1858, by Douglas C. McMurtrie, New York, 1927), John P. Young, *Journalism in California* (San Francisco, 1915), and William B. Rice, *The Los Angeles Star, 1851–1864* (Berkeley, 1947).

Franklin Walker, *San Francisco's Literary Frontier* (New York, 1939), is a brilliant discussion of the gold-rush writers. See also John Walton Caughey, "Shaping a Literary Tradition," *Pacific Historical Review*, VIII (1939), 201-214, Ella Sterling Mighels, *The Story of the Files* (San Francisco, 1893), George R. Stewart Jr., *John Phoenix, Esq.: The Veritable Squibob* (New York, 1931), and *Bret Harte: Argonaut and Exile* (Boston, 1931), Prentice Mulford, *California Sketches* (edited by Franklin Walker, San Francisco, 1935), and Francis J. Rock, *J. Ross Browne* (Washington, 1929). The writings of a substantial number of these craftsmen are available in various printings.

Assay

The world-wide history of gold strikes may be followed in W. P. Morrell, *The Gold Rushes* (New York, 1941); those of the North American continent are described in T. A. Rickard, *History of American Mining* (New York, 1932), and Glenn Chesney Quiett, *Pay Dirt* (New York, 1936). E. H. Hargraves, *Australia and Its Goldfields* (London, 1855), points up the California background for his discovery; for an incisive survey of Australia's mining history see the chapter by G. V. Portus in the *Cambridge History of the British Empire* (Cambridge, 1933).

For the modern pilgrim to the diggings—whether by armchair or sedan—several excellent handbooks have been prepared. The most satisfactory is Joseph Henry Jackson, *Anybody's Gold* (New York, 1941). C. B. Glasscock's *A Golden Highway* (New York, 1934) describes the old mining country as seen during the revival of placer working in the depressed 'thirties. Philip Johnson, *Lost and Living Cities of the California Gold Rush* (Los Angeles, 1948), and Rockwell D. Hunt, *California Ghost Towns Live Again* (Stockton, 1948), stress the centennial motif. The Wilson-Erickson reprint of Delano's book titled *Across the Plains and among the Diggings* (New York, 1936) is notable for the Louis Palenske photographs, while Otheto Weston, *Mother Lode Album* (Stanford University, 1948) is a more elaborate pictorial souvenir.

Supplement to the 1948 Bibliography

Carl I. Wheat, *Books of the California Gold Rush, A Centennial Selection* (San Francisco, 1949) is a useful bibliography, which Dale L. Morgan enriches in his introductions to the M'Collum and Gardiner books listed below. John Caughey, ed., *Rushing for Gold* (Berkeley, 1949) is a select miscellany. Theressa Gay, *James Wilson Marshall* (Georgetown, 1967) is a robust biography. Erwin G. Gudde, *Bigler's Chronicle of the West* (Berkeley, 1962) contains the account of an eye witness. In *The California Gold Discovery* (Georgetown, 1966) Rodman W. Paul meticulously assesses the evidence, good, bad, and uncertain, on the time, place, and circumstances.

Seeing the Elephant: Letters of R. R. Taylor (Los Angeles, 1951), edited by John Caughey, and William M'Collum, *California as I Saw It* (Los Gatos, 1960), edited by Dale L. Morgan, are vivid accounts by forty-niners via Panama. On the rush by Cape Horn see Raymond A. Rydell, *Cape Horn to the Pacific* (Berkeley, 1952); Oscar Lewis, *Sea Routes to the Gold Fields* (New York, 1949); John E. Pomfret, ed., *California Gold Rush Voyages* (San Marino, 1954); and Robert Samuel Fletcher, *Eureka: From Cleveland by Ship to California* (Durham, N.C., 1959).

Dale L. Morgan, ed., *The Overland Diary of James A. Pritchard* (Denver, 1959); Howard L. Scamehorn, *The Buckeye Rovers in the Gold Rush* (Athens, O., 1965); Helen S. Giffen, ed., *The Diaries of Peter Decker* (Georgetown, 1966); and Thomas D. Clark, *Gold Rush Diary: Being the Journal of Elisha Douglass Perkins* (Lexington, Ky., 1967) are extraordinarily informative overland narratives. The Pritchard volume is noteworthy because Morgan made a chart for 132 diarists via South Pass showing when they passed 61 check points en route. On the Wyoming section see John Caughey, "The Transit of the Forty-niners," *Essays in Western History* (Laramie, 1971), 7-17.

George P. Hammond, ed., *Digging for Gold Without a Shovel* (Denver, 1967), the letters of a gold buyer, relates mainly to San Francisco. Doyce B. Nunis, Jr., ed., *The Golden Frontier: The Recollections of Herman Francis Reinhart* (Austin, Texas, 1962); Charles C. Camp, ed., *John Doble's Journal and Letters from the Mines* (Denver, 1962); Dale L. Morgan and James R. Scobie, eds., *William Perkins' Journal* (Berkeley, 1964); and Dale L. Morgan, ed., *In Pursuit of the Golden Dream: Reminiscences by Howard C. Gardiner* (Stoughton, Mass., 1970) graphically describe life in the diggings. Rodman W. Paul, "In Search of 'Dame Shirley'," *Pacific Historical Review* (1964), 127-146, reveals much about the premier writer on this subject. On how gold was mined a most informative reference is Otis E. Young, Jr., *Western Mining* (Norman, Okla., 1970). On hydraulic mining and its consequences see Robert L. Kelley, *Gold vs. Grain* (Glendale, 1959).

On the art of healing (so-called) in the gold rush see George W. Groh, *Gold Fever* (New York, 1966). On the vigilantes the debate continues: Alan Valentine's *Vigilante Justice* (New York, 1956) has serious reservations about the San Francisco Committee of 1856; George R. Stewart's *Committee of Vigilance* (New York, 1966) is an encomium for the Committee of 1851.

Index